MONEY
&
PROMISES

Paolo Zannoni

MONEY & PROMISES

Seven Deals that Changed the World

Columbia University Press
Publishers Since 1893
New York   Chichester, West Sussex
cup.columbia.edu
First published in the UK in 2024 by Head of Zeus Ltd,
part of Bloomsbury Publishing Plc

Cataloging-in-Publication Data is available from the Library of Congress.

ISBN 9780231217132 (hardback)
ISBN 9780231561587 (ebook)

To my wife

Contents

Introduction: Lady Debt   9

1. Pisan Promises   21

2. Venetian Ledgers   47

3. English Tallies   83

4. Neapolitan Charity   113

5. The Écu de Marc   155

6. American Dreams   193

7. Bolshevik Bank Money   229

Conclusion: Indebted   265

About the Author   270

Acknowledgements   271

Bibliography   272

Image Credits   296

Chapter Openers   297

Index   298

Lady Debt

LLOW ME TO BEGIN WITH A CONFESSION: I am a banker.
I have devoted most of my life to the business of banking –
to working with governments, corporations and individuals,
advising and assisting them to raise capital and to manage risks. In
turn, this has allowed them to preserve and grow national, corporate
and personal assets. There are worse ways to spend your time.

I am also a student of the development of banking and monetary
systems. I have spent years trying to understand exactly what money
is, how banking works, and, in particular, the relationship between
banks and states, between my world and the world of everyday politics,
between actual money and hard reality, and the impact of economic
policies and decisions on society as a whole.

My interest in banking began while studying political science at the
universities of Bologna, Florence, and Yale. Back then, in the 1960s and
'70s, my research focused on worker–management relations. I was not a
communist, but nor was I exactly a capitalist. Then, as now, I wanted to
understand how things worked. I was interested in the fundamentals.

After Yale, abandoning an academic career, I joined Fiat in Turin in 1979. In 1985, I moved to Washington DC to run Fiat head office there. In the early 1990s, as president of Fiat USSR in Moscow, I had a front-row seat to the collapse of the Soviet Union.

From there, I joined Goldman Sachs International in London, before heading up the Italian and Russian branches of the bank. After two decades as a Partner at Goldman Sachs, I now serve as Chairman of the Board at Prada and as an International Advisor to the Executive Office of Goldman Sachs International.

✳ ✳ ✳

As a financial insider, I have been privileged to see up close the workings of banks, governments and businesses. *Money and Promises: Seven Deals that Changed the World* is, in part, my attempt to make sense of these experiences. It is my *apologia pro vita sua*. It is also, more importantly, an attempt to describe the complex, intimate relationship between banks and states, and to put into historical context our recent experiences of turbulence in financial markets and in political institutions and systems.

In seven chapters, dealing with seven historical periods, from twelfth-century Pisa to the Bolsheviks in Russia, I explore how vastly different regimes at different times and in different cultures have worked with banks to achieve their purposes and goals.

We begin our journey in twelfth-century Pisa. Chapter 1 describes the development of modern banking and how bank debts first became the currency of the state. The chapter examines the ledger of a private bank, the Compagnia di Parazone e Donato, and shows the importance of promises in banking; the promises that customers make to pay their bankers, and the promises that bankers make to their clients.

We then travel to seventeenth-century Venice to see the establishment of a new kind of bank, Banco Giro. It made money available, first to the state's institutions, then to the whole population. This chapter details how Banco Giro turned the floating debt of state agencies into purchasing power and how bank money became the main currency of the Venetian Republic.

From Italy to London, Chapter 3 delves into the infant years of the Bank of England, the model on which most modern central banks are based. Founded in 1694, it was built on a system of tallies, a type of debt security issued by the English Exchequer for more than 700 years and which represented the financial obligations of the state to its citizens.

As well as sustaining countries, financial systems had to support global empires too. In Chapter 4 we see how the Kingdom of Naples developed its own approach by establishing banking charities. They were built to help the poor, and support the Kingdom and the Spanish Empire.

Chapter 5 examines the strange case of the écu de marc, the ancestor of the Euro, an international private currency that moved seamlessly across borders in early modern Europe. It was a supranational currency of remarkable stability, used to great effect not only by bankers, merchants and investors, but also by Spanish emperors in pursuit of their national and international interests and ambitions.

Chapter 6 features an all-star cast – Thomas Jefferson, Benjamin Franklin, and Alexander Hamilton – and tells the story of how the Continental Congress established the first public bank in North America against the historical backdrop of the limited use of coined money in the colonies.

And finally, Chapter 7 tells perhaps the most extraordinary story of all: the unlikely development of Bolshevik bank money in the 1920s, a unique combination of capitalist banking practices and Bolshevism. *Money and Promises* tells the story of how and why these various banks, in different cultures and at different times, created money for the benefit of the state. The book offers new and original insights into some of the fundamental features of our modern banking system and their impact on public policies. It describes and analyses the deals, the actual transactions, between banks and states that have shaped the modern world.

It explains exactly how, for example, over the years, states have paid for public goods – services for the poor, officials' salaries, metal for armour and weapons, all of the goods and services necessary to the functioning of a nation – with banks' promises to pay. And it reveals how the debts of banks have not only increased the purchasing power of states but have also granted banks extraordinary powers that persist into the twenty-first century, influencing every feature of modern economies.

The research underlying the book's analysis is based on original sources from archives in Venice, Naples, Philadelphia, Medina del Campo, Pisa, and the vaults of the Bank of England. Many of these sources have never been examined before and no one volume has brought together this range of research to provide an historical analysis of the emergence of modern states and modern banking for the general reader.

My hope is that the book will enable readers to better understand banking, and in particular the nature of bank debt – because so often we get it wrong. We say that we go to the bank to get money, or that we borrow money from the bank. We believe that banks earn income by lending us money, something of value, which we then return at a later date. In fact, whether we are paying by cheque, digital transfer, debit or credit card, the goods and services we purchase are bought with our banks' debts, or bank money. This is not a pile of cash in the vaults of an institution, but simply the bank's *obligations*, its *promises* to pay.

And what is true for us as individuals is true also of nations and states: today, sovereign currencies everywhere are made up mostly of bank debts, backed by clients' promises and obligations. This is the true nature of modern money, which is debt. I am not the first and won't be the last to make this simple observation, that modern money is debt; debt backed by debt. But it is an essential point and one that people sometimes fail to grasp. Understanding this simple point helps to explain a lot.

It helps to explain, for example, why banks fail: they fail because bankers are and forever will be debtors. Banks are in the business of debt; they owe to their clients, their fellow bankers, their partners, their competitors. And their clients and competitors owe to them. One might argue that a business that is based entirely on the exchange of debts – that earns its income by exchanging debts, and therefore has it as both assets and liabilities – is actually destined to fail. And when banks do fail, governments will always seek to bail them out.

Let's take two brief examples to illustrate this important point. On October 16, 2008, my old boss at Goldman Sachs, Hank Paulson, then U.S. Treasury Secretary, asked the leaders of America's nine biggest financial institutions to accept an injection of equity by the federal government. At over six-and-a-half feet tall, and a former defensive lineman for Dartmouth's football team, and still known today as 'Hank the Hammer', when Hank Paulson asks you to do something, he can be pretty persuasive, as I know only too well.

The banks did what Hank asked.

In response, the frantic selling of shares in the nine institutions that had been taking place over the previous weeks ceased abruptly. Though the stock market still suffered, and the financial crisis was far from over, the run on the equity of the banks came to an end. The hedge funds that had led the charge were forced to retreat, recognising that even they could not attack the banks with the government supporting them, acting as a shareholder.

In the process, the banks were saved, the American banking system became more stable, and the economy recovered, at least until the next cycle of expansion, bailout, and retrenchment.

It was ever thus. Nearly 500 years earlier, on November 18, 1513, in Venice, the Priuli Bank opened for business on the Rialto. Gerolamo

Priuli, the Managing Partner, placed the bank's ledger on a bench in the square, next to which he piled up stacks of gold and silver coins.

Unfortunately for Priuli, the day did not start well. As soon as the bank opened, clients lined up in front of the bench to swap their bank credits with coins from the stacks. Priuli knew he would soon run out – his debts outnumbering the gold and silver at his side – so he sent a messenger to the Council of Ten, the highest governing body of the Republic, which met nearby.

When the Ten learned of Priuli's predicament, they dispatched the official standard bearer with the Council's flag to the Rialto. The bearer placed himself and the flag behind the bench, next to Priuli. The message was loud and clear: the Republic would make sure the bank had enough coins to meet the demands of its customers. Reassured, Priuli's clients dispersed and went about their business. The bank was saved. For the time being.

The similarities between October 16, 2008, and November 18, 1513, are striking. Facing a banking crisis, the Treasury Secretary of the United States, a modern democratic nation, behaved much like the Council of Ten, the executive body of an ancient aristocratic republic. As *Money and Promises* will show, over the course of 500 years, nations have become richer, financial technology has evolved, and governments have discovered new and different ways to manage their economies. Yet banks still run into trouble, the same now as then, and governments continue to stand by them; eventually, they bail out the banks. Indeed, research has shown that in the roughly 200 years between 1800 and 2008 alone, banking crises and state bailouts took place precisely a dozen times in the UK, thirteen times in the US, and fifteen times in France. No other industry in the world can claim a similar record of recurring crises and government backing.

Why is it that when banks face crises, states always seem to be willing to bail them out? Is it some kind of grand conspiracy, as some claim? Is it something rotten at the heart of capitalism? Some structural defect in the system?

No. This book suggests that the answer lies in the nature and function of the debts of banks; because the debts of banks are the currency of nations. We should not, therefore, be surprised or shocked that states bail out the banks when they periodically face crises and occasionally fail.

In a paper published in the wake of the 2007–2008 global financial crisis, 'Banking Crises: An Equal Opportunity Menace' (2008), the economists Carmen Reinhart and Ken Rogoff observed that 'while many now-advanced economies have graduated from a history of serial default on sovereign debt, or very high inflation […] graduation from banking crises has proven, so far, virtually impossible.'

Why is it impossible? Because bankers are *always* debtors. They are forever in debt; to their clients, customers, other bankers, and, most importantly, the state. In return, these clients are indebted to the bank, creating both a virtuous circle and a Catch-22. The never-ending exchange of debts between banks and states, as we shall see, presents great opportunities – and is fraught with dangers.

There is a long and distinguished history of misunderstanding not only this profound and fundamental relationship between banks and states, but also of misinterpreting the very nature of banks and banking, and indeed the very nature of money and of debt. *Money and Promises* is intended, therefore, not only as a history of banking but also as a necessary corrective to some common fallacies and misconceptions.

Daniel Defoe, for example, the author of that great portrait of economic man, *Robinson Crusoe* (1719) – or to grant the book its magnificent full title, *The Life and Strange Surprizing Adventures of Robinson Crusoe, of York, Mariner: Who lived Eight and Twenty Years, all alone in an un-inhabited Island on the Coast of America, near the Mouth of the Great River of Oroonoque; Having been cast on Shore by Shipwreck, wherein all the Men perished but himself. With An Account how he was at last as strangely deliver'd by Pyrates. Written by Himself* – was an indefatigable commentator on all matters relating to trade, commerce, finance and politics. But even Defoe gets it wrong. In 1706, he published an article on one of his favourite themes, 'Of Credit in TRADE', which begins:

> Money has a younger Sister, a very useful and officious Servant in Trade, which in the absence of her senior Relation, but with her Consent, and on the Supposition of her Confederacy, is very assistant to her [...] Her Name in our Language is call'd CREDIT, in some Countries Honour, and in others, I know not what.

Defoe's personification of Money's younger sister as Dame Credit is undoubtedly brilliant and memorable. But he misses something: Defoe fails to account for another important member of Money's large and complicated family. According to Defoe, Money has a younger sister. I believe that Money also has a twin. I shall call her Lady Debt.

Much has been written about Money and about Dame Credit. There are thousands of books devoted to understanding and interpreting their every aspect. They dominate our thinking and our fantasies about our financial lives. But Lady Debt goes either unacknowledged or despised and anyone who consorts with her is regarded with contempt. 'What is a debt, anyway?' asks the anarchist anthropologist David Graeber in his book, *Debt: The First 5000 Years* (2011). Graeber's 500-page jeremiad is a bold attempt to challenge our ideas about money and banking, but it is perhaps more moral outcry than argument, a long curse against all those he regards as usurers and money lenders. 'A debt', according to Graeber, 'is just the perversion of a promise. It is a promise corrupted by both math and violence.'

I beg to differ. Unlike Graeber, I believe that states and institutions have used a special kind of debt, the debts of banks, to enable themselves and their citizens to survive and prosper, rather than as a tool of domination and destruction. *Money and Promises* seeks to demonstrate not only that modern money *is* bank debt – it seeks to explain why this is no bad thing. As a banker and a businessman, I – like many others – have spent a lifetime in service to Lady Debt. I believe that it is high time that she was given her due.

CHAPTER 1

Pisan Promises:
The Growth of Obligations

Within the surface of the fleeting river
The wrinkled image of the city lay,
Immovably unquiet, and forever
It trembles, but it never fades away …

Percy Bysshe Shelley
'Evening: Ponte al Mare, Pisa' (1824)

THE STORY OF BANK MONEY begins in Pisa in the twelfth century. By studying the history of money and finance in this ancient maritime republic, by examining in detail the ledgers and transactions of its pioneering banks and corporations, and by attempting to understand the complex trades between individuals and institutions in this great city state, we get to witness the development of many of the fundamental financial instruments of modern banking and can also perhaps begin to understand the profound relationship between money, states and promises.

Coin Trouble

Known today for its leaning tower – the bell-tower, the campanile, of the old cathedral, *Cattedrale Metropolitana Primaziale di Santa Maria Assunta* – and as the birthplace of both Galileo Galilei, the father of modern science, and Leonardo da Pisa, known as Fibonacci, who introduced modern arithmetic to the West, the ancient city-state of Pisa was one of the great maritime republics. The chief harbour of Tuscany, Pisa had acquired the island colonies of Elba, Corsica, Sardinia, and Menorca, and had set up entrepôts on the coasts of France, Spain, North Africa, and the Levant, with vessels moving their precious wares of spices, silks and dyes among them. Pisa was thus at the very centre of medieval Europe. It was a powerhouse.

Coalition governments ruled the city. Merchants, ship owners, and manufacturers, along with artisans and workers, were among those involved in government, with certain groups rising to greater prominence over others at various times. Crucially, whoever led the coalition had control of the Mint, which was used to coin the heavy silver pieces needed for the international trade that kept Pisa afloat, as well as providing the small change needed for everyday use. The silver mined in the colonies of Elba and Sardinia flowed into Pisa, and full-weight silver coins flowed out in return, coins that are still being found in troves all over the Mediterranean today.

But Pisa had a problem: the Mint could not supply enough coins to meet the demand of its citizens, the needs of its merchants and its vast ongoing sea trade.

* * *

There were a number of reasons why the Mint couldn't keep up with demand. First, the peculiar practice and principles of minting – the process of manufacturing the coins – determined the money supply, to the disadvantage of both the citizens and the Mint. The Mint would purchase bullion, precious metal, gold and silver, from private citizens at a fixed price, and would pay for that bullion with the very coins, minus a fee, they had minted from the bullion. The supply of coins thus depended on the metal available, and the metal available was determined by the supply of coins; the less precious metal available to the Mint, the fewer full-weight silver and gold coins that were created and the greater the demand for them. It was a vicious circle. The need for coins and the price offered for bullion drove citizens to sell their precious metal to the Mint, but if the Mint offered too low a price, citizens simply sold their bullion and the local coins abroad. It was a precarious system: there was no secure guarantee of supply.

The second reason the Mint was unable to meet demand was that the actual act of minting coins was a highly regulated activity. A closed and secretive guild, made up of skilled artisans known as coiners, manually produced the coins using hammer and chisel. More like a caste than a guild, the ranks of the coiners were closed, with membership handed down from father to son. The coiners' guild was independent and powerful, maintaining strict rules and procedures governing every aspect of how the coiners lived and worked, which drastically slowed coin production.

Political and social conflict also inevitably contributed to problems of production. Though the merchant class generally held sway in the governance of the city, their role could be fraught and fragile. When a new coalition came into power, the leaders would tailor the coinage to meet the demands of their own interests and the interests of their supporters and constituencies. Labourers, artisans, retail businesses and farmers tended to prefer coins of small denomination, containing little precious metal, which provided them with a cheap means of payment suitable for retail trade and workers' wages. Merchants, big businesses and manufacturers preferred the heavy silver and gold coins that were better suited for international and wholesale trade. Debates and disputes about which coins to mint, how many and by whom, were frequent – and sometimes bloody.

It was this crisis of coins in Pisa that paved the way for the development of banking as we know it today.

But first – before the complex systems of banking could fully emerge – a number of other factors had to be in place. And they just happened to be in place in Pisa.

Fibonacci and the New Mathematics

As one of the great maritime republics, alongside Venice, Genoa and Amalfi, Pisa had become a centre not just for the trade of goods in exchange for coins, but also for the trade of ideas. This was true for one man in particular, Leonardo da Pisa, better known by his nickname, Fibonacci.

Fibonacci's story has been told many times before. The son of a Pisan official based in the North African colony of Bugia, Fibonacci had spent time travelling and trading in the southern Mediterranean, which is where he learned about

Leonardo da Pisa. Fibonacci.

Fibonacci's *Liber Abaci*. Dating from 1290. The oldest copy known, now at the Biblioteca Riccardiana in Florence.

Arabic and Indian mathematics. In his *Liber Abaci, The Book of Calculation*, published in 1202, Fibonacci outlined the advantages of the Arabic numeral system and Indian mathematics over the Roman system, introducing ideas such as *zephirum* (zero) and algorithms. His ideas quickly caught on, locally and far beyond. In recognition of his brilliance and influence, in 1241, the city of Pisa began paying Fibonacci the princely sum of 20 lire per annum. He was a local hero.

It is important to note that Fibonacci's was no mere theoretical enterprise. He was interested in showing how the new maths could help business. *Liber Abaci* was a book made for merchants and bankers: it is a guide to making money from money. Indeed, as Will Goetzmann of the Yale School of Management has argued, *Liber Abaci* might be understood as a kind of textbook for aspiring financiers. It shows how

A *Liber Abaci* from the Republic of Venice. One of the most successful manuals for merchants, written by Girolamo Tagliente, was reprinted 20 times. This copy is from the early sixteenth century.

to price money accurately, on a daily, monthly and annual basis, using simple and compound interest. It also presents a simple method for calculating the present value of money accruing in the future. And it explains how to calculate the purchasing power of different currencies in different jurisdictions.

Fibonacci's ideas became the new standard not only for understanding numbers but also for understanding the practice of commerce; they became a method. Cities and guilds – including those in Pisa – set up schools of *abaci* (arithmetic and accounting), based on Fibonacci's principles, to train apprentices for merchant houses. Students would learn, among other skills, how to keep track of debts using appropriate entries on a firm's ledgers. A typical manual of practical instruction for merchants and bankers, published in 1292, for example, now held at the Biblioteca Riccardiana in Florence, is pure Fibonacci.

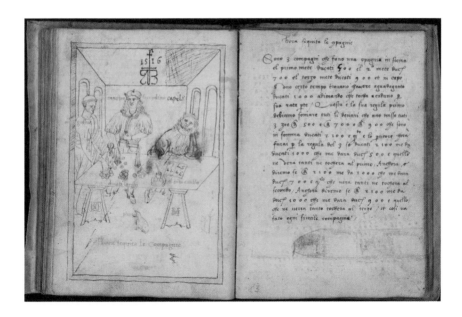

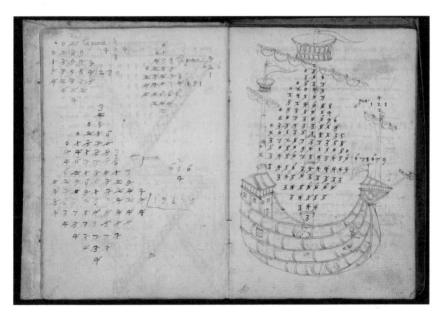

A *Liber Abaci* from the Republic of Genoa (1512). The manual teaches arithmetic and bookkeeping with words, numbers and images from the daily life of merchants: the counting house and the merchant's ship.

So, it was the emergence of new knowledge and institutions, and the need for a new kind of money that made the Republic of Pisa the perfect place for the development of banking. There was also the small matter of the Catholic Church.

The Leaning Tower and the Power of Debt

The best illustration of how banking practices began to emerge in Pisa with the tacit blessing of the Church can be found in the history of the city's most famous landmark: the leaning tower.

Over time, Pisa and the people of the city-state had become wealthy. A small, modest church in the centre of Pisa had served as its cathedral for centuries, but by the twelfth century the citizens were keen to show off their wealth. They wanted to build a grand temple close to the sea, so that any ships docking or passing through would be awed by the city and its church's magnificence. The local church and the republican government handled the construction, setting up a corporation – the Cathedral Foundry – to complete the job. Private citizens endowed the foundry with coins, agricultural land and buildings.

But the project was costly and income from the endowment inevitably fell short of the project's needs. Given the Catholic Church's traditional prohibition on usury, which restricted the practice of lending and borrowing for business purposes, there was a problem. What to do?

The corporation started doing business. Its ledger for the year 1153 alone lists dozens of real estate deals. Pisa's cathedral and its leaning tower owe their very existence to these extraordinary deals.

If we take just a couple of the corporation's transactions as examples, we can see the elegance and brilliance of the Pisan model.

The ledgers show that in 1153, the Cathedral Foundry sold a tract of land to someone called Lanfranco, a local squire, for 1,240 shillings. In another trade, in the same year, and for the same price, the foundry bought an estate from the local bishop, Averardo.

A few months later, it bought back the tract of land from Lanfranco for exactly the same price – 1,240 shillings. At the same time, in another trade, the Foundry sold the estate back to bishop Averardo again for 1,240 shillings.

A few other transactions show a similar curious pattern: the foundry buys and sells back, and sells and buys back, with nobody seeming to make money in any of these transactions. So, what on earth was the point of them?

The answer is that although legally the trades were sales, financially they functioned as loans. The sequence of sale and buyback delivered all the economic rewards of borrowing and lending at interest, because during the entire period between sale and buyback, the properties were being put to productive use. Thus, the foundry effectively 'borrowed' from Lanfranco by selling him the land and returning the capital when it bought the property back from him. And it was effectively 'lending' to Averardo by first buying the estate and then selling it back to him.

The true but unstated business of the Cathedral Foundry was, therefore, unregulated lending, or what is known today as shadow banking. The Foundry, Lanfranco and Averardo all benefitted from this arrangement, in the same way that borrowers and lenders benefit today. The purchasers enjoyed the fruits of the properties while they owned them – Lanfranco receiving the products of the land and the Foundry the yield from the estate. No-one was violating the Church's prohibitions against usury. Everyone was a winner.

This system of shadow banking worked because the risks of lending to the Foundry were so low. The corporation was half-church, half-state, making it a pretty safe bet for the likes of Lanfranco and Averardo.

Similar trades in the Foundry's ledgers are all basically lending in disguise. Since the church leadership in Rome had banned lending at interest, this useful loophole allowed everyone involved to avoid the wrath of Rome.

The benefits of the corporation's lending were not at all insignificant: with all the money and benefits from the transactions, the cathedral was soon finished. And with the cathedral finished, work soon began on the construction of the bell tower and the baptistry, which remains today the largest in Italy, and the whole of what is now Pisa's Cathedral Square, the Piazza del Duomo. The citizens of Pisa viewed this extraordinary feat as nothing short of astounding, eventually renaming the square Piazza dei Miracoli, the Square of Miracles.

The real miracle – as so often – was not so much spiritual as financial.

The Beginning of Corporate Banking

Yet despite these miraculous innovations and developments, by the beginning of the fourteenth century, Pisa's fortunes were declining. The city-state lost its overseas colonies to rival Genoa and its inland expansion was checked by neighbouring Florence. Long-distance trade dwindled and the inflow of precious metals slowed. By the mid-fourteenth century, workers and artisans had become more influential in the city government and had convinced the Mint to coin fewer heavy silver and gold coins, thus creating coins with less intrinsic value, which were still limited in number. As the Mint coined fewer and fewer of the heavy silver and gold pieces that were necessary for wholesale trade and industrial production, entrepreneurs and merchants were unable to buy goods and commodities abroad. Starved of coins, Pisa's economy stagnated.

But this was by no means the end of the golden age of the city. The economic downturn didn't last long and in a short time the economy revived. Manufacturing picked up and trading resumed. Goods made in Pisa travelled by land and on local and foreign ships to southern Italy, Spain, northern Europe and France, despite the fact that the Mint was still turning out mostly small-denomination pieces with low precious metal content in small number.

How was this possible? Trade cannot function without money, so how was Pisa able to experience a scarcity of coined money and economic growth at the same time?

Census data points us towards the explanation, what we might think of as the second great Pisan miracle: the development of corporate banking. In twelfth-century Pisa, money changers had set up shop to trade coins for local currency. Soon they started trading money and debts. By the second half of the 1300s, about fifty bankers were active in the city – a high number in a city with a population of only 15,000 people.

The records of these bankers show that their business had changed from that in the twelfth century – bankers were no longer just money changers, but true merchant-bankers, trading money, debts and, occasionally, goods. Bankers had become treasurers and financiers for local and foreign businessmen. They made and received payments on behalf of clients and supplied means of payment to manufacturers and traders. In Pisa – home to the Cathedral Foundry, to Fibonacci, to the schools of abaci, and always desperate for money – the complex, interrelated systems of modern banking were emerging.

The Compagnia di Parazone e Donato

At the centre of this network was a small bank, the Compagnia di Parazone e Donato (literally, Company of Parazone and Donato), which operated for just three years, from 1373 to 1376. From the economic historian's point of view, this small, short-lived company is significant for one important reason: it kept meticulous records. And, crucially, one of its ledgers, a binder of about 200 loose sheets, survives. *Libro dell' a di Parazone Grasso e Donato del maestro Pietro* – the Ledger of the Parazone and Donato Bank – was just one of several books in which the partners recorded the bank's transactions. Trades are only summarised in the ledger. Other books, not extant today, would have offered more detailed descriptions of each transaction. But the ledger contains just enough information to reveal the secrets at the heart of banking practices at the Compagnia, the same secrets at the heart of banking as we know it today.

The bank was managed by two men, Parazone Grasso and Donato di Pietro. We know little about them. Parazone was a businessman who came from a wealthy, well-connected local family who were engaged in a range of business activities and held important public positions in Pisa. Donato was a well-educated, experienced finance professional who had worked in other local banking houses before joining forces with Parazone. Of the two partners, Donato showed the best grasp of finance and banking. Their complementary skills made them an ideal team.

Established as a partnership on June 1, 1373, the Compagnia's capital structure reflected the different roles of the partners. To start, each initially provided capital of 150 florins, but they soon found this was not enough. Parazone, with money and connections, bridged the shortfall with a loan to the partnership of 600 florins, at 10 per cent yearly interest. With enough capital, the partners went to work making the Compagnia into one of the world's first corporate banks.

The Ledger is the Key

To understand how the Compagnia worked, one needs to understand its ledger; then, as now, the ledger is the key. Money is a kind of witness, and a ledger, literally and metaphorically, is a form of accounting.

We know from the Compagnia's ledger that it offered its services to businesses, partnerships and individuals. Clients included manufacturers of wool, cloth, leather and ships, and service providers, such as innkeepers, tailors, retailers, cobblers and tavern owners. Merchants, seafarers, and other bankers were also on the client roster. But these clients of the Compagnia di Parazone e Donato did not deposit coins at the bank for safekeeping. The Compagnia wasn't that sort of bank. Instead, the Compagnia's clients used the bank's debts to make their payments and to grow their business. The ledger reveals exactly how this process worked.

Like other businessmen and bankers who had perfected their bookkeeping skills at the schools of abaci, inspired by Fibonacci, the

Compagnia and its clients entered the details of transactions into a ledger. But the Compagnia's ledgers were fundamentally different from those of its clients. Clients who bought and sold goods would settle their debts with entries in the bank's ledger. When they sold their wares, they received book entries as payment. And when they bought goods, they paid with those book entries. Clearly, the bank's clients viewed the Parazone and Donato ledgers as unique, and the entries as essentially a form of money. Not only that, the state also viewed the bankers and their ledgers as special, and watched them accordingly – the first banking regulations by the republican institutions of Pisa date as early as 1162.

In Pisa and other republican city-states, such as Barcelona, Genoa and Venice, banks and their ledgers held a unique status. Bankers were not quite public officials, but their ledgers were public documents. The courts accepted them as proof of transactions, debts and claims, and they viewed entries in the bankers' books as evidence of the contracting parties' intentions. Public authorities strictly supervised the records – and actively prosecuted sloppy or corrupt bankers who fiddled with their books. No data survives to document instances of counterfeiting in banking ledgers in Pisa, but such data is available from Venice, where bank ledgers were widely used and also considered public documents.

(In Venice, special magistrates – called *provveditori sopra i banchi*, or 'banking supervisors' – controlled and oversaw the ledgers. Magistrate records show that supervision was effective. There are only a few instances of bankers altering the inscriptions in their books. Over the fourteenth and fifteenth centuries, only two violations are known, one in 1349 and the other in 1468. In these cases, the various violators were promptly punished: they were exiled, jailed or executed.)

The Compagnia's surviving ledger can be hard to decipher, but it offers crucial clues to the partnership's operations. The biggest obstacle to understanding the ledger is to piece together the individual bank accounts which are spread over a few hundred loose folios. Fortunately, some pioneering work was undertaken by a team of scholars from the University of Pisa in the 1950s. Headed by the renowned economic historian Federico Melis, the team analysed and reorganised all the entries in the ledger of the Compagnia and from 200 folios, the scholars reconstructed thirteen complete bank accounts. For an economist, for an historian, and for a banker, they make fascinating reading. The thirteen account holders were an active bunch; one of them had more than eighty entries in his account in less than a year. So even though the ledger tracked just a few individual accounts, it summarised hundreds of transactions.

Making Promises

The Compagnia's surviving ledger uses numbers more than words, but there is one word that gives the numbers their true significance: *impromettere*.

To understand the monetary basis of society, we must understand the language and the grammar of banking. And in order to do so we must grasp the meaning and use of promises. *Impromettere*: the archaic Italian verb means 'to make a promise'. In the case of the Compagnia, that promise was a debt of the bank or of a client. The verb is used in the first person, singular and plural, and in the third person, singular and plural: *I promise; we promise; he promises, she promises; they promise.* The verb's four inflexions provide all the necessary information to describe the Compagnia's activities.

In the first person, *impromettere* was a promise of the Compagnia to pay a client. The Compagnia recorded a claim of the client against the bank and its reciprocal obligation. The claims and the corresponding obligations were entered in the ledger at the same time. One was written above the other on the page, a precursor of double-entry bookkeeping.

In the third person, *impromettere* was a promise by the client to pay the Compagnia; the promise created an obligation of one or more customers to pay the bank. The clients' obligation and the bank's reciprocal claim were also written in the ledger together, one above the other. These entries detailed the clients' debts to the bank and the bank's debts to its clients.

Trading Promises

To take a specific example, many clients of the Compagnia were in the textile business. Six such clients figure prominently in the ledger: a group of individuals named Giovanni, Arrigo, Matteo, Michele, Pietro and Betto.

In the Middle Ages, the textile industry was a crucial component in Pisa's economy. Merchants bought yarn and fabric in France, England, northern Europe and other parts of Italy, and shipped it to the city. The local mills turned the yarn into cloth. Merchants then sold the cloth across the Mediterranean.

One of the Compagnia's clients, Giovanni, owned a mill. Arrigo, Matteo and Michele supplied the mill with yarn, which Giovanni turned into fabric. He then sold it to Pietro, the dyer. Pietro knew the chemical processes and dyes that gave the cloth the desired hue, a valuable skill since the colour of the fabric made its price. Red cloth, for instance, sold for more than the same cloth dyed black. Pietro's skills and knowledge allowed him to run his own shop. He would buy cloth from Giovanni's mill, dye it, and sell it to Betto, a wholesale merchant, who marketed and sold the final product overseas.

The flow of deals among these partners created a vast web of obligations.

For example, at one point, Pietro, the dyer, owed Giovanni, the mill owner, 36 gold florins; and Betto, the merchant, who had sold the final product, owed 36 florins to Pietro. Giovanni owed money to the suppliers of his yarn too: 20 florins to Arrigo, 4 to Matteo and 10 to Michele. As gold coins were still hard to come by in Pisa,

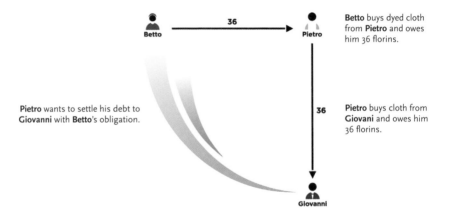

Betto buys dyed cloth from **Pietro** and owes him 36 florins.

Pietro buys cloth from Giovani and owes him 36 florins.

Pietro wants to settle his debt to **Giovanni** with **Betto**'s obligation.

Paying for goods with other people's debts, not coins.

merchants often paid their partners with debts instead. As these debts, or promises, circulated, the need for physical money was lessened, as long as accurate records were kept and the partners periodically cleared reciprocal indebtedness on their books.

So, Pietro wanted to pay Giovanni with Betto's debt, since the two debts were for the same amount. And 36 florins was more than enough to cover Giovanni's outstanding obligations. Giovanni could then do the same and transfer Betto's debt to his associates to pay for supplies he needed at the mill. Since the six partners were in the same industry, paying everyone with Betto's debts seemed easy. Pietro, the dyer, and Giovanni, the mill owner, would be debt free, and the mill and dye shop could keep working. But there was a hitch.

In Pisa, the transfer of debts outside a close circuit of business partners could be a challenge. Social and political conflicts were bitter, and often became violent. Members of rival guilds behaved like enemies, not business associates or competitors. It was group affiliation and identity that established and enabled trust. Members of opposing groups were unlikely to accept the promises to pay – the debt – of an affiliate or associate of a rival faction. In this turbulent and uncertain environment, Giovanni might not be able to pay his creditors with the debt of Betto. They might not trust him. His promises might mean nothing to them. The production of cloth might then slow to a halt.

So, Giovanni approached Parazone, the banker, for help. Sorting out the round-robin of debts took several steps, but the Compagnia's ledger spells them out. It is a beautiful solution to a complex problem.

The first step was an exchange of debts between Pietro and the bank, which was entered into the ledger (italics added for emphasis):

Pietro *owes us* the 36 florins he *promised us* for Giovanni's benefit.

We owe Giovanni the 36 florins Pietro *promised us* for the benefit of Giovanni.

At that point, Pietro still owed 36 florins, but to the bank, *not* to Giovanni. And the bank, *not* Pietro, owed Giovanni the 36 florins. The balance of claims and obligations remained unchanged. But the exchange of debts between Pietro and the bank got the ball rolling. Right away, Giovanni paid his associates with the debts of the bank. This payment represents one of the early recorded uses of what we think of as 'bank money', which is to say bank debt, or bankers' promises to pay. But the role of the bank and its money was not yet done. Pietro, the dyer, also wanted to clear his debt to the bank with the merchant Betto's debt to him. Parazone therefore entered another exchange into the ledger:

Betto *owes us* the 36 florins he *promised us* for the benefit of Pietro.

We owe Pietro the 36 florins he *promised* for the benefit of Pietro.

With this entry, Giovanni and Pietro become debt free.

Thanks to the intervention of Parazone, the production and sale of dyed wool cloth could continue because everyone accepted the bank's debts, even though not everyone was a client of the bank. Arrigo the

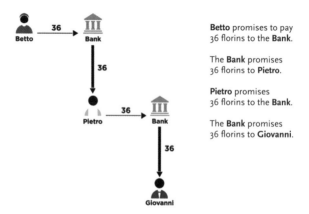

Betto promises to pay
36 florins to the **Bank**.

The **Bank** promises
36 florins to **Pietro**.

Pietro promises
36 florins to the **Bank**.

The **Bank** promises
36 florins to **Giovanni**.

Dealing in debts.

supplier was a client of the bank, so he was happy with a book entry. So was Michele. But Matteo demanded coins from the Compagnia, so Parazone handed four gold coins to Matteo.

And it is this last crucial entry – recording the handing over of the florins to Matteo – that shows how the debts of bankers are different from those of ordinary businessmen. The debts of banks become shining gold coins *on demand.* The belief and certainty that this would happen, *every time,* was the secret formula that made banking work then and continues to make banking work today.

✳ ✳ ✳

The thirteen bank accounts in the ledger list a few hundred banking transactions. Many are similar to those described. Clearly, dozens of merchants, traders, and manufacturers valued the promises of the Compagnia di Parazone e Donato. They must have believed that Parazone and Donato would exchange their promises to pay with gold coins on demand, every time.

Of course, the only way anyone would possibly believe this was if the bankers bought or rented enough coins to give substance to their promises. But full-weight gold coins were scarce in Pisa.

So, the next obvious question arises: how did Parazone and Donato reassure their demanding customers?

Acquiring Cash with Promises

The account of another merchant named Migliore illustrates how the Compagnia acquired enough coins to earn their clients' trust. A citizen of Amalfi, another maritime republic on the southwest coast of Italy, Migliore sold spices and foodstuffs in Pisa. He also bought textiles and tanned leather locally before peddling them around the Mediterranean. Banks became critical in such long-distance trading. With the help of bankers, merchants could travel less and spend more time managing their business.

A minor client of the bank, Migliore's accounts had just fourteen entries. Most payments were made and received with transfers between accounts, but some of the entries represented trades for cash. On July 20, 1374, for instance, Lapo di Tommaso, a cheesemaker, bought a large amount of foodstuffs from Migliore. Lapo paid cash, giving 135 gold florins to the Compagnia for the benefit of Migliore. The bank promised those florins to Migliore, noting them in the appropriate ledger entry, and Migliore was satisfied.

In Pisa, Migliore sold more items than he bought, selling to traders coming into the harbour as well as locals, and the cash stayed in the coffers of the Compagnia. A few months later, the account was closed. At the time, Migliore had a positive balance of 200 florins and 6 denari. This sum was transferred to Migliore in Amalfi with a bill of exchange (a written payment order used mostly in long-distance trade) to his local banker. No coins left the Compagnia's coffers as a result of this transaction.

Satisfaction was mutual; Parazone and Donato were also happy to be indebted to Migliore. At first glance, the relationship might not seem profitable for the Compagnia – the account doesn't show any fee to the bank. Unlike Giovanni, the mill owner, Migliore didn't pay the bankers to receive their promises. Still, his account was important for the Compagnia's business.

With cash scarce, coins were a valuable resource for the bankers; the bank needed them to back up their clients' claims for cash, should they be made. This allowed the cycle of trust to continue.

Trading Promises Pays

These ledger entries and the transactions they represent belie the image of the banker as the quaint, risk-averse figure portrayed in popular histories, especially those of a particular English system of banking, in which wealthy people deposited their valuables with a goldsmith-banker they trusted. Custodians of other people's valuables and cash, goldsmith-bankers were understood to be prudent individuals who lent only excess cash, a far cry from the likes of Parazone and Donato.

For the Compagnia, safekeeping was not the point of the banking business. They were, in fact, aggressively seeking debt – they continually strove to become indebted because they gained financially for doing so. Nor were the local entrepreneurs and merchants who were their clients interested in keeping their coins safe; they wanted to get bank money to use in making payments and settling debts. The more promises the Compagnia made to its clients, the more their clients could grow their businesses.

The ledger of the Compagnia di Parazone e Donato reveals two features of banks that have endured for centuries.

First, the ledger is a key component of any system of banking. The ledger's form, whether on parchment or electronic, matters less than the exchanges it records and the role it plays. The ledger lies at the centre of the banking business and the supply of money. Debts circulate smoothly and safely as entries in the bank ledger. Second, the ledger, under government supervision, promotes the active trading of debts. Banks not only enter into obligations; they also exchange them like traders at a bazaar.

Up until Parazone's death in 1376, the Compagnia di Parazone e Donato was quite profitable. Individual clients were willing to pay to become creditors of the bank. The bank earned fees equalling between 8 and 10 per cent per year of what it promised to pay on their client's behalf. The ledger shows that its clients used the entries in its ledger regularly as means of payment. Alas, no other ledgers of banks have survived to show how extensively this bank money was used in Pisa.

But there are clues. Federico Melis and his research team at the University of Pisa, for example, looked beyond the scanty thirteen accounts in the Compagnia's surviving ledger and analysed the bank's clients' records. The books of one of these clients, the Lanificio San Casciano, one of the largest wool manufacturers in the region, offer useful insight into the wider functioning of business and commerce in Pisa at the time.

Lanificio San Casciano used bank money from several local banking houses to purchase almost three-quarters of the material it needed to make cloth. Bank money also paid for the labour and facilities necessary for production, as well as the operations and the expansion of the woollen mill. A major user of bank debts, the Lanificio San Casciano was willing to pay the price needed to put them to work. The company paid between 8 and 13 per cent annually for the use of bank debt, in line with the cost of the fees reported in the Compagnia's extant ledger, representing about one-third of the firm's total cost of doing business, showing that banking fees were one of the company's major expenses. It was worth it – bank money was cheaper and more plentiful than gold florins.

Though it's difficult to generalise from this single case study, it suggests that in fourteenth-century Pisa many businesses used bank money frequently and paid handsomely to do so.

Bank Money and Economic Growth

Bank money made it possible for businessmen and consumers to pay for goods and services with debts instead of gold, which explains how the republic was able to experience economic growth while being plagued by a scarcity of coined money. For the business community of fourteenth-century Pisa, bank money offered an easily available substitute for scarce coins, and the most enterprising businessmen used it often, as did several public offices and church institutions. The trading of promises, as registered in the ledger, affected not only the bank and its clients but also the whole of Pisa's political economy and the wider community.

The Compagnia was not the only bank active there in the late fourteenth century. The team from the University of Pisa tracked down at least forty-nine more. Their ledgers have not survived but, no doubt, they behaved like Parazone and Donato. And many of the coins minted in Pisa ended up in the banks' coffers. From there, coins backed the bankers' promises, money that fuelled the economic growth of the last quarter of the 1300s.

Parazone and Donato 'made money' in the same way as the coiners and the engravers at the public mint. In fact, they produced and circulated money faster and more freely than the coiners. It was therefore easier to create bank money than coins. For the bank's clients, paying with bank money instead of coins made economic and financial sense. If a business in fourteenth-century Pisa needed ready money, getting gold florins was slow, expensive and sometimes impossible. Bank money, on the other hand, was easily accessible and circulated well. Widely used by local businesses, the promises of bankers at fifty institutions affected the purchasing power of traders, workers, and local and foreign entrepreneurs.

Thus, Pisa operated with two kinds of money. To use the terminology of John Maynard Keynes, money in Pisa comprised both 'money proper', coins from the public mint, and 'bank money', bankers' promises to pay. And bank money was used more often than money proper. The same, in fact, still holds true today for states and banks.

Creating money is one of the key prerogatives of sovereignty. In Pisa, that prerogative was split between the republican institutions and banks, which limited the state's monopoly over producing and managing money. Still, debts with the purchasing power of gold coins could also be useful to the state. For example, Pisa's government could have done as Pietro, the dyer, did and exchange public debt for bank debt. Doing so would increase the purchasing power of government offices. The republic did just that, supplying public goods with the debts of the banks instead of coins from the Mint. States and banks have always searched for ways to make money out of public debt, quickly, cheaply and safely. The specific nature of the tools and transactions have varied, but the result is always the same: every state exchanges bundles of public debt for bank money in order to increase their purchasing power. And it all began in Pisa.

CHAPTER 2

Venetian Ledgers:
News on the Rialto

Shylock, we would have moneys.

William Shakespeare
The Merchant of Venice, Act I, Scene III (*c.* 1596)

V ENICE WAS AND ALWAYS WILL BE an inspiration. The history of banking and of bank money in Venice is, like the city itself, truly something to behold: a maze of alleyways and dead ends, of extraordinary vistas and sunlit squares. In *Death in Venice*, Thomas Mann has Gustav von Aschenbach arrive in Venice from abroad, noting in wonder the 'dazzling composition of fantastic buildings'. We shall approach Venice neither as Aschenbach from afar nor as tourists gazing in wonder, but from the inside, from the very centre, the heart of the city and its trade – the Rialto.

Rialto is one of the oldest wards in the city of Venice. Down from the famous bridge, on the left bank of the Grand Canal, there is a small square, Campo di San Giacomo di Rialto. There is nothing remarkable about it. It is not St Mark's Square or Thomas Mann's Venice, with its grand hotels and its 'flattering and suspect beauty'. The square is modest. There are narrow porticoes casting shade, a small fountain in the centre, and dominating the eastern side, the tiny church of San Giacomo, which gives the square its name. It may be understated but Campo di San Giacomo di Rialto has its own very special place in history. This unlikely spot was once the financial centre of the Republic; Wall Street and the City of London squeezed into just a few square yards. This was where the deals were done. This was the heart of both local and international trade, of import and export, where merchants would meet to do their business and where bankers and money changers would lease benches around the portico from the city authorities to facilitate that business. It was a place of intrigue, gossip and news. It is no coincidence that in *The Merchant of Venice*, Salanio asks Salarino, 'What news on the Rialto?' The Rialto was where it was happening.

In 1619, Zuane Vendramin was well known in the Rialto square. Vendramin was not a banker but a bullion dealer and in Venice, bullion dealers performed an important public service. The Venetian monetary system relied on the Mint to be able to supply, for a price, coins on demand. Merchants and consumers who wanted coins would sell bullion to the Mint for a fixed price and they would then get paid with the coins minted from that same bullion, minus a charge, which consisted of the cost of minting expenses and a small seigniorage. For the Mint, the difference between the price it paid for gold and silver and the price of the coin it gave back was income. For the merchant or consumer, that difference was the cost of turning bullion into money, legally sanctioned purchasing power.

If the Mint price was significantly lower than the price of bullion on the market, the merchant or consumer lost value by selling to the Mint. When that happened, the flow of precious metals dwindled or stopped and so did the supply of coined money. But the Mint price of bullion was not the only variable affecting the money supply; the timing and speed of supply were also important factors. When the Mint was slow in returning the minted coins, citizens and merchants lost value. They would suspend sales and the supply of coins would dwindle further. Which is what you would expect in a market subject to the laws of supply and demand. But whatever the vicissitudes of the market, Venice's citizens, merchants and public offices still needed a steady supply of coins. This is where someone like Vendramin came in. Bullion dealers like Vendramin set out to meet the needs of Venice's citizens and public offices. They would purchase precious metal on the world market and sell it to the Mint. Then, like any other citizen or merchant, they would get paid with the coins minted from the bullion they had sold.

Not surprisingly, Vendramin and his fellow dealers were big clients of the bankers in the Rialto square. In order to pay for all that gold and silver bullion, they used bank money, which meant that the supply of coins in Venice effectively relied on the supply of bank money. When Vendramin wanted to sell bullion, the Mint promised to pay the bank the price of the bullion, for the benefit of Vendramin. The bank then credited the sum to Vendramin, who delivered the bullion to the Mint. When the coins were created, the Mint delivered them to the bank for Vendramin's benefit and all remaining debts were cleared. While

Vendramin waited for the coins to be delivered he could spend the debts of the bank. Therefore, banks, the Mint and public offices all benefitted from Vendramin's use of bank money.

We shall return to Zuane Vendramin and his pivotal, pioneering role in the development of Venice's banks later. But first we need to understand the functioning and long, complex history of bank money in the Venetian republic. And in order to understand that history, we need to begin by talking about tax and public debt.

Forced Loans

Buying from bullion dealers was not the only way the Venetian state procured its coins. Taxing and borrowing were routine. Venice was a republic run by an oligarchy of the wealthy. The rulers did not much like taxing themselves or their fellow citizens, so they relied instead on debt to fund state expenses. The Venetian republic started borrowing long-term from its citizens early on in 1164. It was not voluntary. The state assessed the financial wealth of the individual and then a percentage (2 per cent or 4 per cent) was simply appropriated. This loan was meant to be long term or even permanent. The lender, the individual, did not expect to receive their principal back. But there were advantages to the system: forced loans paid interest at around 5 per cent, providing a predictable cash flow for the life of the loan. Each loan was packaged, with individuals holding shares in the loans, and the shares themselves could be transferred and sold, so cash could be easily obtained and profits made by trading in them. All in all, for the merchant elite, forced lending to the state was actually much more attractive than paying taxes. Compliance was high and so were public revenues.

A secondary market in shares in the loans quickly developed and they became a major asset class, offering a popular investment for individuals, businesses and banks, who invested heavily in them. The few bank ledgers that survive in Venice show that shares in the

Republic's debt feature prominently among the assets of private banks in the city. Forced loans were a brilliant, simple invention and a great financial tool for the state.

However, funding state activity with forced lending had its limitations. It was difficult, for example, to finance the unexpected short-term obligations of government by raising long-term debt and, in difficult times, long-term public debt traded at deep discounts to face value. Issuing loans under those circumstances was a challenge. At such times, under such circumstances, the state paid for goods and services neither with the money from the coins procured from bullion traders nor with the money made from forced loans, but with the money made by private bankers. And in Venice, as in Pisa, bank money was made with inscriptions in bank ledgers, those inscriptions being viewed as bankers' promises to pay, promises that held the purchasing power of coins.

The Venetian state therefore relied on bank money and took it seriously, carefully overseeing and monitoring bank money transactions. In 1318, a Venetian law regulated the transfer of balances between accounts through entries in bank ledgers. Cooking the books, using false information in ledgers, carried heavy penalties and offenders were prosecuted ruthlessly; it was, after all, tantamount to robbing a bank or an individual. Venice's merchants, meanwhile, took full advantage of the opportunities and the convenience that bank money offered to them, happily exchanging their debts for those of bankers, and, despite the various regulations and restrictions imposed by the state, the balance sheets of the banks grew fast.

Bank Money – Familiar, Easy to Use and Reasonably Safe

The banks became pillars of the state. The story of exactly how is told by Domenico Malipiero, a chronicler of the history of Venice from 1475–1500. Malipiero's *Annali Veneti* (*Venetian Annals*) provides an engaging insider's account of the most important events in late fifteenth-century Venice – tales of soldiers of fortune, merchants, admirals and ordinary citizens. What is truly extraordinary about the *Annali Veneti* is that banks are the heroes of the story; there seems to have been no aspect of public life in the republic that was untouched by the influence of bank money and bankers' promises to pay. Malipiero goes so far as to describe a handful of Venetian banks – Garzoni, Lippomano, Pisani and Priuli – as 'the four pillars of the temple'. The state was supported by the banks and vice versa.

As an example, let us take defence. This is always a good example, because defence is disturbingly expensive, has an enormous impact on the everyday lives of citizens and tends to loom rather large in any state's financial planning. Freedom may be paid for in blood, but weapons and men are paid for with money.

At the Battle of Motta in 1412, for example, against Hungarians, Germans and Croats, the Venetian army was led by a mercenary captain named Carlo Malatesta, who quickly became the state's biggest creditor. Malatesta needed payment for his own services and to be able to continue to supply men to the republic and lead them into battle, at an estimated cost of around 26,000 ducats. This was a vast sum and the state coffers did not hold enough coins to be able to pay him. So, Venice settled Malatesta's obligation not in gold but with an entry on the books of the Priuli bank, a private institution. Malatesta, like any other good entrepreneur or businessman, was more than willing to accept payment in whatever form was safe and convenient, and he knew he could rely on bank money to pay soldiers and acquire supplies. Bank money was widely used in Venice and the promises of the Priuli represented instant purchasing power for Malatesta at par with gold.

Banks in Venice regularly made money available in this way for the benefit of government agencies that were short of coins. In the second half of 1482, for example, the Venetian Senate authorised borrowing 115,000 ducats from the four major banks in the city. That short-term loan on its own accounted for more than 10 per cent of total public expenses for the year.

This vast amount of borrowing paid not only for war but was also vital to public welfare more broadly. Grain supplies to the city, for example, often depended on bank money. In the late 1400s, the Medici family demanded the guarantee of the bank owned by the Garzoni Family, one of Venice's four major banks, before delivering wheat to the Grain Office to feed the city. Once they had the guarantee of the bankers – their promises to pay – the grain supplies were duly delivered.

Confronting Bubbles

Such convenience brings with it all sorts of dangers. Bubbles created by an excess of debts and bank money were not uncommon in Venice, with the government of the Republic periodically and frantically trying to prevent the next overexpansion of bankers' promises. The history of banking in Venice is therefore one of often hasty regulation and deregulation, as the state attempted to manage the overextension of banks' debts.

One example of this see-saw regulation can be found in the history of Venice's foreign trade. Making bank money from the debts of overseas clients was a widespread practice in Venice. It offered convenience to merchants, as well as a good source of profits for bankers. Merchants would write bills of exchange in foreign cities, which would then be deposited and function as money in Venice. But they did not bring actual coins to the bank or to the city.

So, in 1421, the Senate restricted the ability of banks to accept these bills. This new law sought to maintain an equilibrium between debts in the bank ledger and actual cash in the bank coffers. But the legislature soon eased its restrictions, bowing to the demands of bankers and merchants and, as so often, bank money, the promises of bankers, fuelled prosperity for the bankers and merchants, at least until the next liquidity crunch and debt crisis.

It is worth noting, here, that in the long history of economic booms and busts, bank money almost always plays a part. The decrees of the

Venetian Senate reveal predictable and familiar responses to financial cycles, with the periodic tightening and loosening of regulations on banking activities, no different from our contemporary cycles of regulation and deregulation. In 1496, for example, there were about ten banks in Venice; by the middle of the sixteenth century all of them had gone bust. Savers and citizens suffered. As always, something had to be done. And as always, what was done was to restrict the freedom of the bankers to make money.

In 1585, the Senate decided to establish a public bank, the Banco della Piazza di Rialto. The Banco accepted deposits but could not make money in excess of the coins deposited. Every entry in the ledger of the Banco had to be backed by silver and gold coins of equal value; only full weight coins were accepted as deposits and any form of bank lending was prohibited. Only transfers between accounts were permitted. The bank was established to replace coins with ledger entries, not to increase the money supply. The state closely enforced the law.

The good news is that it worked. After years of boom and bust, the public bank, the Banco della Piazza di Rialto, made bank money safe again in Venice.

But the bad news is, safety can also bring with it uncertainty, insecurity and risk. In banking, nothing is ever quite straightforward.

The Price of War

Boom follows bust, scarcity follows plenty; bankers understand this, particularly when they feel it in their own pockets. I remember when Hank Paulson was the Chairman and CEO of Goldman Sachs, he would always remind the bank's partners when announcing the yearly bonus not to spend it all at once. Banking, he would remind us, is a cyclical business. You're going to need that bonus when the going gets tough. Venetian bankers, senators and citizens would certainly have agreed with Hank – they went through many cycles. But they always came out of them by way of financial innovation.

Wars have often prompted creative problem solving in finance – and in the Republic of Venice, the next evolution in the development of bank money derived from the hard lessons of war and the perils of scarcity caused by safe money.

Venice's last land war, the War of Gradisca, proved a turning point in Venetian banking history. The war, also known as the Uskok War, after the Uskoks, who staged a number of guerilla attacks and acts of piracy against the Venetians, was fought between Venice, the Dutch and the English on one side and the Austrians, Slovenes, Croats, and the Spanish on the other. The fighting took place close to Venice, near the borders of today's Slovenia and Croatia. With the battles raging so close, the Venetians spared no effort on defence. The city hired a large number of mercenary troops and supplied them with plentiful arms and provisions. It also subsidised its allies, the Dutch and the English, often with gold and silver. And eventually, Venice and its well-paid allies prevailed.

After the Uskok War, Venice experienced a shortage of money. This was hardly surprising. Coins had left the city to pay for supplies, weapons and foreign mercenaries. Merchants and citizens were reluctant to bring bullion to the Mint, so fewer coins were produced and since bank money was mostly made by depositing cash at the public bank, the Banco della Piazza di Rialto, fewer coins meant less bank money. The combined scarcity of bank money and coins, the two main means of payment, impacted every activity in the republic. Simply minting more coins with less bullion was not a realistic option; debasing the coinage, the authorities believed, was an illness worse than the cure and they resisted lowering the precious metal content of the principal coins. Things were spiralling out of control.

But Venice's mounting problems were not just monetary. Post-war, the state's fiscal position was absolutely dire. Wars are traditionally financed by borrowing and taxes, in order to raise the necessary revenue, but too much public debt had been issued. Shares in the public loans now traded at a significant discount to face value, which made more borrowing from savers difficult. Taxes did not offer a realistic solution to the shortage of money. The institutions of the state were dominated by a hereditary aristocracy whose wealth was based largely on financial assets. Taxing them was not a good way to enhance a career in the Republic. And anyway, bullion was as scarce as coins both in private and public coffers.

Post-war Venice was therefore facing a triple threat: scarcity of bullion, restrictions on making bank money and a reluctance to tax. Altogether they curbed the state's ability to provide public goods. A creative way out of the predicament was urgently needed. Someone needed to cut the proverbial Gordian knot, once and for all.

Which brings us back to our bullion trader, Zuane Vendramin, the man in the Rialto square.

A Brilliant, Self-Serving Proposal

Vendramin had a suggestion, a modest proposal. His day-to-day business was selling precious metals to the Mint with the help of banks, so he knew first-hand about the shortage of money in the Republic of Venice. Low prices and long delays made the selling of bullion to the republic difficult. And fewer coins meant less bank money. And the war had made things much worse.

On May 1, 1619, Vendramin wrote a letter to the Senate: 'I have silver worth 600,000 ducats and I am willing to sell all of it to the mint.' With that bold opening sentence, Vendramin had the senators' attention. His supply of silver could quickly ease the money shortage and stimulate trade. Trade would bring Venice greater tax revenues and this, in turn, would lead to a recovery in public finance.

Of course, Vendramin's offer came at a price. He was a bullion trader, after all; he wasn't a charity. He expected to be paid immediately and in full for his silver, he explained, but was prepared to be flexible on the exact terms of payment. For half of the value of his silver, he said, he expected to receive gold on delivery, but he would release the remainder, the balance, in exchange for 'a special kind of credit' at a 'new type of bank'. His letter to the Senate set out the main features.

Here was Vendramin's proposal. An official elected by the senate would need to keep the new bank's ledger: this would keep everything above board. The debits of this new institution should be freely transferable, and no one should be able to refuse them as payment for goods or for settling existing debts above 100 ducats, thus guaranteeing ease of transfer and exchange, to both Vendramin's and others' advantage. And the debts of the institution would become legal tender, just like coins from the Mint, guaranteeing security and peace of mind for everyone.

It was a cunning plan. And it came at exactly the right time. As it was, the Banco della Piazza di Rialto could only make bank money with coins; the coins stayed at the bank while merchants and consumers spent bank money, which did not increase the money supply of the republic and was in effect a system that merely replaced the coins in its coffers with book entries. Vendramin's new type of bank would actually make money for the use of the state, which could then be used to buy bullion and mint coins, thus producing both bank money and coins. Public offices, merchants and consumers would be able to spend both, and the total money supply would grow.

The Bank of Transfers for Grain

Vendramin's proposal was not entirely original. It was, in fact, inspired by a previous shortage of cash in the city.

In 1607, with the war in Gradisca far on the distant horizon, money in Venice was already running low. It was a crowded city with a large urban population, 200,000 inhabitants, who all needed feeding. A government agency, the Grain Office, was in charge of procuring foodstuffs. Seven wheat merchants had accumulated huge credits with the Grain Office. These merchants resisted supplying yet more wheat on yet more promises that they would, at some point in the future, be rewarded. The merchants argued they could not pay traders and workers with the debts of the Grain Office, but they could pay them with bank money.

Everyone who did business in Venice accepted the debts of local banks – the debts of the Grain Office, however, not so much. The reason was simple. Venetian merchants knew how the bank made money through its balance sheet. The Grain Office was not a bank and its debts were not money. So, the senate quickly established a special purpose bank, the Banco del Giro delle Biave, literally the 'Bank of Transfers for Grain'. The Banco made money the way private banks do. The Grain Office promised to pay the Banco for the benefit of the grain merchants, the Banco credited the merchants' accounts and the merchants used the Banco's debts as money.

The Banco opened accounts for each of the seven wheat merchants. In order to do so, it debited the Grain Office and credited each merchant with the amount the Office owed him. The merchants could now make payments transferring the bank debt between accounts; the alchemy of banking had made money out of the debt of the Grain Office, a state agency. The debts racked up by the Office to buy wheat had become actual buying power. The Banco created the money, the Grain Office spent it first and then a wide range of people in Venice spent it. Everyone benefitted.

The Banco del Giro delle Biave experiment was a success; it stayed open for seven years. When it eventually closed in 1614, it held hundreds of accounts. The original merchants had used their credits at the Banco to pay workers, partners and suppliers. The initial large debts were split in the bank ledger and assigned to hundreds of citizens and businesses; when the Banco closed, many of the accounts were for sums of less than ten ducats. In those seven years, wheat was plentiful in Venice and more money changed hands.

Vendramin basically wanted to revive the Banco del Giro delle Biave experiment but on a much larger scale to increase the money supply of the Republic. The new bank would issue Vendramin with its special kind of debts in order to buy his silver; this bank money would then circulate freely as a means of payment; and the Mint would make coins out of Vendramin's silver, further relieving the shortfall of money. The proposal nicely blended public spirit with self-interest.

The offer was more than tempting; it was like an answer to prayer. The Senate agreed to Vendramin's terms and asked the Mint and the Pien Collegio to proceed.

Pien Collegio: The Overseers

Pien Collegio, the Full College, was one of the most important executive bodies of the Republic of Venice, made up of senior members of the various other executive bodies and the judiciary. Like any fully developed state, a vast bureaucracy and multiple institutions governed Venice. The Maggior Consiglio, the general assembly of all the city's noble families, was the highest legislative body. Every important piece of legislation had to be approved by the Consiglio. In 1293, membership became restricted and hereditary, so only the original aristocratic families and their descendants held legislative power. This effectively meant that the aristocracy took charge of all the policies of the Venetian republic. Over time, due to demographic changes, membership of the Consiglio fell, with numbers reducing from 2,500 to under 2,000 noblemen, but it was still far too large a body to wield executive power effectively. Smaller executive bodies were therefore established under the control of the Consiglio. By the end of the sixteenth century, the Senate had taken over most of the legislative and executive functions. With more than 300 members, the Senate was certainly smaller than the Consiglio, but the state's complex procedures limited even its effectiveness. Hence the Pien Collegio.

The Collegio was an even smaller body than the Consiglio and the Senate, made up of a group of experienced men of state who implemented the Senate's decrees and managed public administration. It held most of the executive and legislative powers of government, it met in session every day and it was exactly the right state institution to supervise Vendramin's proposed new bank.

The Start-Up Bank, Banco del Giro

The new bank, the Banco del Giro, like any good start-up, was established with just two employees, the 'depositario', the official keeper of the ledger, and a journalist, the scribe who recorded all transactions. The debts of the Banco, entries in the ledger, could be transferred from person to person. Two copies of the ledger were kept. One was at the Banco; the other was at the Pien Collegio.

Members of the Collegio played an extremely important part in the development and supervision of the new bank. They were mostly financiers who were keenly aware of both the benefits and perils of bank money. They understood the advantages of the alchemy of banking for the state: a bank that made money out of floating public debt and increased the purchasing power of public offices. In Venice,

The main branch of Banco Giro, now a restaurant. (A pretty good one.)

private bankers had made money exchanging their promises to pay with those of their clients for centuries. But the new bank would be making money only out of the promises to pay of the agencies of the state. The leadership of the Collegio did not know how merchants and consumers would value this new type of bank money and they were keen to keep tight control over the Banco. They didn't want to give public offices an unrestricted licence to create bank money by simply exchanging debts and becoming indebted with the Banco. So, they set up a strict set of procedures that public offices had to follow. First, the Senate had to approve any transaction that required bank money. Once the trade had been approved, both the government office and the Banco were required to follow strict rules and regulations to be able to make and spend it. To make sure that the public offices followed the rules, Pien Collegio kept a copy of the ledger.

A Marvellous Book – An Incredible Find

The decree of May 3, 1619 establishing the Banco del Giro marked the beginning of a bold experiment in the history of banking and public finance. This experiment lasted not for years, as with the Banco del Giro delle Biave, nor for decades, but for almost *two centuries*, until the brutal end of the Venetian republic in 1797 at the hands of Napoleon and the armies of Habsburg Austria.

Obviously, the best way to understand how the Venetian Senate and Pien Collegio used the alchemy of banking to the advantage of the state for so many years would be to study specific transactions between the government offices and the bank. The records of these transactions would reveal exactly what the state was trying to achieve and how they did it. These records would also reveal the precise nature of the role played by the bank in paying for public goods. Such records would be absolutely priceless.

Fortunately for us, these records do exist, thanks to the Pien Collegio. Although the members of the Collegio were few, they employed a vast bureaucracy that recorded everything for their scrutiny and on their behalf. These records are stored today in an old convent, the Convento dei Frari, in the centre of Venice, a beautiful compound of cloisters and courtyards that now houses a branch of the state archives. Inside there are more than 70 kilometres (40 miles or more) of shelf space that show the inner workings of Venetian public bodies, businesses and private citizens through its extensive files of laws, regulations, wills, petitions, patents, cargo manifests and financial records, including thousands of private and public contracts, and the records of the Pien Collegio.

I have studied these records. Bear in mind, I am not a scholar. I am a banker and businessman; my work involves doing deals and making things happen. The work of research, in contrast, requires patience and calm; it requires hours and hours of working alone in archives. Yet I love it. For me, sifting through the records of centuries-old trades brings its own rewards and satisfactions: transactions do not lie, they

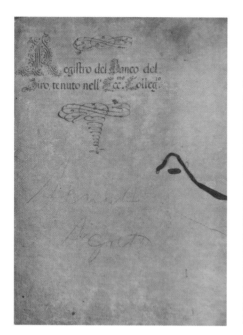
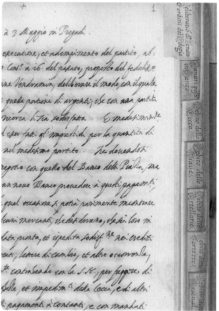

The ledger for Banco Giro's first six months of operation.

disclose the true goals of each party, how they tried to achieve them and the final outcome. Locked away in the archives, you get to see the big picture. You get to see the truth.

Working in archives can also present tremendous challenges. There are always gaps and holes; the historical record is incomplete. Archives offer answers yet at the same time often withhold their secrets and the state archives in Venice are no exception. But what the Venetian archives do reveal are the workings of the long-term relationship between the Banco Giro and the Republic of Venice.

We know the general picture of the workings of the Banco Giro. We know, for example, that the bank was managed by a *depositario*. The senate did not want bankers – even public bankers – to become too powerful, so a new depositario was elected every quarter, and when he took office, he received from the incumbent a small logbook summarising the current state of the bank. A few of these logbooks have survived in the archives. They are indexed notebooks, long and thin. They are like little snapshots of the state of the bank at given points in time. But, alas, the logbooks reflect only the liabilities and cash reserves at that moment. That's all they list: the bank's liabilities and its creditors, with their names and the amount the bank owes them and the coins in the coffers of the bank. The notebooks give no details of the actual deals the bank did to create money. To properly understand how the state used the alchemy of banking, we would need to know much more. We would need to be able to consult the Banco Giro's actual ledger.

Now, remember, officials kept two ledgers: one at the Banco and the other at the Pien Collegio. Most of the records of Banco Giro have long since been lost, stolen, ransacked or destroyed, Venice having been conquered and plundered by Napoleon and the forces of Habsburg Austria in 1797. While the records in Pien Collegio are our best hope for being able to understand the great Banco Giro experiment. While in the state archives, I knew exactly what I was looking for – the Banco ledgers kept at the Pien Collegio. The staff encouraged and supported my searches. But the ledgers could not be found. Among all the records of the Pien Collegio – mile after mile after mile of priceless material – they just weren't there. But I kept looking – and eventually I got lucky. Filed away – or rather, misplaced – was the one and only ledger that seems to have survived. And it happens to be the ledger covering the first six months of Banco Giro's operation, from May 1619 to January 1620. It was an incredible find, and perhaps the single most fascinating document I have ever studied.

It is an elegant, leather-bound book, divided into nine sections. The first section repeats, word for word, the Senate decree that established the Banco Giro, spelling out the procedure the bank had to follow in order to create bank money. The last section is the summary of the debits, credits and cash at year end January 1620, the current state of the Bank. The most interesting material lies in the seven chapters in between.

Each chapter lists all of the transactions between a given government agency, its suppliers and the Banco Giro for 1619. Tabs separate the chapters. Each tab is inscribed with the name of a government agency – and every trade between the public offices and the bank that created the money for the benefit of the state is detailed there. Of course, what happened to that bank money once it was made and spent by the merchants and citizens of Venice will forever remain a mystery, but those first trades are the blueprint of the foundations of Banco Giro.

Rules and Regs

The very first transaction in the ledger, the trade between the Mint, the Banco and Zuane Vendramin, usefully demonstrates the first principle of banking: the books have to balance.

Vendramin's sale of 600,000 ducats was split into four tranches. On June 3, 1619, as soon as the Banco opened its doors, Vendramin delivered silver to the value of 150,000 ducats. In payment, he received 100,000 ducats in gold and 50,000 ducats in a ledger entry. The bank 'made' those 50,000 ducats the way private bankers had done for centuries. Remember, bank money is bank debt and in order to issue debts, any well-run business must first have enough assets. And the main assets of a bank are…? The clients' promises to pay. The Mint was the Banco's first client, so its debt was the bank's first asset. With the Mint as its client, the Banco Giro had enough assets to issue debts in order to begin to make money. The scribe debits the Mint, credits the sum to the Banco, then transfers it to Vendramin. So, the ledger balances and the institution has 'made' 50,000 ducats for Vendramin to spend, bank debts backed by the obligations of the Mint.

The trade benefits many: the state agencies and Vendramin first, of course, but then the 50,000 ducats soon spreads out to merchants and consumers. And the coins minted from Vendramin's silver add much-needed coins to the money supply. The ledger describes in detail the alchemical process: a trade that only needs a few lines on a register takes up more than two handwritten pages. The meticulous description is not meant to show the accounting prowess of the scribe but to create trust in the Banco Giro. Everyone can see how bank money has been made, how the assets and liabilities on the ledger balance perfectly, so merchants, businessmen and consumers can understand and trust the process.

There was just one little hitch. The promises of banks have the purchasing power of coins only because they can be exchanged with coins on demand at par. The Banco did not begin life as a deposit bank – like the English goldsmiths or, say, the Bank of Amsterdam – so it had no coins to exchange its debts for. This might mean that clients who needed cash and could not exchange book entries with coins at the Banco would sell them on the market at a discount, causing the bank money to lose its purchasing power.

So, what did the Pien Collegio do? They allocated some of the silver pieces minted from the Vendramin bullion to the bank to be exchanged on demand with bank debt. And when the Banco used that first allocation, the Mint provided liquidity to the Banco through a monthly transfer of new coins. And with this regular supply from the Mint, the Banco could exchange bank money for coins. This meant that the Banco, with assets made of debts of the state agencies *and* a small supply of coins, could go ahead and make money out of public debt for the use of the State efficiently, securely and regularly.

And with that, the way ahead was clear. The bank's books were open.

Beautiful Cannons

The next entry in the ledger, June 5, is taken up by the trades between the bank and the Grain Office. It reveals how the state managed to use bank debt to supply foodstuffs both to the vast Venetian metropolitan area and to Venice's many ship's crews.

The third trade in the ledger is perhaps more interesting, detailing the exchanges between the Banco Giro and the Artillery Office. Artillery pieces cast by the Republic of Venice between the fifteenth and eighteenth centuries can be found today in many cities all over the Mediterranean. These cannons – mostly in bronze, sleek and elegant as well as powerful – grace old forts and local museums; they are like works of art. Back in the day, they were the most advanced and lethal artillery available, essential to the Republic's survival. Venice was a fighting state; it had been at war almost continuously from its inception to its demise in 1797. For most of that time, its foes vastly outnumbered its own forces; its beautiful cannons helped even the odds.

Venice armed itself early, from 1378. Huge efforts went into the design and production of artillery. Casting the best cannons became a top priority for the state, with the Artillery Office being put in charge of making and supplying the cannons to both the state's armed forces and private vessels. And so, naturally, in 1619, with the founding of the Banco del Giro, the Artillery Office was given its own separate section in the ledger. Here's the Artillery Office deal from the ledger: on July 13, the Senate authorised the Artillery Office to pay a certain Flemish merchant named Pietro de Voghet with debts of the Banco

Giro. Why? At the beginning of the seventeenth century, the cannons of Venice were still made of bronze. They were more expensive to make than those of iron but performed much better. Quality copper was needed to produce bronze artillery and Venice acquired most of that copper from as far away as Antwerp. Over many years, the Artillery Office had carefully nurtured a network of trusted Flemish suppliers of copper and in the early 1600s Pietro de Voghet was one of the biggest. In July 1619, he delivered 12,000 ducats' worth of high-quality copper to the Artillery Office and demanded immediate payment. The republic needed Pietro, so he had to be paid quickly and in full.

On July 13, the Senate authorised the Artillery Office to become indebted to the Banco to pay Pietro. The procedure to turn Pietro's credit into bank money differed from the previous two transactions insofar as this time around the Mint was not involved. The Banco simply debited and then credited 12,000 ducats to the account of the Artillery Office, and transferred the sum to Pietro's account. Clearly, the Senate and the Collegio had agreed to give the Artillery Office the power to acquire bank money without the intervention of the Mint. It was now enough for state agencies to become directly indebted to suppliers and then exchange that debt for an equal amount of bank money. Without the involvement of the Mint, central control on the creation of bank money was slipping. Public offices turned debt into money more freely. But at the same time, the Banco Giro was more effectively fulfilling its mission: it was making money out of the floating debt of the state.

Leasing New Ships

There's more. Public debt bought not only silver, and bread and dry biscuits, and some nice-looking cannons for the Republic of Venice at no discount to coins, it also bought the Venetians an entire modern navy.

In the republic of Venice, two agencies of the state managed the navy and the merchant marine. The Arsenale built ships and the

Piazza San Marco.

Armamento equipped them to be ready to sail. In its first six months of trading, the Banco Giro made bank money for them both – the trades between the Armamento and the Banco Giro take up the fifth section of the ledger. Unsurprisingly, these are by far the most numerous and most complex trades in the book; shipping was one of the industries crucial to the welfare and survival of the Republic, as important as, if not even more important than, the manufacture of artillery. Enabling the financing of the Republic's shipping was a major undertaking of the bank.

At the beginning of the seventeenth century, Venetian shipping faced some significant challenges. New oceanic routes disrupted established patterns of international maritime trade. The new routes lowered the volumes of goods traded through the Mediterranean. The spice trade was hit especially hard. The wealth of Venice shrank, and in the process, the republic became more vulnerable. The new oceanic routes also prompted the development of new types of ships, capable of crossing the Atlantic and beyond. The vessels developed for these new transatlantic journeys were bigger and faster than those used in the Mediterranean. Large ships with round hulls powered by square sails were more efficient at moving goods and people – they carried more cargo and more cannons and required more people to man them. Venetian shipping still used the smaller galleys for the purposes of trade and in battle, powered by oars and less powerful sails. The new vessels, mostly English and Dutch, soon moved south and competed with the Venetian galleys on traditional Mediterranean trade routes and in war.

The Republic did not have the technology, capital or the manpower needed to build ocean-going ships quickly. But the new round ships were much better than the vessels out of the state shipyards and they threatened Venetian sea power and commerce in the Mediterranean and far beyond. Waiting was simply not an option – Venice was in danger of being outdone and outstripped as a maritime power. The Republic urgently needed these ships to support trade and to strengthen its defences.

The international market offered a solution. Round-hulled ships with square sails could be leased from their owners in the Netherlands and in England. Leasing ships was expensive, so the Venetian government decided to use bank money in order to save its precious coins. But leasing ships in Holland and in England and paying for it in Venice with entries in the ledger of the Banco Giro was a deal not without its challenges. The Republic was able to overcome these obstacles by combining the use of bank money with bills of exchange.

The details of the trades are fascinating. Syndicates of local financiers would lease the ships in Holland and in England, paying the ship owners, captains and crews. Venetian agents in the Hague and London would give the financiers bills of exchange payable at the Banco Giro, so that the debts raised in Holland and England could be settled in Venice without using coins. The Banco credited the financiers the amount of the bills on its ledger and they then used those credits as they pleased. The section dedicated to the Armamento in the Banco's ledger lists many of these kinds of trades. The consortium headed by a certain Melchior Neirot, a Flemish businessman, was extremely active and accumulated large credits at the bank. Another man in London named Rodolfo Limes was not far behind. On July 16, the bank paid a bill of exchange for 8,000 ducats to Limes. In England, Limes had leased six ships for the Republic of Venice. He paid the owners, the captain and the crews, and received from Venetian agents a bill of exchange for 8,000 ducats, payable in Venice at the Banco Giro. Limes or his agent then presented the bill in Venice at the bank for payment. But the Banco Giro could not make money without debiting a public office – that would violate the rules of banking as practised by the Venetian state. So, the bank first debits and then credits the 8,000 ducats to the account of the Armamento, and transfers the sum to Limes.

The state first raises debt in London or Amsterdam from private financiers, then pays it back in Venice with bank money made out of the floating debt of the Armamento. These trades, using different currencies and different means of payment, are some of the most complex international financial transactions undertaken during the period. The ingenuity needed to structure and execute them is remarkable: the Republic of Venice was combining bills of exchange and bank money made by the Banco Giro to increase the purchasing power of the state, reducing the need to coin and export gold or silver, with the promises of the Banco Giro replacing the need for large quantities of gold and silver bullion. And the entries in the ledger allow us to follow every step of the process.

These types of complex transactions became so important in the life of the republic that in 1623 it became mandatory to make *all* bills of exchange payable at the Banco Giro in bank money.

It is difficult to overestimate the importance of these and similar trades for the Republic of Venice as a maritime state. Perhaps just one startling instance will suffice. In 1645 the Ottoman Empire invaded Candia, an important Venetian possession in the southeastern Mediterranean. The war between Venice and the Ottomans was expected to be short, given the Empire's overwhelming superiority of men, ships and weapons. The logistics were also unfavourable to Venice; Candia was 1,800 km from Venice. Yet the fighting lasted for over twenty-five years, a quarter of a century, with astronomically high costs for both sides: scholars have estimated that the total cost of the war of Candia for Venice was around 125 million ducats. The annual revenues of the Republic were a long way short of these sums; a vast amount of public debt had to be raised. And in order to authorise the Banco Giro to make more money, the Senate issued thousands of decrees – literal and metaphorical licences to print money.

But the debts of Banco Giro were not only used to pay for the war; medicines, bread and commodities were procured abroad, paid with bills of exchange and then settled at the Banco. State pensions to individuals serving the State abroad, in war and peace, were paid with bills payable in bank money. The combination of bank money and bills of exchange, illustrated in those early complex transactions with the Armamento, with the likes of Rodolfo Limes, became indispensable to the state.

The Last Tab

And so now to the very last section: the last tab in the ledger kept by the Collegio. This lists the assets of the Banco Giro, the liabilities issued and the cash it received from the Mint. This final section makes it possible to estimate *in total* the contribution of the bank to the purchasing power of the Venetian state and the total money supply.

The ledger shows that in the first seven months of operation, the Banco Giro issued debt (created money) worth 780,000 ducats. And remember, the assets of the bank were only the promises to pay the four public offices: the Mint, the Artillery, the Grain Office and the Armamento. To give liquidity to the debts of the Banco, the Mint deposited coins at the bank for 130,000 ducats. That means that the state received instant purchasing power for 780,000 ducats at the cost of 130,000 ducats of silver coins. Not a bad deal for the republic and for merchants and consumers. The experiment with the Banco Giro had instantly succeeded; entries in the ledger quickly created more means of payments than the coins minted with the silver of Zuane Vendramin.

Of course, this sudden expansion in purchasing power had consequences: the republic's monetary system became more complex overnight. Two legally sanctioned means of payment were now available: coins or bank money made out of public debt. But the state could reap the full benefit of the alchemy of banking only if the bank money had the purchasing power of coins. So, the big question in Venice was: the purchasing power of which coins, exactly?

Mint Money vs Current Money

This is because there is a basic problem with money made of coins. In the words of Sir Robert Cotton, advising King Charles I of England in 1626:

> I must distinguish the monies of Gold and Silver as they are bullion or commodities and as they are measure. The one the extrinsick quality, which is at the King's pleasure, as all other measures, to name: the other, the intrinsick quantity of pure metal which is in the merchant to value.

It's nicely put; the obvious difference between the intrinsic and the extrinsic value of coins. Even then, there are all sorts of differences to be accounted for in both intrinsic and extrinsic value: coins can lose weight, for example, their intrinsic quality and value, through the general wear and tear of exchange. This means, as Sir Robert Cotton rightly intuited, that kings and merchants – or Venetian senators and merchants – are bound to disagree on the price of coins. Therefore, trading becomes difficult and ordinary life is disturbed as consumers and citizens lose faith in money and indeed in the King, which is the problem that King Charles I was dealing with.

Fortunately, Venetian senators were practical men and they had devised a pragmatic way to deal with the difference between intrinsic and extrinsic value. They had split the money of Venice in two: so-called 'mint money' and 'current money'. Only gold and silver coins of good weight and high purity newly minted in Venice were counted as 'mint money', the prime example of mint money being the sequin, which consisted of exactly sixty-seven grains of pure gold; silver coins in so-called 'mint money' also contained mostly pure metal. 'Current money', on the other hand, was made up of coins containing much less silver and gold and which were worn or chipped specimens. The value of each kind of money as legal tender bore out the difference in weight and purity of the metal in the coins by way of an average: all mint money was legal tender at 20 per cent more than all current money. The arrangement may seem rather odd and convoluted but it worked reasonably well in practice. Debts and prices were expressed in either mint or current money. A debt for 100 ducats contracted in mint money could be settled legally with mint coins worth 100 ducats or current coins worth 120 ducats. Debtor and creditor did not need to weigh every ducat.

Bank money was valued at par with mint money. This made perfect sense when the only public bank was the Banco della Piazza di Rialto because its promises to pay were fully backed by deposits of coins formed of mint money. But from 1619, with the establishment of the Banco Giro, bank money made only out of public debt became instantly worth 20 per cent more than current coins; the strange alchemy of banking had magically given floating public debt the purchasing power of newly minted gold and silver.

Bank money has the purchasing power of coins only because it can be converted into coins on demand. That may have been easy to do with the promises to pay of Banco della Piazza di Rialto, but it was not so easy with those of the Banco Giro, which had a limited number of mint coins. An excess of bank money or a scarcity of newly minted coins could easily destroy the 20 per cent premium on bank money and thus weaken the purchasing power of public debt.

Wily Arbitrageurs

Anyone with even the most rudimentary understanding of the principles and practice of arbitrage can perhaps guess what happened next. Venetian merchants were already highly skilled in currency arbitrage. They traded in many different markets, where the same coin might have two completely different prices. Merchants exploited these differences to their advantage, buying a coin where extrinsic value was lower than the intrinsic value and selling where the price of the metal was high. Classic arbitrage.

This was also practised at home in Venice. A currency that was now made of three kinds of money – current money, mint money *and* bank money – offered entirely new opportunities for arbitrage. And

The inside of a medieval bank.

bank money with no precious metal content and the limited backing of mint coins? That was particularly vulnerable to those wily Venetian arbitrageurs. If the creditors of public offices received more bank money than they could spend, they exchanged it with any coin on the market. If full-weight silver and gold coins were scarce, clients of the Banco would aggressively sell bank money for current coins and drive its price down. This made individuals wealthier, but the state poorer.

The Heady Years

In 1619, Banco Giro's experiment had started with a bang: its promises quickly grew to above 500,000 ducats. Concerned about the rapid increase and the threat of arbitrage, the Senate, by decree, very quickly imposed a ceiling of 500,000 ducats on the debt of the Banco Giro. This decree worked well at first. The price of bank money hovered around the official parity with newly minted gold and silver coins until about 1623. But then the various government agencies pushed the Senate to allow the Banco to make more bank money. And the Senate yielded.

Public spending and bank money started to spiral out of control. Too much floating public debt, too much bank money, threatened the bank money premium. The Senate and Pien Collegio were determined to defend bank money: they increased the transfer of coins to the Banco, but that was not enough. The promises of bankers were on the way towards permanently losing their 20 per cent premium.

So, ever flexible and adaptable, the Senate and Pien Collegio changed tack yet again. The Senate made taxes and custom duties payable in bank money. This helped the situation, but the bank ducat still traded at a discount to the mint ducat. Then the state started borrowing bank money and coins together. Public loans at the time yielded 7 per cent per year: lending unwanted bank money to the state was a much better deal than selling it for current coins. This move strengthened the bank ducat, at first. But it didn't last long.

By 1630, the obligations of the Banco Giro had risen to an eye-watering 2.6 million ducats and bank money was routinely exchanged in the market for current coins, at a discount to mint money. Too much public debt had simply put too much bank money in circulation. The Mint could not supply enough coins to guarantee liquidity at the bank at the official price. The whole grand experiment was in jeopardy.

So, what did the Senate do next? They put on the brakes. The size of the liabilities of the Banco was stabilised slightly below 1 million ducats. But as always, everywhere, government departments just needed more money. They demanded more money. And the pressure mounted as before and so the Banco Giro issued yet *more* promises. And in response, in 1643, the Senate prohibited Banco Giro from exchanging bank money with any coin, mint or current. Debt became simply the word of the bank: bank money and the purchasing power of public debt sank.

Finally, the Senate and the Pien Collegio paused, took a deep breath and reexamined the whole system. It took them some time to survey and assess what had been happening.

From 1619 to 1637, the republic of Venice had enjoyed the privilege of having not one but two public banks, the Banco del Giro and the Banco della Piazza di Rialto. The Banco della Piazza di Rialto, remember, was a bank of deposit and issue; it made money issuing its obligations to clients who deposited coins; it could not make money in excess of the value of the coins deposited; each bank ducat of the Banco della Piazza di Rialto was backed by a mint ducat. The Banco del Giro, in contrast, was a bank of transfer; it made money out of the floating public debt. Businessmen did not deposit coins or exchange debts with the Banco Giro. The bank exchanged the public debt for bank debt. This arrangement where different kinds of banks made money in different ways worked reasonably well.

But in 1637 the Banco della Piazza di Rialto was closed, and so the Banco del Giro became the only institution in Venice making bank money. The deposit of coins by private parties was not allowed at first and the Banco Giro simply kept making money out of the floating debts of agencies of the state, with the consequence, as we have seen, of the price of bank money slowly eroding.

And so it was that in 1666 the Venetian Senate and Pien Collegio reached the conclusion that the state could not support restrictions on the Banco Giro any longer. Yet more bold action was needed. The only way to keep the 20 per cent premium on bank money was to have the Banco Giro make money out of public debt *and* coins *and* the debts of business and consumers. So, for the first time, individuals and businesses were permitted to deposit coins and exchange debts at the Banco Giro. Cash and debts from private individuals flooded into the Banco Giro and it became possible again to convert bank money into mint money. The deep discount on bank money at first diminished and then disappeared.

Banco Giro now made money out of floating public debt, private obligations and the deposits of state agencies, individuals and business. The assets were a mix of private and public debts and the coins in private hands gave liquidity to the debts of the bank. Under this new system, bank money was made by the choices of consumers, businesses and the state.

The Banco Giro had become an entirely different beast to that which had originally been conceived by the enterprising Zuane Vendramin: it was now a bank of deposit *and* issue, serving not just the state but also businesses and individuals. And in this new form it happily operated as the only public bank in Venice until Napoleon ended the Republic of Venice in 1797, an incredible record of longevity.

The Venetian Example: Great in Despite

For all the ups and downs, and despite the enormous pressures and various emergencies that beset the Republic of Venice and the Banco Giro, the great Venetian banking experiment can be judged a success.

As we have seen, partly as a consequence of war and inspired by the innovative proposal of Vendramin, the bullion dealer, concerned citizen and shrewd businessman, the Venetian leadership managed to use the alchemy of banking for the benefit of the state for decades, throughout the seventeenth and eighteenth centuries. And, as we have seen, the only surviving copy of the Banco Giro's ledger, hidden in the state archives and detailing the secrets of the first six months of its trading in 1619, shows exactly how the process worked.

It was a bold experiment and an extraordinary achievement, and we know that it was watched closely by other innovators elsewhere. In 1753 Frederick II of Prussia, for example, wanted to establish a public bank. Frederick was a man who liked to do his homework and relied on his extensive personal network for information and assistance. Fortunately for him, Hugo Streit, a German merchant in Venice, was part of his network. On March 23, 1753, Frederick wrote to Hugo, asking him to send to him a trader from Venice who knew how Banco Giro worked. The King wanted someone from whom he and his advisors could learn how to make money out of the floating debts of government, since the master of the Prussian Mint was busy working on a Royal Edict to set up its own 'Royal Gyro and Exchange Bank' in Berlin. Barthold Georg Niebuhr, a banker and one of the great early scholars of banking, writing in 1854, emphasises the important advisory role of Italian and Dutch experts in setting up the Prussian scheme. The charter of the Royal Gyro certainly shows distinct similarities with both its Venetian and Dutch fore-runners: the obligation for merchants to pay bills of exchange at the Banco, the use of a special currency as bank money. Prussia learned from Venice.

In banking, lessons hard learnt are lessons worth learning. To return to Thomas Mann, as we leave Venice – there is an insight he grants to Aschenbach in *Death in Venice* which applies to endeavours artistic, romantic and indeed financial:

almost everything conspicuously great is great in despite: has come into being in defiance of affliction and pain; poverty, destitution, bodily weakness, vice, passion, and a thousand other obstructions.

CHAPTER 3

English Tallies:
Documentary Promises

*All money, properly so called, is an acknowledgement of debt;
but as such, it may either be considered to represent the labour and
property of the creditor, or the idleness and penury of the debtor.
The intricacy of the question has been much increased by the
(hitherto necessary) use of marketable commodities, such as gold,
silver, salt, shells, etc., to give intrinsic value or security
to currency; but the final and best definition of money is that it
is a documentary promise ratified and guaranteed by the nation
to give or find a certain quantity of labour on demand.*

John Ruskin
Unto This Last (1860)

A TALLY IS USUALLY A STICK, or a bone, or a piece of ivory – some kind of artefact – that is used to record information. Palaeolithic tallies include the Lembombo bone, found in the Lembombo Mountains in southern Africa, reported to date from around 44,000 BC; the Ishango bone, which consists of the fibula of a baboon, from the Democratic Republic of the Congo (the former Belgian Congo), thought to be 20,000 years old; and the so-called Wolf bone, discovered in Czechoslovakia during excavations at Vestonice, Moravia, in the 1930s, and estimated to be around 30,000 years old. Marked with notches and symbols, these tallies are ancient recording devices, means of data storage and communication. Not merely artefacts, they are important historical documents.

In England, from around the twelfth century, and for over 600 years, tallies became important financial instruments, a key part of public finance and an answer to a perennial problem for money-lenders, merchants and those involved in commerce and trade: how to both facilitate and record the exchange of goods, services and commodities. Reading these English tallies, understanding their history and their

The stocks of early Exchequer tallies.

changing use, provides us with an understanding not only of the nature of individual financial transactions during the late medieval and early modern period, but also of the development of banking practices in England and its relationship to the English state.

Tallies as Financial Tools

Usually made of willow or hazel-wood, tallies were used to record the key information of a financial exchange. The name of the parties involved, the specific trade and the date were written on each side of a stick. Notches of different sizes – which stood for pounds, shillings, and pence – were also cut on both sides. Then the stick was split in two along its length, creating a unique jagged edge; only those two pieces could ever fit perfectly together again. When someone presented one side as proof of a transaction, the parties could check for the right fit.

The potential uses for such a simple tool are obvious.

To begin with: an example of the early use of tallies as a record of debt repayment. John D'Aber-non was the Sheriff of Surrey. His portrait in brass, in Stoke D'Aber-non Church, Cobham, shows him as a knight in full armour, wield-ing a broadsword. When he died,

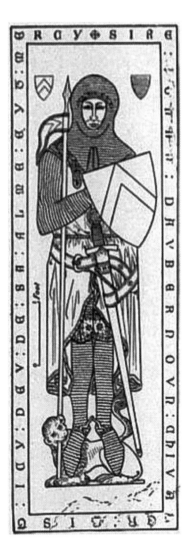

Brass rubbing of the image on the tomb of John D'Abernon.

D'Abernon left his title, possessions and debts to his son, also named John. In 1293, we know that John D'Abernon gave two pounds and ten shillings to the Exchequer to pay a fine on behalf of his father. How do we know? Because at the time of payment, the official tally cutter made a series of notches on a stick: two cuts for the two pounds and one smaller notch for the ten shillings. The stick was then split, with the longer end going to John, and the shorter end staying with the Exchequer. The following words were inscribed on both sides: 'From John D'Abernon for his father's fine' and 'XXI year of the King Edward'.

John could thus prove to anyone that he had paid the fine of his father – simple and convenient.

Tallies also enabled the functioning of the tax system in medieval England, which was a rather more complex affair. The process took months to complete. It worked roughly like this. Tax receivers collected revenues from the King's subjects at Easter. They then passed them on to the Exchequer, which completed an audit in late September or early October. At the time, the Exchequer had two branches: the Lower and the Higher. The Lower Exchequer received and disbursed the revenues. The Higher Exchequer audited the process. They used tallies to track who had paid whom. As soon as the Lower Exchequer received the revenues, the tally cutter recorded the payment on the tally and split the stick. The tax receiver – the debtor – got the longer part, called the 'stock'. The Exchequer – the creditor – kept the short end of the stick, called the 'foil'. And once a year, at Michaelmas, the Higher Exchequer audited the whole process by matching stocks and foils. The stock was the proof that the collector had not merely pocketed the tax revenues.

Sticks as Public Debt Securities

Over time, both the use and appearance of the tallies began to change: in the early years, tallies were 3 to 5 inches long; later, they grew to be 1 to 2 feet long, and sometimes much longer. More money meant more notches; more notches, in turn, required longer sticks. One of the last issues of tallies made by the English Exchequer was in 1729, for £50,000: the tally is a whopping 8 feet, 5 inches long, visible proof of the growth of public spending, taxation and inflation.

As the appearance of the tallies changed, so too did their uses. Inside the Exchequer, they served as receipts for money paid by taxpayers. Outside the Exchequer, they began to be put to entirely different purposes.

The business of the Exchequer simply could not work without the tally sticks. They were essential for auditing and controlling public finances, which obviously made them excellent collateral for a loan.

The longest tally issued for the value in the vaults of the Bank of England. Issued for £50,000. Length: 8 feet, 5 inches.

The tally was not a mere generic promise to pay, but a strong, unique claim on the proceeds of the Exchequer's revenue stream. It identified the cashflow and the individual in charge of paying; the creditor gave the stock to the indicated tax receiver to get coins from a specific revenue stream, and a lender was sure to get his coins sooner or later. The humble English tally stick was therefore ripe to become a veritable public debt security, not merely a receipt. They functioned just like paper public debt securities, except instead of being written on paper, the transactions were instantiated and inscribed on sticks.

To take an early example: Richard de la Pole was a merchant who traded wool, wine and corn with France and central Europe

Paying taxes to the Exchequer.

in the early 1300s. He had a reputation for using debts aggressively to grow his business, which appealed to King Edward III and his advisors, who thought they might be able to make use of his skills. So, they appointed him Royal Butler. The job of butler was to supply all sorts of goods – food, wine and arms – to the royal household and to the army. We know that in 1328 Richard bought some wine from the French. As a good businessman, as Royal Butler, did he pay for the wine in coins? He did not. Rather, in order to pay the bill, the Lower Exchequer cut eight tallies, which were addressed to the collectors of taxes for West Riding in Yorkshire, listing the tax revenues earmarked to settle the debt. The Lower Exchequer gave the foils – one half of all the eight tallies – to Richard, who handed them to the merchants who sold him the wine. The merchants then exchanged the tallies with coins from the taxes paid in West Riding, and finally, a few months later, the Higher Exchequer called upon the tax receivers to account for the shortfall of cash, whereupon they presented the eight foils, which had been first given to Richard, as proof of the payments made.

To be clear: unlike coins, tallies did not actually settle debt. By accepting a foil, a vendor was effectively agreeing to a delayed payment from the Exchequer; the tally was a kind of guarantee that they would get coins. For the state, meanwhile, the tally was a convenient way to borrow from its suppliers, or a form of what we would now call vendor financing – the citizens and merchants who sold goods and services for tallies were effectively financing the state, in much the same way as those who lent actual coins to the Exchequer.

Sol and Pro Tallies as Private Debt Instruments

Over time, financial tools and instruments develop. Their uses change and become refined. And so in England, eventually, the increased use of tallies led to the development of two kinds of tallies: so-called *sol* tallies and *pro* tallies. Sol tallies continued to act as simple receipts for cash paid to the Lower Exchequer. They had the date of the payment, the amount and the name of the tax receiver making the payment, with the word 'Sol' (from the Latin *solutum*, for 'paid') concluding the inscription. Pro tallies, however, had two functions. First, they worked effectively as orders of payment from the Exchequer to the receiver. Second, once the payment was made, they simply reverted to being receipts for the purposes of audit; in the inscription, the word 'Pro' (Latin for 'in favour of') replaced the word 'Sol', with the tally cutter simply adding the name of the party due to receive payment.

Sol tallies continued to play their record-keeping role inside the Exchequer, and it was the pro tallies that began changing hands as private debt instruments. Not surprisingly, the Exchequer became addicted to the power of tally sticks.

Traditionally in England, private debt instruments did not circulate well until the seventeenth century. The courts of law typically refused to uphold the rights of the bearer of a bill of exchange or a promissory note not in his name – but a bearer of Exchequer tallies could transfer his rights in full to third parties. If a merchant needed cash, he could, for a price, exchange tallies for coins or bank notes with a banker. Most English bankers were goldsmiths who simply kept the coins of wealthy clients safe. They would issue their own notes – written promises to give back those coins – and would in turn buy tallies. But not all pro tallies offered the same level of security. The cash flow from some taxes often fell short of expectations. Tallies cut on less predictable revenues were worth less; those cut on taxes that were sure to yield plenty of cash traded at higher prices. And the time to payment also influenced how much the stick was worth; tallies cut on revenues that accrued later were worth less than those cut on ready cash. Goldsmith bankers therefore bought sticks at different rates.

Assessing the true value of tallies was a skill that could lead to great wealth – indeed, by the seventeenth century, the emerging London financial houses, like Hoare, Child and Blackwell, established their fortunes based largely on their ability to assess the true value of tallies.

Within a few hundred years, tallies had become the backbone of the English money market – records of debt repayments; auditing and accounting instruments; public debt securities; and private debt instruments.

Tallies and Institutional Change

But there were problems ahead. For centuries, the English state borrowed on the security of the King. Lenders advanced cash to the Exchequer in exchange for the King's promise to repay them. Suppliers sold goods to him on credit. Yet despite the King's standing, and the widespread use of tallies, lenders did not always see those promises as reliable, and royal borrowing required elaborate dealings. Kings and queens often sought money or guarantees from the City of London Corporation (the governing body of the city and its financial centre), but the Corporation was reluctant to accommodate royal requests.

In 1392, for example, the City refused to make a loan to King Richard II for the relatively modest sum of £1,000.

Since the authority to tax resided with Parliament, kings realised that a joint promise between them and Parliament would carry more weight with lenders. In partnership with Parliament, they could borrow more money, and at lower rates. Some kings did their best to borrow with the permission and sanction of Parliament, but the relationship between kings and Parliament was not always entirely smooth. Indeed, as every English schoolchild knows, tensions between them eventually grew to the point that the two sides went to war.

The English Civil War lasted for nearly a decade, 1642–1651, with pro-Parliament forces on one side, the so-called Roundheads, and the Royalists, or Cavaliers, on the other. There were, of course, other matters at stake in the Civil War besides the right to borrow and spend – religious, civil, constitutional – but after the turbulent years of what became known as the Interregnum (the period in English history from the execution of Charles I in 1649 to the Restoration of the monarchy in 1660), the financial settlement was a necessary part of the eventual compromise between the returning Charles II and the so-called Convention Parliament, with Parliament retaining the sole power to tax and most of the power to spend, and Charles being granted tax revenues of about £1.2 million per year, which he was at liberty to spend largely unchecked.

It seemed like a solution. But the compromise soon faltered: receipts from Parliament's levies did not meet requirements; the King spent more than his allowance; foreign wars greatly increased the government's expenses; and Parliament was unwilling to raise more taxes. The figures did not add up. Some creative accounting was required in order to balance the books.

Here's an example of how it was done. We know that in 1664, a number of the Royal Navy's ships required maintenance. The navy naturally turned to the Lower Exchequer for cash, but the department had no coins, so instead the treasurer recorded a payment from the receivers of the customs tax and a cash disbursement to the navy. No actual cash came in or went out of the Exchequer, but a sol tally was cut and given to the navy, who handed it to the shipyard as payment for the work. From the shipyard, the tally went from hand to hand until a goldsmith banker exchanged it with his notes and finally swapped the stick with the tax receiver for coins – a full three years after the initial issue of the tally.

Paying with receipts of fictitious cash remittances worked, but not for long. The tally sticks started being discounted at every exchange until finally being exchanged for silver or gold coins: as the sticks moved from hand to hand, they became worth less. Eventually, a banker would acquire them at a heavy discount with his own promises to pay – bank notes – and would wait for the designated receiver to have enough tax revenues to be able to exchange coins for the sticks. So, bankers grew richer, the holders of the tallies poorer, and unfunded public debt simply grew and grew. As the worth of tallies declined, so too did the willingness of merchants and citizens to accept them as payments.

For years, the utilisation of wooden sticks had proven useful, but the system was in crisis.

Parliament Takes Charge

And things got worse: English public finances were set for further great upheaval. After the Glorious Revolution of 1688 – the deposition of James II, and his replacement by his daughter Mary II and her husband, William III of Orange – all expenditure, tax and borrowing was to be sanctioned by the now sovereign Parliament. The Nine Years' War (1688–1697) – that epic conflict, sometimes described as the first global war, fought in Europe, North America and India, between France and a European coalition including England, Spain, Portugal, the Holy Roman Empire, the great Dutch Republic and the Duchy of Savoy – then put incredible demands on the new Parliament's finances. Before the war, public expenditure had been around £2 million a year. By the end of the war, expenditure had tripled to almost £6 million and public borrowing was forced to keep pace with expenditure: between 1688 and 1697, state borrowing rose to over £32 million.

Expenditure was spiralling, taxes could not keep up with borrowing, the tally cutter was working overtime, the discount on tallies kept increasing, and yet all the while goldsmiths, banks and the finance houses continued to trade in tallies to make their profits. Something had to change.

And it did – with the founding of the Bank of England in 1694.

The Bank of England and the Projecting Age

The Bank of England was one of the great inventions of the seventeenth century, the age of the *grand project*. In his 1697 book *An Essay Upon Projects*, Daniel Defoe, the author of *Robinson Crusoe*, merchant, pamphleteer and the man responsible for first identifying Dame Credit as the true sister of money, described his century as the great 'Projecting Age', a period in which innovators from various walks of life were busy proposing projects for every conceivable purpose. Defoe himself promoted projects for highways, banks, pension offices, academies for women and mutual societies. He wrote in praise – and with some scepticism – of the inventors of diving bells, turnpikes, windmill-makers, stock traders and bank promoters. One such 'pedlar', 'tub-preacher' and 'whimsical projector' was an ingenious, charismatic Scot named William Paterson. It was Paterson who masterminded the creation of the Bank of England.

Paterson was a man of his age, a visionary and a buccaneer. Early in his career, he had travelled to the West Indies, where he had set up as a trader. He later became the promoter and projector of both the Hampstead Water Company and the failed Scottish attempt to colonise Panama. The Bank of England was by far his most ambitious and successful scheme.

Subscribing to the shares of the Bank of England.

By the late 1600s, the British nation was facing serious problems: revolutions and wars require massive reserves of cash, and the state desperately needed to be able to benefit from the business of banking and the trading of public debt. Paterson had some interesting thoughts on how to solve these problems.

Between 1691 and 1694, he submitted three different schemes to Parliament designed to secure long-term public borrowing funded by future cash flows. All three schemes revolved around the same basic structure: the Treasury would guarantee a steady stream of future tax revenues to a fund managed by Trustees, the Trustees would then borrow money against the future cash flows, and with that money they would make big up-front payments to the government. Paterson had made all the necessary calculations: the Trustees could pay the Exchequer £1 million in exchange for £65,000 of tax revenues a year. Trustees would raise permanent capital with a loan. They would not return the principal to the lenders; they would only pay them interest with the cash from the Exchequer. If the lenders wanted the principal back, they would have to sell the shares in the market. Paterson had found a way of introducing permanent public debt to England.

The idea was not new – the Republic of Genoa had done the same when it set up the Compagnia di San Giorgio in 1390 – but it was certainly ingenious. When Paterson submitted his schemes to the new Parliament, the Exchequer turned them down not once, not twice, but three times.

Not a man easily discouraged, Paterson sought help and advice. Michael Godfrey was a financier with widespread support in the City: he had access to capital. Charles Montague was the Chancellor of the Exchequer, and an influential networker. Both Godfrey and Montague believed there was merit in Paterson's idea, but they suggested a few changes. Most notably, Godfrey advised Paterson that it would be a better idea to raise permanent capital by selling equity in some kind of corporation. The corporation would then lend its whole capital to the Exchequer. It was a simple but profound adjustment to Paterson's original scheme: risk capital was available in London, and many members of the moneyed class were sitting in Parliament; a chartered corporation that sold shares in its equity would be sure to attract both money and much general support. Subscribers would have to pay coins for their share of the equity, but the corporation would not have to pay coins to the state: it would simply provide its own promises to pay in the form of bank notes and the coins would stay in the corporation's coffers in order to be able to swap notes for coins on demand.

Paterson's amended scheme was a winner. Parliament approved it as part of the Tonnage Act of 1694, which had the aim of raising new taxes of £1.5 million and authorised borrowing on those taxes of £1.2 million. Instead of borrowing from the public, the state would be borrowing from a corporation that had been funded by selling its own equity to the public. The corporation's charter, blessed by Parliament, spelled out the privileges and obligations of the new corporate entity and of the state: the agreement was to expire in 1705, when the Exchequer had to pay back the loan. If Parliament wanted to withdraw the charter before 1705, it had to settle the debt with the corporation first.

The corporation was permitted 'to trade in gold and silver bullion, to deal in bills of exchange and to loan on pledges and on mortgages'. Shareholders in the bank could transfer or sell their shares on the market, and they seemed like a good opportunity for profit. Godfrey began taking subscriptions for the corporation on June 21, 1694. The King was one of the first to purchase shares. By July 2, investors had subscribed all the £1.2 million, and had paid 60 per cent of the capital in gold and silver. The corporation could start operations. The corporation's charter was approved by Parliament on July 24 and sealed on July 27. The following week, the shareholders selected the board of directors, known as the General Court. The corporation – the Bank of England – was in business.

In the first week of business, the Court met daily to set up operations. The directors chose a place of business, hired key personnel and established procedures. The Exchequer then demanded its money and the new bank duly obliged, paying the whole £1.2 million with sealed notes by the end of 1694.

Exchequer Tallies and the Bank of England

Many contemporary observers thought the project would fail spectacularly. The plan was sketchy. The partners had executed it in a hurry. Public offices got a lot of notes within a short time, and spent them right away. All that debt would sink the fledgling start-up. But – against the odds – the scheme worked.

The standard popular histories of the bank tend to claim that it was simply trust and credit that enabled Paterson's experiment to succeed. In reality, the bank owed its success to exactly how the Exchequer and the directors structured and executed their early trades: using tallies.

Parliament had chartered the bank to execute a simple trade: to exchange public debt for bank debt. But subscribers had paid only 60 per cent of the share price when they signed up, meaning the directors had just £720,000 in coins to back their promises of £1.2 million. In banking, assets and liabilities need to balance. If not, the systems of trust and credit soon break down. As shown in the previous chapter, Venice took pains to make sure every debt on the ledger of Banco Giro had a corresponding asset. So how did the directors of this new Bank of England balance their books?

There was only one public debt security capable of meeting the needs of the directors: tallies. To understand exactly how this system worked and how English public debt became money, the evidence of the tallies is crucial. Alas, very few of the actual tallies survive today. Public creditors only returned the sticks when they got their coins back and the Exchequer stored all of the returned sticks in the cellars of the House of Parliament, most of which were destroyed in a fire in October 1834. Some of the few surviving tallies are locked away in a long wooden case in the vault at the Bank of England's Museum.

There are thirty-nine in all: they cover a period between 1694 and 1816. Miraculously, six of the thirty-nine tallies relate to that first trade for £1.2 million between the Exchequer and the bank. Most of the tallies are fragments, but one of them is almost complete, and readable. The inscriptions, in Latin, are clear and succinct. In a few lines, the official tally cutter sums up the very first trade between the corporation and the English state:

> From the governor and Company of the Bank of England part of twelve hundred thousand pounds (L 1,200,000) payable by them for securing certain recompenses and advantages mentioned in a certain act of parliament of the 5th and 6th year of William and Mary, by the hands of the commissioners appointed to receive subscription towards the sum of the said payment, in full payment of L 300,000 by them first received. /england [sic]
> *Easter (Exchequer term) 1 September, 6 William and Mary.*

With the evidence of the tallies, we can begin to reassemble the pieces of that first deal. As discussed, on July 27, 1694, Parliament approved the corporation's charter. We know that on the same day, Montague, the Chancellor of the Exchequer, responded to the most pressing needs: the navy had asked for £24,000; gunmakers £5,000; the Irish army £3,000. The army fighting on the continent wanted much more: £80,000. Montague therefore demanded bank debts amounting to a total of £112,000.

The bank directors had to balance their books: they needed assets in hand in order to issue the debts. So, the tally cutter cut five tallies – four for £25,000 each and one for £12,000. The tallies went straight to the bank. Usually, under the old system, as with Richard de la Pole, the old Royal Butler back in the fourteenth century, the Exchequer would give the tally to a public officer in charge of procurements. The public officer would then give the stick to a supplier, and the supplier would exchange it with the notes of a banker, and the banker would finally exchange the tally with the tax receiver for coins. One of the problems with this system was that each time the tally changed hands, the holder had to trade, and the tally lost value. But now, the Exchequer simply exchanged the sticks for notes, at once and at par. And then the bank, when asked, would exchange its notes for coins. The state lost none of its purchasing power in the straight tally-for-notes exchange and the bank got paid a fee to manage the swap, a fee that covered the risks and costs of banking – efficient, and worthwhile for all concerned.

On August 1, the General Court met at the bank's new headquarters to keep its part of the bargain. In order to meet the Exchequer's

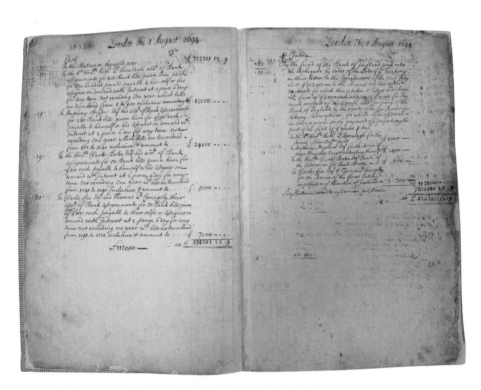

The first page of the general cash book of the bank, July 27, 1694.

demands, they agreed to issue sealed interest-bearing notes. Some directors had favoured issuing notes that paid no interest, but the board wanted to keep the notes in circulation and not have to redeem them with their few coins in the coffers. Paying interest seemed the best way to induce their holders to hang on to the notes for as long as possible. Further, to discourage counterfeiting, the notes were numbered and the beneficiaries named. Once all of these details were agreed, the Court ordered the cashier to enter the trade on the first page of the ledger, a trade that set the pattern for over 300 years of transactions between the Bank and the English state.

We can see here the fine details of that first deal. The single page shows the two faces – assets and liabilities – opposite each other. The five tallies received – the assets – appear on the right folio. The liabilities – the bank notes – appear on the left: 1,120 notes for £100 each. Lord Ranelagh, the Commissioner of the army, received the first 800 notes. Antony Stevens, the commissioner of the navy, got the next 240. Charles Bertie, the head of the ordnance department, ended up with fifty, and Charles Fox, of the Irish army, got his hands on thirty.

It's just numbers in a ledger, but it is an absolutely historic deal.

As in Venice in 1619, the bank had made money out of public debt, exchanging its own promises with the promises to pay of the state. For the state, exchanging tallies for notes directly with the bank was a better use of tallies than the age-old custom of paying for goods and services with the sticks. The Exchequer exchanged tallies wholesale, at par, and the debt securities it received had the purchasing power of coins: the tallies had become bank money. Public offices had got their £1.2 million in purchasing power for an equal amount of public debt, and each party to the trade had got something out of the deal. The Exchequer got more money, at no loss; the bank got fees and the right to conduct the business of banking. Paterson's scheme had worked.

Many transactions followed. Government offices spent the notes as soon as they got them. Some of the notes came back immediately to the bank in exchange for gold and silver, but most circulated for longer, adding to the quantity of money in England, pleasing both merchants and consumers. The shareholders of the bank were happy, too – they had paid coins for only 60 per cent of their stake but now received the benefits of 100 per cent of their share of equity. Everyone was a winner.

Fractional Reserve Banking

And winners like to win. The bank notes continued circulating and some of the coins from the corporation's subscribers stayed in the coffers. These coins were a great temptation to the bank's new board of directors. They knew they could use them to issue interest-free notes, reaping even greater profits. There were plenty of tallies in private hands and issuing bank notes was a cheap way to finance assets. The board wanted to profit from the abundance of outstanding public debt by swapping the sticks in the hands of the public for more promises to pay from the bank. They knew that if they were to swap private tallies for bank debt, the bank could grow its business and profits.

The only problem was, the original charter of the corporation prevented them from doing so. Members of the legislature did not want the bank to practise what is now called fractional reserve banking, in which only a fraction of a bank's deposits are backed by the cash available in its vaults. They viewed the practice as dangerous to the safety of a public bank. Parliament had therefore limited the amount of debt the bank could issue to £1.2 million – the exact and entire capital of the bank – to ensure that the assets, capital and liabilities all matched. The Exchequer and the court disagreed with the legislators. The court viewed exchanging bank debt for public debt as the best way to grow the bank income and profits. Chancellor of the Exchequer Montague wanted more tallies in the vaults, where they would stay put until the bank turned them over to the tax receivers, meaning the sticks would not depreciate further in value; tallies were good assets for a financial institution only as long as their price was stable. And finally, consumers, businesses and public offices wanted an end to the scarcity of money; they wanted means of payment with the same purchasing power of gold or silver coins from the Mint.

Basically, everyone wanted the bank to issue debts for more than its capital, and far in excess of the coin reserve. The court saw its opportunity and moved fast. On August 8, 1694, the board of directors approved printing notes for 'the use of the house'. Soon after, the bank issued notes for £500,000 more than its total capital. It was a bold move. Some doubts were raised. But the Exchequer lobbied Parliament and, as it turned out, the charter's wording was rather dense and ambiguous, which meant that Parliament could not stop the bank from issuing debt for more than its capital and more than the coins in its coffers. The directors, free to issue more debt, now turned their attention to the assets they needed in order to do so – the existing tallies already in private hands.

Safe Sticks, Safe Debts

At a meeting of the court, the directors debated which tallies were a good asset for their purposes. They knew that different tallies had different values – and that over the years, kings had issued plenty of tallies without Parliamentary approval. Could they really be a proper and reliable asset for the newly founded Bank of England? It was a delicate issue, at the heart of political, financial and constitutional debate. The directors knew they needed to make their position clear: which tallies would they accept, and why? On August 30, 1694, the Court told the *London Gazette* that the bank would only accept tallies that represented 'a credit on loans by acts of Parliament'. It was a smart move: the bank had effectively sided with its biggest client and regulator, Parliament.

But the 'right' authority alone was not enough to make a tally safe enough to be a good asset. Even Parliament-approved tallies entailed risk and traded at different prices. The court therefore set strict guidelines on which tallies they would accept as security. As a general rule, the directors favoured 'sin taxes', those that resulted from the purchase of tobacco and alcohol – they allowed a high £660,000 limit on tallies supported by wine and tobacco taxes. (Interestingly, they were rather more sceptical about the revenues of the East India Company – they would discount no more than £460,000 worth of tallies backed by the Company's duties.) No one in the court opposed swapping Exchequer tallies for the bank's promises to pay. And the Exchequer was very keen indeed for the bank to get as many tallies as possible out of circulation; tallies were a solution, but they were also a problem.

Why? To take another tally as an example: one of the surviving sticks in the Bank of England's Museum dates from early in 1695. The Exchequer had issued the tally to a citizen who bought annuities. Traditionally, the English state had sold annuities to finance government expenditures. An individual would make a payment to the Exchequer. In return, the state promised them a fixed sum every year for the rest of their life, or for the life of a designated individual. Investors could buy annuities for one, two or three lives. The state would continue paying the beneficiary as long as one of the selected individuals was alive. For the owner of the annuity, the odds of receiving payments for longer were better. For the state, it meant more money up front, but the obligation to make payments lasted longer. To balance the interest of the two parties, annuities for more than one life carried different interests. Annuity on one life carried a 14 per cent interest per year, two lives 12 per cent, and three lives 10 per cent. At the time, most European sovereigns borrowed by selling annuities, but the practice in England was unique.

When the individual bought an annuity, he received the stock of a tally. The investors' ability to exchange the tallies with coins directly with the tax receivers made the English annuities a reasonably safe investment. If the annuity's beneficiary wanted to swap the future stream of payments with cash up-front, he could simply exchange the stick for bank notes or coins. Both before and after 1694, the Exchequer sold millions of pounds' worth of annuities – but these kept changing hands, and in the process lowered the sticks' market value. The Exchequer was therefore very happy to see them stored in the vaults of the bank, where they could wait to be cashed.

The Charter Renewed

By the end of 1696, the bank held tallies for no less than £3.3 million. But the assets on its books – other than public debt – amounted to only £121,000. The bank had effectively made money out of public debt. The trouble was, it simply could not buy enough sticks to raise the price of existing public debt to the Exchequer's satisfaction; in 1697, tallies traded at a discount of more than 40 per cent of their face value, the bank had already issued a lot of notes in order to get tallies, and these notes were changing hands for 20 per cent less than their face value. The bank was profitable – it was continuing to pay high dividends to its subscribers, but the alchemy of banking was not working quite as the state might have hoped.

So, the Treasury leaned on the bank to sell more shares in its equity by purchasing the tallies in private hands. Public creditors would be able to buy equity with their tallies and thus share in the bank's profits – and the price of tallies would increase. But the bank's directors did not want to short-change existing shareholders, so they negotiated and drove a hard bargain. Eventually, the state and the bank reached a compromise: the bank agreed to sell new equity for £1 million, with new shareholders able to pay for their shares with 80 per cent in tallies and 20 per cent in bank notes.

It was a good deal for both the holders of tallies and the holders of bank notes, but perhaps not so much for the state. In order to do the deal, the bank's original shareholders had extracted major concessions from Parliament. On June 24, 1697, Parliament extended the bank's charter for five years. The amended charter gave the bank a stronger monopoly on banking, at least in London. The new charter also increased the government's yearly payments to the corporation. However, by September 1697, the discount of bank notes to coins was just 1 per cent – and by the beginning of the new year, it was gone. So, shareholders could anticipate fat dividends, the price of the bank's stock rose, the state was profiting, and more bank money could fuel economic growth – the alchemy of banking was working for everyone again.

The Treasury Challenges the Bank

By the beginning of the eighteenth century, two institutions were creating money in England. The public mint made coins with silver and gold bullion; the Bank of England made money by swapping debts with the state. Parliament was grateful to the Bank for exchanging tallies with bank notes at par because the notes had the purchasing power of gold coins from the Mint, and the price of existing public debt securities was stable. Public finance was on the mend.

Still, Parliament was reluctant to give the Bank of England a complete monopoly on creating money from public debt. Creating money is, after all, one of the state's essential prerogatives. In 1707, Parliament therefore asked the Exchequer for a plan to make public debt work as money, without asking for help from the Bank of England. Tallies did not work well as money: they were strong claims on future tax revenues, but the sticks did not have the purchasing power of coins – only the debts of banks had that. So, the Exchequer basically decided to copy the notes of the bank and issue its own Exchequer bills – essentially, bank money without a bank.

This was not the first time the Exchequer had tried to function as a bank. Attempts to issue debts that could work as money had failed in 1672 and 1696. A third try in 1697 had fared rather better. The Exchequer had arranged for a consortium of private financiers to cash its own bills on demand, for a fee – in effect, creating a bank without bank notes. The government issued close to £2.7 million of these Exchequer bills, which circulated as well as the notes from the Bank of England. The experiment not only worked – better still, it did not break the law. The charter amendment in 1697 may have given the Bank of England a monopoly on the issuing of bank notes in London, meaning that competitors could not issue their own bank notes, but they could still cash the Exchequer bills. By issuing its own bills, it looked very much as though the Exchequer was nurturing a rival to the newly formed bank.

It was the War of the Spanish Succession – triggered by the death of the childless Habsburg King Charles II of Spain in 1700, which led to a struggle for control of the Spanish Empire and drew Spain, Austria, France, the Dutch Republic, Savoy and Great Britain into conflict – that rescued the Bank of England and guaranteed its long-term fortune. The English had fielded a large army on the continent. The campaign, led by the Duke of Marlborough, was successful, but hideously expensive. The Exchequer doubted whether private financiers had enough coins for the costly war. The best solution was to once again strike a deal with the Bank of England. The bank's directors agreed to exchange Exchequer bills with bank notes, but not with coins. The Exchequer believed the proposal could work; bank money was, after all, now widely accepted at par with coins. And so, the bank and the Exchequer agreed to swap tallies for bank debts once more.

In March 1707, tallies for £1.5 million were cut and delivered to the bank as security for the loan. In exchange, the bank would cash the Exchequer's bills on demand. The execution of the trade copied the first transaction of 1694. After the Exchequer delivered the tallies to the bank, the bank had the assets to issue enough debts to cash the Exchequer's bills. And of course the bank got paid well to create this money out of public debt: the Treasury agreed to pay the bank 4.5 per cent interest on Exchequer bills cashed at the bank.

The government kisses the bank.

The directors wanted more. They wanted no more rivals, state-sanctioned or otherwise. They wanted a guaranteed monopoly on banking. Parliament agreed. The bank's new amended charter banned:

> any body politic or corporate whatsoever, erected or to be erected (other than the said Governor and Company of the Bank of England) or for any other person whatsoever, united or to be united in covenants or partnerships exceeding the number of six persons, in that part of Great Britain called England, to borrow, owe or take up any sum or sums of money on their bills or notes payable at demand, or at any less time that six months from the borrowing thereof.

Only the Royal Bank of Scotland, the Bank of England's northern sibling founded in 1697, was exempt.

The 1707 loan, like that of 1694, was never returned and the tallies stayed with the bank. Again, one of these tallies has survived in the bank's vaults as evidence. At 7 feet, 2 inches long, it has fifty notches, each representing £1,000: a debt of the Exchequer to the bank for £50,000. The stick is a witness to the trade that guaranteed the future of the Bank of England and sealed the dominance of bank money as the national currency of England, and is witness to the English government's admission that its debts could not compete with those of the bank as money.

The English Disease

In the end, the trade between Parliament and the bank wasn't about pounds, shillings, and pence. It was about the sovereign power to create money. Using the alchemy of banking to make money with public debt proved a great benefit to the state and to its citizens, and over many centuries the tallies worked their magic. Businesses exchanged promissory notes and bills of exchange with bank debt. Merchants and citizens deposited their coins to get bank debts. The bank made money from the obligations of consumers, businesses and the government. And so the debts of the Bank of England became a true national currency, the problem of the centuries-old scarcity of money was finally solved and the country prospered.

But as we've seen before, the system of exchanging public debt for bank debt has its drawbacks.

In England, it was public spending alone that drove the money supply of the nation. For several years, the only assets on the books of the bank were the tallies, and bank money made solely out of sovereign debt is fragile. Plus, the growth of public debt encouraged the bank to make more money that the economy could use, making the bank yet more vulnerable. The following three centuries certainly proved that though bank money is convenient, it is not always safe, and that dividing the power to make money between the state and banks requires constant vigilance and continual adjustments to find the best trade-off between safe money and the adequate supply of money.

As we shall see again – in America, in Russia and elsewhere – the problems faced by the English were also faced by others.

CHAPTER 4

Neapolitan Charity:
The Good Bank is the Bank
that Doesn't Pay

If it is true that a good bank is one which does not pay, it is also true that an accredited bank is one which is not unwilling to pay.

Ferdinando Galiani
Della Moneta (*On Money*)
trans. Peter R. Toscano (1751; 1977)

THE BANKING CHARITIES OF NAPLES are unique financial institutions, quite unlike anything else in the history of finance, just as Naples is quite unlike any other city in modern Italy. In early modern Naples – which was then the largest city in Europe, after Constantinople – there developed a peculiar type of bank money which was neither a simple inscription on a ledger, as we have seen in Venice, nor a bank note, as in England. Tracing the development of this unique bank money and the history of Naples's banking charities is like walking the narrow, crowded streets of Naples itself: thrilling, fascinating, occasionally bewildering, a story of multiple twists and turns and populated by unlikely characters and canny operators who tested the very limits of what was possible in finance, both practically and theoretically. Examining in detail the ledgers of these banks – extant today in one of the most extraordinary archives in the world – illustrates how bank debt can be essential to the prosperity of both a state and its citizens, and also illustrates some of the risks involved in public debt financing.

As we have seen, public banks exchange public debt for their own, enabling the institutions of the state to make payments with those bank debts. The banking charities of Naples are a particularly interesting example of this practice, because over many years a number of different regimes governed the Kingdom of Naples and the banking charities were there to support them all, even after the Kingdom became part of the new Italian state in 1861 and different regimes once again rose and fell. Over the years, the Spanish Empire, the democratic republics, the fascists, they *all* exchanged public debt for the debts of the banking charities. The story of the so-called 'good banks' of Naples is therefore both unique and indicative, an extraordinarily long-lived experiment from which perhaps we can all learn.

But in order to get to Naples, we must start in Rome.

The Warrior Pope

In the early 1500s the Catholic Church, as so often, was in chaos, split between reformers and traditionalists. A few rebellious cardinals, supported by Louis XII, King of France, had met in Pisa in September 1511 in an attempt to undermine the authority of Pope Julius II. In response, in 1512, Julius – Giulio, Giuliano della Rovere, the Warrior Pope, the archetypal warrior-statesman, who had personally commanded a number of bloody campaigns against rebellious republics and the French – fought back by convening an ecumenical council, the Fifth Lateran Council, held at the Lateran Palace in Rome.

At the very first session of the council, on May 10, 1512, the battle lines were clearly drawn. Giles of Viterbo, an Augustinian ally of Julius, delivered a fierce address attacking the various evils of the Church and the schismatic cardinals. At the second session, a week later, the quasi-council at Pisa was roundly condemned and all its decisions declared null and void.

The battle between reformers and traditionalists at the contentious Council – which lasted for five years, until 1517, outlasting Julius II and extending into the reign of his successor, Pope Leo X – was not just a matter of theological niceties or a clash of personalities. Many of the arguments raging at the time related, inevitably, to money. The Dominicans, for example (motto: *'Benedicere, Laudare, Praedicare'* – to pray, to bless, and to preach) were embroiled in a long-running argument with the Franciscans (motto: *'Pax et bonum'* – peace and the good) about the matter of renting coins. The outcome of this argument – what might at first appear to be rather recherché – was to determine the shape of banks and banking for centuries to come, and in particular the development of a unique kind of bank, the so-called 'good banks', the banking charities. In order to understand the genesis of these extraordinary institutions, we must stay awhile in Rome and with the factious Fifth Lateran Council.

The Monti: Renting Coins

The Franciscans had a long tradition of sponsoring charitable financial institutions. Their method was admirably simple: Franciscan charities would collect coins from the wealthy and pious and would lend them, free of charge, to the deserving poor, those who had fallen on hard times, the old, the disabled and the sick. While they waited for the deserving poor to come and collect the coins, the charities would literally and metaphorically pile the coins into mounds, which gave the institutions their name: *Monti di Pietà* (*Mounds of Compassion*).

By the early fifteenth century, Franciscan congregations had established Monti di Pietà in many cities. The system everywhere was simple and the same: the coins came in and the Monti loaned them out. As demand for the coins increased, the size of the mounds decreased; there were never enough coins to go round. More and more communities wanted more and more coins for their sick artisans, their unemployed labourers and their small farmers who had suffered a bad harvest – or whatever other temporary misfortune – and who were in a position both to both borrow and return the coins. Demand outstripped supply. So, at the Fifth Lateran Council, the Franciscans asked to be allowed to charge the borrowers of the coins a small fee. They also wanted to reward the businessmen and wealthy members of the community who deposited their coins with them, thus enabling the stacks of coins to grow again: a truly virtuous circle, or mound. So the Franciscan argument went.

There was only one problem. At the time, the Catholic Church deemed lending at interest to be usury: a mortal sin.

> And if ye lend to them of whom ye hope to receive, what thank have ye? For sinners also lend to sinners, to receive as much again. But love ye your enemies, and do good, and lend, hoping for nothing again; and your reward shall be great, and ye shall be the children of the Highest: for he is kind unto the unthankful and to the evil. (Luke 6: 34–35.)

The front page of *La Tabula della Salute*. A pamphlet by Marco da Montegallo on the Monte di Pietà. The stack of coins rules the scene.

Charging borrowers was forbidden. What the Franciscans were seeking was essentially an exemption from these rules and interdictions for their brand of what we would now call microfinance. The growing number of deserving poor, they argued, deserved financial help and theirs was an elegant and effective solution. The Dominicans, on the other hand, among others, strongly opposed weakening the prohibition against usury – a sin, they argued, is a sin.

The Franciscans had a ready comeback. They argued that the income from lending coins was not really interest at all; it was, rather, a *rent* paid by the borrower to the Monti for the temporary use of the coins. They granted that charging interest on a loan may have been usury and a sin, but charging someone a rent for the temporary use of one's property was not. In order to establish their point, the Franciscans argued that lending coins in fact consisted of not one transaction, but two. The first transaction consisted of the giving of the coin: this transaction was entirely gratuitous and not a loan at all; of course, no one should charge for a gratuitous act. But the second transaction in this exchange consisted of allowing the borrower to use the coin as they pleased: this use, the Franciscans argued, should not be free of charge. The Monti should be able to charge a small rent to the borrower to be able to use the coins received however and howsoever they pleased.

This was devilishly clever. (William of Ockham, lest we forget – famous for his *lex parsimoniae*, the heuristic Occam's razor – was a Franciscan.) But the logic of the Franciscans extended even further. They applied their reasoning not only to the borrowers but also to the depositors. Deposits, they argued, also consisted of two transactions: safekeeping and use. The safekeeping of the coin should be free, of course, but the Monti should be able to pay the depositor for the use of the coin while in its possession; this was only fair.

The Dominicans completely rejected these arguments – which are either entirely specious or utterly brilliant, depending on your point of view. Fortunately for the Franciscans, the Lateran Council clearly admired the brilliance and sheer audacity of their assertions;

An illustration from a medieval, fifteenth-century manuscript, showing customers with their account books.

the Dominicans lost the case and in his Papal Bull *Inter multiplices* of May 4, 1515, Leo X blessed the renting of coins and the charging of a fee by the Monti.

At first, rents were charged on the coins, not to earn profits for the Monti but merely to cover their operating expenses – this was not usury, after all – but it is just a short step from charging rent for coins at no profit to the exchanging of promises to pay with customers and establishing a fully functioning banking system. And soon the Monti di Pietà did indeed became banks – the 'good banks'. And among the good banks, it was the banking charities of Naples who were the best example of their kind.

Un pezzo di cielo caduto in terra

And so at last from Rome – the eternal city, home to theological debate – to Naples, the great siren city, '*un pezzo di cielo caduto in terra*' (a piece of Heaven fallen upon earth), according to Jacopo Sannazaro, the great Neapolitan poet and epigrammist. Naples, with its narrow, crowded streets, the great beauty of the Bay, of Ischia and Capri. Naples, renowned for the many opportunities that it once afforded sailors and foreigners, and known forever for its poverty, corruption and misgovernment. Naples, a place of wonder and delight, filthy, crowded and depraved. (It was after the cholera epidemic of 1884 that the then-Prime Minister of Italy Depretis declared that Naples should be disembowelled – *Bisogna sventrare Napoli*.) 'The foreigner knows a great deal about Naples without visiting it,' writes Peter Gunn in his *Naples: A Palimpsest* (1961), 'the view of the bay, the music, in turn both lively and sentimental; the flamboyance of its colour; the poverty and slums […] he knows something of its chequered history.'

A reminder of the history: Spain had annexed the Kingdom of Naples in 1507 and the city of Naples became the center of public administration, finance and commerce. From 1507 until the end of Spanish rule in 1707, the Kingdom of Naples was run by a Viceroy sent from Madrid with the assistance of a locally elected council. As Naples grew as a city and as a centre of government and administration, people left the countryside to live and work there, the process of urbanisation thereby accelerated, and inevitably there was a rise in

Naples's population of the unemployed, the unskilled and the poor. And the city's religious institutions and charities were keen to help in any way they could.

There were seven great benevolent associations in Naples: three of them ran hospitals; two of them cared for orphans from poor families; and two of them, the Monte di Pietà and Monte dei Poveri, rented coins to the deserving poor. All of them needed coins to pay for their work. As Naples continued to develop and expand, and the population ever increased, the demand for coins grew even greater – and soon, the seven charities ran out of coins. Merchant bankers were numerous in Naples, but they catered only to the wealthy businessmen. They were no help. So, the charities decided to borrow a trick or two from the merchant bankers, once again challenging the status quo, just as the Franciscans had at the Fifth Lateran Council.

The seven charities petitioned the Spanish authorities for licences to establish banks of deposit, issue and circulation. Basically, they wanted to add a banking business to the renting of coins. And the Spanish authorities granted these licences – a small gesture by the Spanish, but with enormous consequences for the charities. Strengthened and enabled, they could now not only accept the deposit of coins, but they could also, much more importantly, issue bank debt – promises that had the purchasing power of coins. We have seen already what this sort of power can enable banks to do – and what the banking charities of Naples did was truly remarkable.

The charitable institutions were now effectively running two kinds of banks. One was the traditional Monti that rented coins to the deserving poor – all well and good. The other kind of bank was now operating not only as a place of deposit but also with the power of debt issue. This bank started attracting an entirely different kind of customer: not the deserving poor, but Naples's affluent society, the city's professionals, merchants and craftsmen. For these new customers, the new bank provided a useful payment system: they didn't want the bank to keep their coins safe; they became clients of the bank to be able to make payments with ease and security and without losing purchasing power. Indeed, in doing so, they could actually gain purchasing power, since the banking charities could make more promises to pay than the value of the coins that clients deposited with them. So, more coins came in, meaning that the Monti got more coins to rent out to the deserving poor, and more promises were exchanged with the bank's new customers. The two banking businesses became mutually sustaining and supportive. The Monti not only got more coins to rent to the deserving poor, but the valuables that secured the loan of those coins – such as precious metals and other artefacts – acted as good assets for the bank. If the borrower did not return the coins, the Monti sold the assets for cash at auctions, securing them another source of profit. And for the banks, issuing promises to pay to their new, wealthier clients was a good way to finance assets that in turn yielded yet more income and capital gains. The charities found that they could help the poor *and* earn profits at the same time. It was a kind of miracle. In Naples, piety and greed seemed to mix well. Perhaps Naples was an exception. Perhaps not.

Don Juan's Warrant

The Spanish authorities certainly understood the advantages of this new type of bank, both for the Kingdom of Naples and for the wider Empire. In 1580, Don Juan De Zuniga, the Spanish Viceroy in Naples, confirmed by royal warrant the banking privileges of the Annunziata, one of the city's seven charities. The Spanish authorities, Don Juan wrote, issuing the warrant himself, approved the bank receiving coins from those who wanted to spend them. The authorities also approved the bank's issuing its own debt to those clients, so that they could continue to make promises to pay, over and over again.

Don Juan was smart. He knew that the Spanish Empire could benefit from an institution that made money by exchanging promises to pay. He also understood that the charities' promises to pay could replace the silver coins that were then the only legal tender in Naples. Coins were scarce throughout the Kingdom. Silver was worth more as a commodity on the world market than as coined money in the provinces of the Kingdom, so the coins inevitably left to go where they were valued more, which meant that economic activities and tax revenues suffered in Naples due to the lack of coins. Don Juan hoped that the debts of the banking charities could supply the means of payment that citizens and public officials desperately needed – and so the great Spanish Empire would benefit from the charitable institutions at least as much as the deserving poor of Naples. It was a case of the state supporting the banks in order to support the state: a win–win. We will return later to the long-running problem of the desperate lack of silver coins in Naples, but Don Juan's warrant was the very beginning of a close partnership between the banking charities and the state that lasted, in many shapes and forms, for more than four centuries. And there is one man who understood that partnership better than any other.

The Foulest Man of his Century

Naples has produced many of Italy's greatest thinkers and writers, including Giambattista Vico, author of *Scienza Nuova* (1725). It has also produced an extraordinary glut of brilliant economists, among them Carlo Antonio Broggia, author of *Trattato de' tributi, delle monete, e del governo politico della sanità* (1743), which offers a complete theory of taxation; Giuseppe Palmieri, with his influential book, *Riflessioni sulla Publica Felicità relativamente al Regno di Napoli* (*Reflections on Public Happiness in the Kingdom of Naples*) (1788); Antonio Genovesi, the very first Professor of Political Economics at the University of Naples; and perhaps the very greatest of them all, Ferdinando Galiani, described by none other than Friedrich Nietzsche, in *Beyond Good and Evil* (1886), as 'the most profound, sharp-sighted and perhaps also the foulest man of his century'.

Ferdinando Galiani. The foulest man of his century.

Nietzsche was a profound contrarian and much given to exaggeration and hyperbole – Übermensch, the will to power, the death of God, etc. – and when he describes Galiani as 'the foulest man of his century' he was in fact offering words of praise rather than blame for Galiani's celebrated cynicism, which Nietzsche greatly admired, rather than as comment on any failings in Galiani's personal habits or character. (Though among his many weaknesses and vices, we do know that Galiani had a rather sweet tooth. He loved sweets, especially chocolate – and he bought his chocolate at the best chocolatiers in Naples. I know because I have seen the accounts. He seldom paid with coins, preferring bank debts.) Whatever his charms or lack thereof, Galiani was someone who understood the workings of the banks of Naples better than anyone before or since.

Born in 1728, the nephew of a cardinal, Galiani became the abbot of a monastery near Naples. But he cut a curious figure and did not fit well in the local curia: only four feet six in height, he was a *bon vivant* and carouser who liked to stay in bed till noon, eating his chocolate and entertaining guests with his wit and wisdom. A free-thinker, open to new ideas and cultural trends, his interests ranged from archaeology to politics, and in 1751, still in his early twenties, he published *Della moneta* (*On Money*), which established his international reputation. At the height of the Enlightenment, in 1759, he moved to Paris as Secretary of the Embassy of the Kingdom of Naples and became something of a sensation, befriending Diderot and the Encyclopedists.

Like a number of other notable writers and intellectuals of the time, including Jean-Jacques Rousseau, he also developed a long-standing relationship with the great *saloniste* Madame d'Épinay. Though he was the author of numerous works on a range of topics, it was *Della moneta* that not only secured Galiani's early fame, but also guaranteed his posthumous reputation, which spread well beyond the salons of the eighteenth century and indeed beyond Nietzsche's honourable – or dishonourable – mention.

Karl Marx, holed up in the British Library, for example, read *Della moneta* closely. He found many things he liked, quoting it in his *A Contribution to a Critique of Political Economy* (1859). In *Della moneta*, Galiani argued convincingly that only human toil gives value to goods. The most valuable wares are therefore those that require the most labour to make them. Gold and silver may represent and measure value, but they do not grant it. If this sounds familiar, it's because it was Galiani who forged one of the first labour theories of value, which Marx then developed as the premise for his own theory of capital.

Galiani was good on money, but he was absolutely brilliant on banks. He grasped intuitively how banks could and should function. He writes in Book IV of *On Money*: 'If it is true that a good bank is one which does not pay, it is also true that an accredited bank is one which is not unwilling to pay.' In other words, the financial institution that has to pay money to its clients will run too many risks, get overextended, run out of coins and ultimately fail. On the other hand, a bank that does not pay money is not forced to return the deposits to clients or its profits to shareholders; such a bank is much less likely to run into trouble and might then prove more useful to businesses and society without risking failures. Such an institution – generous, convenient and safe – is, in Galiani's terms, the definition of a 'good bank'.

The charitable banks of Naples, Galiani pointed out, were exactly these kinds of institutions. They did not pay money to either clients or shareholders. They did not return the coins deposited to their clients; instead, their clients exchanged their coins for the promises to

The chapel of the Sacro Monte dei Poveri with the arms of the De Santis family.

pay the institution, and made payments with them rather than with coins. Also, these banks did not pay dividends to their shareholders, the charities. The charities did not expect to make a profit from the banking business, so the institutions did not return any of their income. Instead, under the direction of the charities, they used the income to pursue worthy goals: the Monti rented coins to the deserving poor and the banks ran hospitals, hostels and hospices, as well as supporting other causes (such as ransoming Catholic citizens captured by Muslim pirates, or posting securities to free citizens who ended up in debtor prisons).

Galiani acknowledged that the banking charities of Naples were not the only banks that did not pay money. Indeed, the Bank of Hamburg, Bank of Amsterdam and Banco Giro did not return coins to depositors or pay dividends to their owners. But these banks were not as effective as the good banks of Naples because they were not profit-making organisations. They may not have *paid* money to their owners, but no money was *earned* either. Their lack of profits limited how much good they could do.

The banking charities of Naples were truly different. They worked hard to be profitable. They acquired assets that yielded income and profits and used those profits not to pay dividends but to support the community and the state. The banking charities were so good, so unusual, that they brought honour to the city of Naples, Galiani argued. (And Galiani was no great fan of Naples – he couldn't wait to leave the place, and when he was eventually recalled to Naples from Paris, he told friends that he had 'rejoined the vegetable kingdom'.) Other nations and communities should copy the example of Naples, he concluded.

Naples's banks were not only good in theory, or merely on the pages of Galiani's book – they *actually* worked. They operated for over four centuries and survived multiple shocks and stressors, including foreign occupations, wars, revolutions and various regime changes, the kinds of things that tend to wipe out even the most stable institutions. Come what may, the banking charities adjusted, adapted and formed partnerships with whoever and whatever was in charge: the Spanish Empire, the French, the republics and the Italian Kingdom. In 1861, the banking charities merged into a single institution, the Banco di Napoli, which remained fully owned by a charity until 1996, when it became a public company. Today, the Banco di Napoli is a commercial bank with the charity as one of the

The archives of the Fondazione Banco di Napoli: full of ledgers and stacks of credit pledges.

shareholders. And in the archives of the Fondazione Banco di Napoli lie the secrets to the intimate workings of the good banks.

Vedi Napoli e poi muori

You know the saying: see Naples and die. For most, this means seeing the bay of Naples, the grand vista that has inspired generations of artists. But for a few lucky people, like me, it means gaining access to the archives of the Banco di Napoli. In the centre of Naples, tucked away in a crumbling run-down baroque building, no fewer than 300 rooms are stacked from floor to ceiling with ledgers and documents, 500 years of history and evidence of the bank money of the good banks, gathered together in a single place. It is difficult to describe; I am a banker, not an artist. But take my word for it – it is simply incredible. Galiani himself would have swooned; rows upon rows upon rows of bank debt securities neatly stacked, one after another, waiting to be deciphered. In order to understand the work of the good banks, there is only one thing to do: examine the archives.

The bank money issued by the banking charities was different from that of the Banco Giro and the Bank of England. The debts of good banks did not circulate as entries in the ledger or as bank notes but as a peculiar type of debt security, credit pledges, which were widely used as a means of payment instead of coins and eventually deposited or cashed at one of the banking charities. For centuries, the clerks of the banking charities filed these debt securities issued to the clients as soon as these were returned to the bank. And this is what we have in the archives. We'll begin with a famous example.

Caravaggio's Money

In early October 1606, a young artist named Michelangelo Merisi arrived in Naples in the middle of the night. Merisi was a fugitive. He had left Rome in a hurry, a court of justice having sentenced him

Michelangelo Merisi da Caravaggio.

to death for killing a man in a swordfight. Officers of the law and friends of the man whom he had killed were out hunting for him; any citizen was authorised to kill him on sight; Merisi was not a man to be welcomed and entertained. And yet every art dealer and patron in Naples wanted to give him shelter and protection. Why? Because

Merisi was possessed of a peculiar talent. He wasn't just any old artist, he was a *great* artist. His unique combination of sacred subjects and profane figures and his innovative use of light was in high demand. He believed that in Naples, with his extraordinary skills and reputation, he would be safe and would find easy employment. He was absolutely right. With his *Sette opere di Misericordia* (*Seven Acts of Mercy*), painted in 1606, he became the first painter in Naples to be paid over 400 ducats for a single work, a small fortune at the time. So, this Michelangelo Merisi, this genius, this fugitive, who was he? He is, of course, better known today by the name of his home town – Caravaggio.

We can gain an insight into the substantial sums that Caravaggio managed to earn in Naples from the archives. We learn, for example, about a certain Nicolo Radolovich, who was a merchant from Ragusa (Dubrovnik), the merchant republic on the Adriatic coast of Croatia. Radolovich did a lot of business with the Kingdom of Naples and had resettled in Naples, where he wanted to gain acceptance into the local elite. Becoming a patron of the arts was then, as to some extent it is now, the best path to the top, providing easy access to society's elite. Radolovich was eager to commission a large oil painting from Caravaggio. He wanted him to paint the Virgin Mary with various saints around her in different poses. Caravaggio, in return, was eager to make money as quickly as possible, so he got to work feverishly and delivered Radolovich's painting.

The two entries in the ledger of the Banco di Sant'Eligio for the lost painting by Caravaggio. On October 6, 1606, Radolovich promises 200 ducats to the bank. The bank promises 200 ducats to Caravaggio.

Yet there is no trace of this painting. To all intents and purposes, it does not exist. But we know that it did exist, and that it was finished and delivered to Radolovich. We know because Caravaggio was paid with a 'credit pledge' of the Banco di Santo Spirito, the peculiar type of bank money issued by the banking charities, and because the evidence remains in the archive in Naples, to this day. The credit pledge was to be cashed by Caravaggio or deposited in his bank account *only* if the conditions for payment were met, if the painting was completed, and sure enough, in the ledger of the Banco di Sant' Eligio, there is an entry that shows that Caravaggio had cashed the pledge. (There was, in fact, no need for Caravaggio to cash the pledge, since most people in Naples accepted the credit pledges of the banking charities as readily as they accepted gold and silver coins. But since Caravaggio spent most of what he earned from his paintings in gambling dens and on women, it seems likely that they may have been less inclined to accept the credit pledges of the banking charities and that in order to purchase exactly what he wanted, whenever he wanted, he decided to cash the pledge.)

Radolovich was not the only patron who paid Caravaggio with a credit pledge by a bank. Another such patron was Tommaso De Franchis. We know that he commissioned several works from Caravaggio, including the masterpieces 'The Seven Acts of Mercy' and 'The Flagellation of Christ'. Tommaso belonged to an old, rich, powerful Neapolitan family, among them the great merchants, magistrates and directors of the banking charities. They were accustomed to using credit pledges to pay for goods and services and so, naturally, Tommaso paid Caravaggio in the same way. The actual pledges he used to pay Caravaggio do not survive, only the entries in the ledgers that show that Caravaggio cashed or deposited them. But a lot of the other pledges used by the De Franchis family have survived and these allow us to see in detail how this unique type of bank money worked.

The Rise – and Rise – of Credit Pledges

In the early seventeenth century, Antonio De Franchis ran the various De Franchis family businesses. He was the patriarch. He would usually make and receive payments in notes. The notes, handwritten on bank paper, were an instruction to the bank to make a payment. The note could circulate when endorsed, but was not in itself a debt of the bank; it was an obligation of Antonio's. Its acceptance relied on the trust that the recipient had in Antonio, not in the bank. The note was much like the modern cheque (though the cheque was not an invention of the banking charities, being already common in fourteenth-century Pisa).

Antonio liked the convenience of writing notes, but not their limited acceptance, so he often found himself paying with a pledge of credit, which functioned effectively like an IOU of the bank. We'll take just one pledge as an example: an elaborate document issued by the Banco dei Poveri, which reads: 'We, the Governors of the Banco dei Poveri, pledge to keep Antonio De Franchis as our creditor. He can do with his pledge as he pleases.' The pledge, with its bank seal and the cashier's signature, *was* a debt of the bank, i.e., true bank money.

The arms of the Banco dei Poveri (Bank for the Poor) in the ledger of the year 1600.

But it was not a bank note: it did not move from hand to hand, but from name to name. The bank paid only the legitimate holder of the pledge, not the bearer. The written endorsement and acceptance of both parties, payer and payee, was needed. And to keep track of these debts, the bank entered all transfers on special ledgers. Because of that, the pledges moved slowly but were safer than ordinary bank notes and increased the money supply in the Kingdom of Naples, allowing someone like Caravaggio, for example, to be able to charge clients and to be paid handsomely by the likes of the De Franchis family for his paintings. The ledgers of the banking charities record a few such payments made to Caravaggio by its clients and from him to various parties using credit pledges. As a means of payment, the pledges were perfect; they just worked.

The citizens of Naples had faith in pledges: the banking charities had effectively established their debts as money with a perfect balance of convenience and trust. At the beginning of the seventeenth century, Naples had about 260,000 residents and approximately 35,000 of them were clients of the banking charities. This means that around one seventh of the city's residents were being issued with the promises of bankers, with most of the rest of the Kingdom's citizens accepting them more than willingly. The pledges certainly added to the money supply of the Kingdom: the question is, exactly how much, and what were the other effects and consequences of their use?

Francesco Balletta from the University of Naples has spent a lifetime studying the circulation of the credit pledges issued by the public banks of Naples. His research spans over 200 years, from 1587–1806. In that period, according to Balletta, the exact quantity of credit pledges being issued by the banks grew and contracted, depending on events such as wars, rebellions, economic cycles, imperial policies, plagues, famines and so on, but in total the newly chartered bank holding charities issued vastly growing numbers of credit pledges. From 1607 to 1622, for example, the number of pledges issued by the Banco dei Poveri alone expanded more than seventyfold, from 4,742 to 343,038.

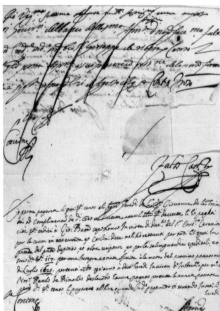

The pledge of credit in the 1600s.

And the value of all the pledges issued by the seven bank holding charities went from 47,000 ducats in 1587 to 7 million ducats in 1622. The growth was not steady – it lurched downward on occasion – but the overall trend was definitely upward. Bank money was being widely used in Naples as a means of payment.

Balletta also usefully estimated the metallic reserve of each bank and of the whole system of bank holding charities. These reserves fluctuated from a high of 55 per cent (1587) to a low of 8.34 per cent (1610), with an average rate of about 20 per cent the amount of circulating bank money. So, we know that the banks' promises to clients made up a large part of the Kingdom's total money supply. This had two main effects: firstly, bank money, using credit pledges requiring entry into a ledger, made the money safe, while reducing the system's reliance on silver as a reserve, so that silver could then move to where it was needed or valued the most. Secondly, the credit pledges massively increased the money supply of the Kingdom. Naples didn't entirely escape the

The pledge of credit in the 1700s (left). The pledge of credit in the 1800s (right).

cycles of boom and bust that one might expect to be caused by large increases in the issuing of bank debt, but the cycles and their consequences were manageable. To understand why these credit pledges worked, why they were trusted and for so long, we have to look even closer at exactly how the banking charities operated.

Behind the Scenes: Sales and Buybacks

Ferdinando Galiani got it absolutely right, as always: he understood that the banking charities of Naples not only *managed* money, as did their counterparts in Venice, Amsterdam and Hamburg; what made them unique and ensured their success was that they also *earned* money.

But how? As we have seen, getting paid to rent coins was permitted, but charging interest on promises to pay was most certainly not. The Franciscans had established their work-around at the Fifth Lateran

Council and over the years the Spanish authorities had granted the banking charities certain privileges, but this was still not enough to establish a fully functioning, highly profitable banking system. In the 1600s, the Kingdom of Naples was a province of Spain, the most Catholic of all the world's great empires. The banks themselves were owned by Catholic charities. And the Roman Curia, the Church's governing body, just 120 miles up the road in Rome, viewed the charging

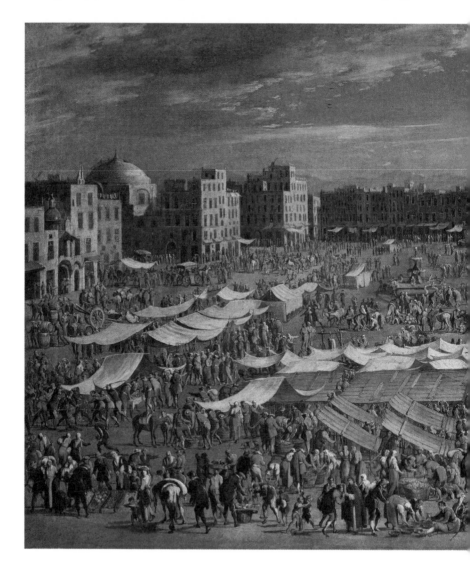

of interest on loans as a form of usury. Renting coins may have been permitted, but the banking charities were now doing much more than just renting coins. They were issuing pledges of credit; they were being paid to become indebted to their clients – which looks and sounds a lot like usury. So how did they get away with it? How *exactly* did

Market in Naples in the 1600s.

they earn income without incurring the wrath of the Church and while working within the strictures of the law? This is a mystery that historians have tried to solve for a long time. Fortunately, again, the ledgers of the banking charities reveal how they did it.

We'll take another example. Antonio De Franchis was not the only aristocrat in Naples in the 1600s who did business through the banking charities. Count Fabrizio di San Severino was another.

The Count was a real estate developer and a client of the Banco dei Poveri. He bought properties in Naples and refurbished them. Then he sold or rented the property. Like the real estate developers of today, the Count financed his business with a lot of bank debt and little equity. In 1616, he wanted to buy a building for 1,200 ducats solely with debt. He already owned a large mansion near the Church of Santa Maria, in the city centre, which he rented for 92 ducats a year, so he sold the mansion to the bank for 1,200 ducats, enabling him to buy the new building. But six months later, he bought back his old mansion for 1,200 ducats – exactly the same price he had sold it for. Neither the bank nor the Count lost or made any money on these trades. But during the period it owned the mansion, the bank had earned 46 ducats from renting it out and the Count had forgone that income. The trades were legally a sale and a purchase, but taken together they were the equivalent of a financial payoff of a loan at about 8 per cent annual interest: in other words, an entirely lawful transaction achieved by sale and buyback rather than by charging interest on a loan. This sort of arrangement met the needs and purposes of both the banking charities' clients and the banking charities themselves. Examining the books of the seven banks in the archives in Naples reveals dozens of such sale and buyback arrangements, providing a ready flow of income for the banking charities, enabling them to conduct the business of banking without breaking the laws of church or state. *That's* how they did it.

So, the complete business model of the banking charities is now clear. Clients of the charities became clients of the bank. They deposited coins and promised to pay the bank to use its debts as means of payment. In exchange, the bank issued them with pledges of credit, a form of debt security, enabling them to make payments that they could effectively use as money. The bank then rented out some of the coins to the deserving poor, creating a social good, and the remaining coins stayed in the bank in order to guarantee the pledges the purchasing power of the Mint. In order to actually earn income, the bank exchanged promises to pay with clients who wanted to use bank debts instead of scarce coins, and engaged in the sale and purchase of assets that yielded an income with bank debts rather than coins. And all without breaching canon and civil law.

A wonderful system. Except for one thing, which is always a problem for any bank: there weren't enough high net-worth individuals like Count Fabrizio di San Severino in Naples to be able to sustain seven banking charities. So, the banking charities started doing business with the state.

Quasi-Perpetual Public Debt

As a reminder: in 1556 Philip II, despot, brilliant administrator, became King of Spain. Naples, Milan, the Netherlands and various overseas colonies were also under his rule. A year later, he added Portugal. This was the grand union of the Spanish empire.

It was an empire born indebted and Philip II – known as Philip the Prudent, who was certainly meticulous, if not always wise – pursued aggressive international expansion that only added to the debt load. Naples had to share that burden.

The public expenditures of the Kingdom of Naples went from 1.3 million ducats in 1550 to 4.7 million in 1626. By 1636, this rose to an eye-watering 7.5 million. Tax receipts lagged, but the Kingdom met the demands of the imperial administration by raising lots of debt. What is truly remarkable is that the Kingdom of Naples, due to highly skilled and efficient financial administration, was able to satisfy the seemingly insatiable appetite of the Spanish conquerors for almost two centuries.

The Kingdom's success in raising debt was a mixed blessing: they were able to meet the demands from Madrid, but they were restricted in their freedom to spend money. At the start of the period, military expenditure took the largest share of the outlays. But over time, the spending patterns shifted. Military expenditures fell from 45 per cent to 23 per cent. Meanwhile, interest payments exploded. The cost of servicing the debt increased from 31 per cent to a whopping 56 per cent of the budget. The Kingdom financed Spanish imperial policies with funded debt for years, but relying on continuous borrowing had created a monster. By the early seventeenth century, the financial machine was working overtime simply to feed that monster. More than 50 per cent of the Kingdom's revenues went towards interest payments.

The share of public expenses that went to the imperial war machine had halved, but the actual amount had doubled. The Spanish Empire benefitted handsomely from the prowess of the financial administration in raising and managing public debt: the citizens of the kingdom benefitted rather less, since military expenses and debt servicing left fewer resources for supporting economic growth and welfare.

Still, we should not underestimate the achievement of the financial administration of Naples. Few nations in Europe were able to borrow so much from citizens and investors and keep doing it for so long. Private investors, both domestic and foreign, kept buying the public debt of the Kingdom even when it became clear to investors that the Kingdom was going to be unable to return the money it had borrowed. Why? And how did the Kingdom do it? Was this an early example of sheer financial folly or was there something else going on? Understanding the history of the management of public finances in the Kingdom of Naples reveals certain fundamental truths about the management of public finances that are not limited to Naples, but which can be applied to the understanding of public debt in any country, in any age.

The Kingdom had seriously started borrowing long-term in 1510, and the debt was fully funded. The financial administration understood that most lenders to the state were not financers after capital gains but simply savers looking for a long-term cash flow for themselves, their immediate families and their heirs. A system of perpetual public debt would be able to satisfy the needs of these smaller investors and the demands of the Spanish Empire, so the financial administration quickly developed a product that was well-suited to the market for public debt, fully funded and long-term; let's call it quasi-perpetual debt. But raising and supporting even quasi-perpetual public debt is not easy; it's not simple now, and it was even more difficult then. In the 1600s, few states had been able to do it, and the Kingdom of Naples only succeeded in doing so because of the assistance, once again, of their friends, the banking charities.

Tax Farming

The Treasury of the Kingdom raised public debt in a rather unusual way. They farmed out the collection of indirect taxes to private entrepreneurs, while the concessions to collect specific taxes were auctioned off, with these concessions usually lasting for five years, with an option to renew. The tax farmers pocketed the tax revenues and paid the Treasury a yearly rent for the privilege. The Treasury had the option to buy back the concession, returning the upfront payment. So far, this is nothing unusual: France and England also farmed out the collection of specific taxes.

But in Naples, tax farming provided a means of engineering a very special kind of public debt security: the Treasury split the future rent payments into shares. Each share was a claim on a given percentage of future rent payments, then the Treasury sold the shares to private investors for an upfront payment. The Treasury could buy back the shares, returning the upfront payment, the capital.

But seldom did it have the resources to do so, and so the debt became perpetual. Most savers viewed this public debt security as an attractive investment. The payments by the tax farmers were predictable and steady, since the tax farmer would keep paying the rent in order to not lose the concession. It was unlikely that the Treasury could buy back the shares, so investors expected a long-term steady stream of payments, a sort of perpetual income. Shares of the rent of specific taxes were often part of an inheritance and of the dowries of daughters. If a saver needed cash, they could easily sell their shares on the secondary market. The demand for long-term streams of payment was always there.

The Kingdom's ability to pay for public goods and to support the Empire relied heavily on this ingenious scheme. Soon, the banking charities realised the opportunities that this peculiar form of public debt offered them. Shares in the rent of the tax farmers were the perfect asset for a bank: they guaranteed a nice long-term stream of payments. So, the bank bought them with bank debt and then, at the right time, sold them to clients. And here's the crucial point. Without the banking charities, raising the vast amount of debt that the Kingdom required would have been impossible, and without trading the rents of the tax farmers, the banks would not have grown so profitable so quickly. In many ways, this is no different to what the primary dealers in public debt securities do today. But there *is* a difference, because the banking charities did much more than the primary dealers of today; the relationship between the state and the banks was even more complex and fascinating and *good* than at first appears.

Each tax farming concession was like a little business – a going concern, a kind of public–private partnership. These businesses hired employees, paid salaries, collected taxes and paid rent to the state. They needed lots of financial support, and in addition to everything else, it was the banking charities who offered this support and were the treasurers and financiers of these businesses. Each tax concession had its own bank account, and the taxpayers paid their dues into these accounts. Sometimes they paid taxes with bank debts; most small taxpayers paid with coins. Those coins stayed in the bank's coffers and became part of the reserve, enabling them once again to rent more coins to the deserving poor. And the bank then issued more credit pledges – so, another example of the banks and the state working effectively together, one supporting and enabling the other.

But the mutual support between the state and the banking charities didn't end there. It went further still, and if we go back into the archives of the Banco di Napoli and look at the ledgers, we can discover yet another aspect of the deep, profound, long-running relationship between banks and the state.

Liquidity, Depth – and the Curse of Public Debt

Altamura was one of the wealthiest regions in the Kingdom of Naples. It produced quality crops in abundance and the local mills turned those crops into wheat. The Kingdom taxed wheat heavily, so the tax bill for the citizens of Altamura was high. Revenues from the region contributed a steady flow of money into the Kingdom's coffers. And these revenues offered the Spanish royal administration an opportunity for some creative financing.

In 1630 the financial administration of the Kingdom rented out the collection of the wheat tax in Altamura to a man named Gaspare Romer, a Flemish financier who had moved to Naples. Romer had deep pockets and profited nicely from keeping on the concession. Shares in the rent he paid to retain the Altamura tax concession were an attractive investment for savers interested in a long stream of steady cash flows. As was standard practice, the investor would buy the shares, paying a sum up front, and in exchange they would receive yearly payments equal to 7 per cent of the sum they'd paid. Not bad.

At the end of Romer's concession, the Kingdom's administration had two options. It could buy back the shares in the concession that had been sold to investors, returning the sum it had received, or it could renew the concession and use the rent to pay interest to investors every year. As it turned out, shares in the Altamura tax concession sold rather well even when, around 1630, it was clear that the Kingdom was not going to have the resources to buy back the shares and most people doubted that the Kingdom could keep up the yearly payments. So why on earth did investors keep buying this particular form of public debt?

The Banco di Santo Spirito bought a large chunk of Romer's rent. Then it split the shares it had bought into smaller portions and resold them to its customers. One of those customers was a man named Carlo D'Aloisio.

The archives of the bank reveal nothing particularly interesting or special about him. He was just an average bank customer, like most of the other 35,000 citizens of Naples who banked with the charities. But the D'Aloisio family were old clients of the Banco di Santo Spirito. His father, Luciano, had opened an account at the bank in 1599. One of his first transactions had been to purchase 200 ducats' worth of shares in the rent for the concession of the wheat tax. And in 1630, Carlo paid 400 ducats to buy more from the bank. The archive shows that the family regularly bought the peculiar public debt of the Kingdom from the Banco di Santo Spirito. If we look at the trades between Carlo and the bank, we can see how the banking charities supported the state and vice versa.

While the Treasury paid 7 per cent of the upfront payment to the Banco di Santo Spirito, the Banco paid Carlo only 5 per cent and charged a spread of 2 per cent. But a close look at the trades reveals that the bank agreed to pay D'Aloisio his return *regardless* of what the Treasury did: it kept crediting his account with the agreed sums even when the Treasury paid late, less than promised, or nothing at all. In other words, in exchange for the spread, the bank guaranteed the state's obligations to its client, and all the banking charities did the same: their guarantees assured the buyer that they would get a steady stream of payments for a long, long time. And it was this guarantee by the banking charities that explains why the demand for public debt never slackened in the Kingdom of Naples.

The banking charities gave the Treasury much-needed flexibility: the state could pay less or late without upsetting the demand for public debt. The Treasury, not surprisingly, took full advantage of this flexibility. The ledgers are full of missed and delayed payments to the banking charities. Those debts accumulated year after year and reached sizable sums; the state's promises to pay stopped being good assets and became liabilities. But the banking charities were 'good banks'. Their ledgers show that they kept paying the shares of the rents purchased by their customers, and they bore the losses. Any capital market needs more than willing buyers and sellers to work well: it needs brokers who buy and sell securities even when demand or supply are slack. When Carlo D'Aloisio wanted to buy or sell shares in the rents, he went to his bank. Thousands of people like him, bank clients, did the same. And bank debts supplied the money they needed to make the purchases, the bank's guarantees making the future streams of payment secure. In the language of finance, we would say that the banking charities 'made the market', they gave the market for public debt both liquidity and depth. Modern securities firms perform this function. But the banking charities did more: they guaranteed the payment of interest and they stepped in when the state did not honour its promises to pay. The spread that the banks charged clients for the service softened the blow, but did not cover their losses. Again, Galiani was absolutely right: these banking charities were good banks, and particularly good to the state.

Public finances that rely on tax farming have many obvious faults. But we should acknowledge that the peculiar scheme in Naples had engineered a market that was able to support a very large and pretty much perpetual public debt. The state did not have to return the capital it received. A steady flow of payments was enough to support the public debt, and the banking charities guaranteed that steady flow. Investors kept buying the debt of the Kingdom, with bank money being the very lifeblood of the scheme. This was no small achievement at the beginning of the 1600s. But the reality was that over 50 per cent of government expenses went to the investors in public debt; in the end, the Kingdom of Naples could do little more than pay interest on its public debt. This is, of course, the curse of perpetual public debt, as true now as it was then. And this problem of ever-present, ever-more-costly and ever-spiralling debt might perhaps have spelled the end for the relationship between the state and the banks.

Isabella, One Sharp Trader

Tax revenues could barely keep up the interest payments on the Kingdom's debt securities. But simultaneously, the issuing of new debts kept the Kingdom afloat. The authorities desperately needed to lower the cost of the debts that had piled up to be able to pay for fresh issues. Upsetting investors by arbitrarily lowering the yearly payments was out of the question. The only way out of the predicament was to buy back the outstanding obligations and issue new ones at a lower yield. Demand for public debt was strong and the Treasury believed that investors would keep buying the public debt obligations despite the lower yields. In order to buy back the large amounts of existing debt, all the Kingdom needed was plenty of cash — which it did not have. So, the Treasury asked the good banks for help.

Back in the archive, the ledger of the Banco della Pietà tells us what happened next. It turns out, fortunately for the Treasury and for the banks, that not all of the banks' clients were thrifty forward-thinkers looking for a long-term guaranteed stream of income. Many clients were canny operators who actively traded from their bank accounts. A number of them were women, of whom Isabella Preite was one. A wealthy dame, she was a client of the Banco della Pietà in the early 1600s. She played the public debt market. And one of the transactions of her account shows how the good banks helped the Kingdom of Naples to reduce the cost of debt without turning away investors.

In 1613, Isabella paid the Treasury 2,500 ducats to receive a yearly income of 200 ducats; a stream of income equal to 8 per cent of the sum paid up front. This yield was much higher than what, say, Carlo

D'Aloisio was getting – but the deal was riskier because in this case the bank did not guarantee the yearly payment. However, Isabella was one sharp trader and she understood leverage. She guessed that if the government wanted to reduce the cost of debt, they would need to buy it back and reissue it later at a lower cost. And she was absolutely right, because sure enough, a year after she had bought her shares, the bank offered to buy them back for 2,500 ducats. She gladly took the money. Now the bank owned the shares, and because it was a good bank, always willing to help the community and the institutions of the state, when the Treasury reduced the yield from 8 per cent to 7 per cent – lowering its payments from 200 to 175 ducats – it was the bank who took the loss but kept on trading in public debt, while Isabella kept her tidy profit from her year of holding the shares.

Isabella's canny trade was not an isolated instance. Many similar trades can be found in the books of the banking charities. They explain how the Kingdom was able to lower interest costs from 8 per cent to 7 per cent without ruining the market for public debt and with no coins in its coffers. It was a very shrewd move by the Treasury: investors got their capital back at no cost to the Kingdom *and* they kept buying shares in public debt, even if the yield was somewhat lower. The archives show that the good banks helped the state in this way, over and over and over again. Indeed, a few years later, the banks executed similar transactions in order to be able to allow the Treasury to slash the interest on public debt yet further from 7 per cent to 6 per cent, with the costs of the buyback once again being borne by the banking charities and not the Treasury or the investors. Galiani was right yet again. The banks acted as you might expect a 'good' bank to act: they purchased large chunks of public debt with bank money and sold it to their customers (in this way earning a spread), while also helping the state when the time came by buying back the outstanding public debt and reissuing it at a lower yield.

Without the banking charities, it would have been simply impossible for the Kingdom of Naples to issue the massive amount of debt

The seal of the Bank of the Holy Saviour (left). The seal of St James (right).

needed to satisfy the demands of the imperial court. The balance sheets of the banks show the impact of the thousands of trades like those done with Isabella and Carlo. Between 1587 and 1622, no less than 50 per cent of the assets of the seven banking charities were shares in the rents the tax farmers paid to the Kingdom. Most of the other assets were the valuables deposited at the Monti by the deserving poor to rent coins. Later, the share of assets on the bank's balance sheets made up by public debt declined but remained substantial. The banking charities made money by exchanging public debt, shares in the rent, with bank debt – and, as always, by helping the deserving poor.

Silver Coins and Bank Money

Bank money thus became a large part of the money supply of Naples. The trouble was that, despite the fact that bank money reduced the need for coins in the Kingdom, it did not solve the fundamental problem of the lack of coins. Even with all that bank debt, coins were a vital component of the money of Naples because for a long time, coins from the local mint remained the only legal way to settle a debt. Silver and gold were used for the large-denomination coins, with small change made from less precious metal.

But the Kingdom was on a silver standard, which meant that it was silver that was the only true measure of the value of all goods and services. The Kingdom's minting process followed the standard pattern of demand and supply: the Naples Mint purchased precious metal from individuals or bullion traders and paid for it with the coins minted from their bullion at the official price minus expenses and seigniorage (the difference between the face value of the currency and the cost to produce it). That's how the Kingdom, just like most European states, made money. And it didn't work. The issue was that if the silver coins minted in the Kingdom of Naples were much sought-after within the Kingdom of Naples, they were even more sought-after outside: silver coins left Naples as soon as they were minted. The Spanish Viceroys, one after the other, had tried to understand why and failed.

The appropriately named Giovanni Turbolo eventually solved the problem of the shortage of coins, while presenting another great challenge and opportunity for the banking charities. Born in Naples in 1570, Turbolo started in business young, first with tax farming, then becoming a merchant and a banker. He was good with money, so good that he eventually got to run Naples's public Mint.

As soon as he got the job, he focused on the silver coinage. First, Turbolo weighed the coins made in Naples against those made by competing nations. (Interestingly, when he was appointed Warden of the Royal Mint in England in 1696, Isaac Newton did exactly the same, literally weighing the coins of England and those of competing nations. Newton, like Turbolo, wanted to understand why newly minted silver coins left England in droves.) He then looked at the rate of exchange of the Kingdom's currency at the European exchange fairs, the foreign exchange markets of the time. This was the real problem. Silver as money was worth more abroad than it was at home, which explained why silver coins left the Kingdom as soon as they came out of Naples's Mint. Merchants became rich by simply buying under-valued coins at home and then spending them abroad. This meant that the working classes back in Naples suffered from the scarcity of a means of payment – and so did the state. Like so many others before him, in order to solve the state's problem, Turbolo turned to the banking charities for help. And again, for the last time, we can trace the history of the banks' good deeds in the archives of the Banco di Napoli. They demonstrate the banks' final secret: how they supported the whole citizenry of Naples, both the bourgeois and the proletariat alike. Solving the problem of silver coins in the Kingdom of Naples was, if you like, the final good act of the good banks.

In response to Turbolo's request and the needs of the administration, the banks bought silver on the international market and sold it to Naples's public Mint. We know this because the Mint had bank accounts in all the banking charities, and the ledgers show plenty of trades between the institutions to support the coinage of the Kingdom. In May 1613, for instance, four banks pooled resources to buy silver worth 250,000 ducats on the market. Using the most complete records – those of the Banco della Pietà – we can see quickly the meaning and nature of the trade: the bank bought silver from foreign bullion traders at the world trade price, then it sold the silver to the Mint at the Kingdom's official price, which was a lot lower.

The Banco della Pietà was a good bank, but it lost big on the trade. They petitioned the Kingdom to use more bank money in payments by public offices: if the authorities would only leave the coins in the banks, they could issue more debts that the public offices could then use. This sort of policy had worked well in a merchant republic like Venice, and it could solve the money problem in Naples as well. The bank had a good argument, if self-serving, but it fell on deaf ears: the authorities ignored the bank's petition. Nonetheless, faithful, unde-terred, the bank kept on supporting the coinage, buying high and selling low, putting silver coins back into the pockets of the people of Naples, proving Galiani right once again: 'If it is true that a good bank is one which does not pay, *it is also true that an accredited bank is one which is not unwilling to pay.'*

Purchasing silver on the market and bearing the cost of a flawed coinage policy; enabling tax farming, making the market for public debt; developing credit pledges and buyback schemes – there seems to have been no end to the ingenuity of the good banks of Naples. The offspring of religious charities, they used their profits to help both the state and the community: good in name, good by nature.

CHAPTER 5

The Écu de Marc:
The Impious Art of Exchange

We invented money and we use it, yet we cannot either understand its laws or control its actions. It has a life of its own which it properly should not have [...] It is impious, being critical of existent social realities, and it has the effect of lessening their degree of reality.

Lionel Trilling
'Art and Fortune' (1948)

TODAY, THE CITY OF DUBROVNIK is where TV and film producers like to go when they want to conjure up images of a glorious imagined past or some strange imperial future – grand Gothic gates and arches, steep stone steps, Romanesque cloisters and carvings, epic fortifications. *Game of Thrones, Star Wars*; surrounded on three sides by the sea, perched high on a rocky ridge, a natural fortress, Dubrovnik is the perfect fantasy location. But its true history is perhaps even more incredible.

Founded by refugees from the Greek cities of Epidaurum and Salona, and with a constitution dating from the thirteenth century – said to have been a model for Oliver Cromwell's grand plan for a commonwealth in England – for centuries Dubrovnik – then known as Ragusa, capital of the maritime Republic of Ragusa – dominated the Balkan Peninsula. A meeting point between East and West, between Slav and Latin cultures, sitting proud on the southern coast of Dalmatia, Ragusa remained both independent and wealthy for over a thousand years. One of its main assets, a source both of its strength and fame, was the argosy, a merchant ship capable of carrying large cargoes over long distances. For centuries, Ragusan argosies were a common sight in harbours throughout the world. (So common, in fact, that Shakespeare uses the word 'argosy' as a synonym for a merchant ship. In his *Etymological Dictionary of the English Language*, Walter W. Skeat notes that the word 'denotes a large vessel, generally a merchant ship [...] the word has been supposed to be a corruption of *Ragosie*, a ship of Ragusa'.)

In its heyday, the Ragusan city-state was governed by a merchant oligarchy, with perhaps the most prestigious among them being the House of Gundulić: in Italian, the di Gondola family, motto: '*Tout ou rien*', all or nothing. And the history of the di Gondolas and their argosies takes us into a realm of financing that transcends time and space, like Ragusa, Dubrovnik itself, a magical kind of financing both fantastical and real, all *and* nothing, used right up to the present by bankers, businessmen and states in order to be able to conduct their affairs.

We shall see how these peculiarly flexible and enduring credit instruments allowed Philip II of Spain to finance an eighty-year-long war in hostile territory with mercenaries who needed regular pay; how they allowed the Queen of England to resolve a rather tricky financial foreign policy challenge posed by the Spanish; and how they enabled the ever-inventive Catholic Church to interpret its own rules and precepts in order to be able to benefit from Spanish congregations' generous tithes and donations.

It is perhaps worth mentioning again at this point that for the past few years, after a long career in banking using inventive credit instruments and financial instruments of all kinds, I have been lucky enough to become the Chairman of Prada, the luxury fashion house, so it seems appropriate to begin this discussion by talking about fine cloth.

Silk and Jersey

In 1540 it was Benedetto di Gondola who ran the di Gondola family firm. Benedetto made particularly good use of Ragusan argosies. He would buy silk in Venice from the firm of Camillo & Lorenzo Strozzi and have it shipped to London to be sold there. In London, he then bought jersey, the much sought-after knitted woollen fabric, and had it shipped to Florence and Rome, where demand for the cloth was high. Benedetto knew how to run a good import/export business: he made sure that his grand merchant argosies never sailed empty; one load in, one load out.

But filling the argosies did not come easy. He had to pay for his silk in Venice at the time of purchase, but his revenues accrued only later, in London, when he sold the silk. And, of course, the same happened in reverse with the jersey: he had to pay in London but was only paid in return in Florence, later. In some ways, of course, this is just a simple logistical problem, a supply chain question. But in financial terms, it raises a much larger question: how does one move value across time and space? What are the mechanisms of complex international financial exchange?

Benedetto couldn't use money to transfer value; money was gold and silver coins, which were scarce and for obvious reasons, including (but not limited to) piracy and theft, did not travel well. With coins therefore out of the question, in order to transfer value, Benedetto had to use something else. So, in Venice he arranged financing with the Strozzi family for his silk purchase. The Strozzis agreed the price and the time and place of payment. To seal the agreement, Benedetto then gave them a note in which he acknowledged his obligation to pay the price of the silk and instructing one of his representatives to make the payment at the agreed time and place.

The note that he gave to the Strozzis was a bill of exchange. A security used all over the world – by the Chinese mostly during the Song Dynasty (960–1279), and long used by Arab merchants and others throughout the Near East – a bill of exchange is usually defined, depending on which dictionary you use, as a short-term negotiable financial instrument, consisting of an order in writing addressed by one person to another, agreeing to pay on demand or at a fixed or determinable future time a certain sum of money to a specified person or bearer of the bill. We shall spend some time unpacking exactly what this means in practice, but suffice it to say that although bills of exchange might not have been a European invention, neither in China nor elsewhere did they come to play the crucial role that they did in the West.

It was the use of bills of exchange that not only allowed Benedetto to transfer value, buying silk in Venice and shipping to London, and buying jersey in London and shipping it to Florence, but which allowed the flourishing of international markets throughout early modern Europe. A bill of exchange is an extraordinary security because it is part order to pay and part debt; and financial debts, as we have seen elsewhere in different contexts, have one very important feature: the debtor does not have to pay money to discharge his obligation. A debt can be discharged by setting it off another debt, which can eliminate the need for coins. So, Benedetto could discharge his obligations to pay for the silk and the jersey by setting them off the promises to be paid by other merchants, and would only use coins to pay the debts he could not offset. Using bills of exchange, Benedetto could therefore not only move value across time and space; he could also increase his purchasing power beyond that of scarce gold and silver coins.

You can perhaps already see the appeal of bills of exchange. Benedetto de Gondola certainly understood their huge power and potential. And he was not alone – international trade came to function increasingly through the use of such bills. Using bills of exchange, buyers could buy more and sellers could sell more, wherever and whenever they wanted. During the early modern period, bills of exchange began to circulate widely, making all things possible for merchants, bankers, states, adventurers and the Catholic Church.

Exchange Fairs

Bills of exchange solved a lot of problems, but they also caused a lot of headaches. Clearing many debts due in many different places and at different times required all sorts of ad hoc processes and arrangements. In order to simplify matters, merchant bankers set up exchange fairs, which were regular gatherings of merchant bankers not only to trade goods, but also to clear bills of exchange. The first exchange fairs were held in the Champagne region, in the north east of the Kingdom of France, in the ancient towns of Troyes, Provins, Bar-sur-Aube, and Lagny.

We have lots of contemporary accounts of how these fairs worked. They were basically a co-operative venture between rulers and merchants: the counts of Champagne guaranteed the attendees' physical security and their equality before the law, and established a legal system for the enforcement of contracts and the protection of rights; and in exchange, the merchants contributed to the royal treasury and to the local economy.

The early exchange fairs were held a few times a year in Champagne according to a fixed schedule: the May fair was held in Provins, the 'hot fair' in June in Troyes, etc. Participants in the fairs bought and sold commodities such as silk, spices, leather and cloth, but mostly they were there to clear bills of exchange. The debts the merchants could not clear were settled with coins or re-issued to be dealt with at the next fair.

Over time, the fairs became rather more formalised, expanded and began to move around, first from Champagne to Bruges, and then to Cologne and Geneva, and by 1420 they had established themselves firmly in Lyon, the ancient capital of the Gauls and a well-established centre of trade in luxury goods. Merchant bankers had long since realised that they could profit more, and more easily, from trading bills of exchange than trading luxury goods. Lyon became not just a centre for commodities trading, a market for goods, but a true financial centre, a market for currency exchange.

And it was to Lyon that our old friend Benedetto di Gondola, the Ragusan merchant with his heavy-laden argosies, went to clear his debts.

Vieux Lyon

Italians were the most numerous among the many traders and bankers who flocked to Lyon to do business at the fairs. Indeed, so many Italians moved to Lyon that the old city acquired and retains to this day a distinctly Italian feeling. Citizens of Lyon built in the Italianate style, in terracotta and stucco, and quite a few streets and squares were named after Italian banking families, in particular in and around what is now the city's extraordinarily beautiful fifth arrondissement, Vieux Lyon.

In Lyon, Benedetto had opened an account with a merchant bank, the local branch of Banco Salviati, a Florentine house. When he bought silk from the Strozzi, Benedetto gave them a bill instructing Salviati to pay the local branch of the Strozzi. When the silk was sold in

London, the buyer gave Benedetto a bill where he ordered his banker to pay the Salviati in Lyon for the benefit of di Gondola. Then at the next fair, Salviati and the bankers of the buyers and sellers of silk cleared the debts of their clients and settled the outstanding balance, if any.

By the time Benedetto di Gondola was frequenting the exchange fairs in Lyon in the mid-1500s, the structure and organisation of the fairs and the processes by which bankers used to clear, exchange, and settle debts there had become even more formalised and regulated. There were now fairs throughout Europe – not only in Lyon, but in Antwerp, Medina del Campo, Lisbon and Frankfurt, and they were all connected by mail and courier, with bills regularly travelling within the network. The fairs lasted a week and were supervised by special authorities.

Only a certain number of exchange bankers were permitted to attend. First, the bankers had to register their attendance. Then they had to list all the debts of their clients, their partners and themselves, and at the same time they had to declare the exact value of the coins they had available to settle the debts that could not be cleared. Next, the exchange bankers would set the rate of exchange of the currency of debts and remittances in the bills of exchange. Then, and only then, with everything in order and the exchange rates set, could the bankers start clearing the debts. Those that could not be cleared were paid with coins or reissued to be dealt with at another fair.

Over time, in Lyon and elsewhere, the use of bills of exchange had expanded far beyond their initial use to merely trade goods: they had become instruments which bankers, financiers and investors could use to profit from dealing in debts. Governments had also started raising short-term financing at the exchange fairs; the demands and requirements of kings and princes swelled the demand for debts and thus the dealing and clearing bills of exchange had become an even bigger business. Merchant bankers profited much more from trading

Overleaf: Vieux Lyon. The city in the sixteenth century.

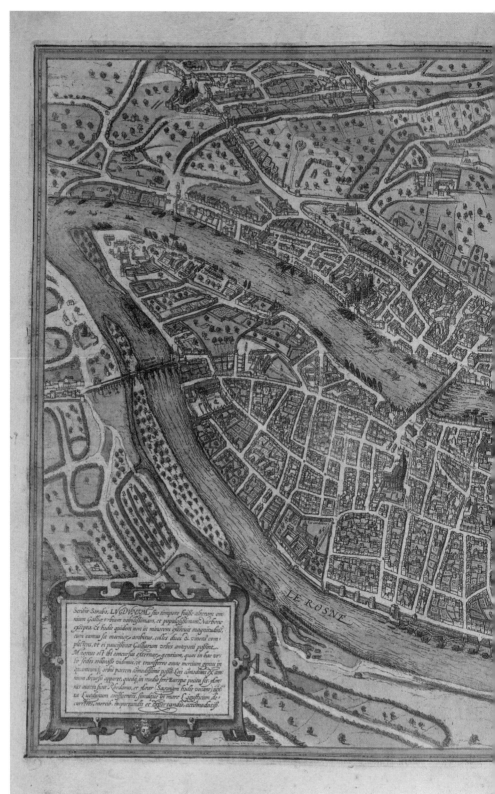

LE ROSNE

Scribit Strabo, LVGDVNVM, suo tempore fuisse alteram omnium Galliæ vrbium nobilißimam, et populoßißimam: Narbone
exceptâ. Et hodie quidem non in minorem creuit magnitudinẽ,
cum tantus sit mœnior̃ ambitus, collesq́ duos & cineat com:
plectens, vt ei paucißimæ Galliarum vrbes antepni poßint.
Magnus est ibi concursus externar̃ gentium, quas in hac vr:
be sedes collocaße videmus, et transferre omne mercium genus in
iquattuorci, orbis partem commodißimè poßit. Loci commoditas & am:
nium decursu apparet, quodq̃ in medio ferè Europæ posita sit: q́m:
nes autẽ sunt Rhodanus, et q̃r̃ Sagonam hodie vocant; vtrõ:
ta Lucduuum conssuentes, simulq̃ ut mare Cogofficium de:
currẽtes, mercib. importandis et exportandis, accommodatiß.

ONVM

Lyon. Qui de la France
Sers de force & rempart,
Lyon, qui de plaisance
Reluis de toute part.
La Riuiere du Rhosne
doucement decoulant
Qui embraße la Saone
Te rendent opulent.

bills of exchange than from trading goods, and so over time these 'merchant' bankers – bankers who financed the trade in commodities – gradually became 'exchange' bankers, bankers who traded debts in many currencies. Times were changing, roles were changing, and in many ways, the nature of finance was changing.

The Eyes of the Mind and the Eyes on the Forehead

Probably the best way to be able to understand exactly what was happening in Lyon is to be able to visualise it. A good diagram is not just an illustration; it is itself an argument. It has explanatory force. And the argument for bills of exchange, *the* diagram both explaining and advocating for bills of exchange, was most clearly drawn over 500 years ago by an Italian named Bernardo Davanzati.

Davanzati was a bit of an odd duck, but a man very much after my own heart: he was a banker who liked literature and ideas almost as much as he was fascinated by finance and money. After a few years of banking in Lyon, Davanzati settled down in Florence to write full time, translating the work of Tacitus and writing on viticulture. It is said that Davanzati's fellow Florentines thought he was conceited, arrogant and a bore, but he was also ferociously smart and wrote with great clarity and simplicity, including on the art of exchange, setting out his ideas about bills of exchange in a twenty-two-page essay, *Notizia de cambi* (1582). Gloriously wide-ranging in his learning and interests and renowned locally during his

Bernardo Davanzati Bostichi. Banker and writer.

Bills of exchange moving between Florence and Lyon.

lifetime, Davanzati may be little-known today, but the impact and influence of his ideas should not be underestimated. In 2017, to celebrate the sixtieth anniversary of the signing of the Treaty of Rome, which established the European Economic Community, a museum in Brussels – the great Bibliotheca Wittockiana, devoted to the art of the book – mounted an exhibition of first editions of the 'Books that made Europe'. One hundred and forty works of economics, politics, finance, history and philosophy that formed the foundations of European identity were proudly displayed, including the works of St Augustine, Xenophon, Tacitus, Hobbes, Locke, Mill, Voltaire, Bentham, Marx, Ricardo: everyone and everything one might expect. Plus, Davanzati's *Notizia de cambi*. The book deserved its place.

Davanzati's essay remains today by far the best explanation of how exchange trades work. It should be essential reading for any course in trade and international markets at any twenty-first-century business school, as significant to the history of finance as, say, Machiavelli's *Il Principe* is to the history of ideas. Davanzati may have been an arrogant bore, but he was both a brilliant thinker and an innovator, and crucially one of the first to understand that images and illustrations can reveal and explain the complex narrative of financial transactions better than words alone.

The combination of text and image was arguably one of the great innovations of the Renaissance. Galileo Galilei famously used the technique in his *Istoria e dimostrazioni* (1613), written in the form of letters to Marcus Welser of Augsburg, reporting his discovery of Saturn's rings, with the words followed by a small drawing illustrating how the rings encircle the planet. Reading Galileo, it might be said that we use two sets of eyes at once: the eyes of the mind and the eyes on the forehead, all the better to understand his ideas.

Similarly, at the core of his essay, Davanzati inserts a graph so that we can understand with the eyes of the mind and the eyes of the forehead. In some ways, the twenty-two pages of actual text are a mere footnote to Davanzati's very simple drawing, which consists of just four lines: two parallels, two diagonals – four lines which explain bills of exchange in their various dimensions, across space and time, their price, everything – the entire story. Like Galileo, Davanzati understood that to understand some complex things, a diagram might say more than words, revealing aspects of a story beyond language. In Davanzati's case, his diagram reveals the story of how bankers and their clients made money with bills of exchange. The diagram looks like this:

In Florence, Bernardo (B) borrows from Giulio (A) 100 écus de marc and promises to pay him back in Lyon. Bernardo gives Giulio a bill of exchange acknowledging the receipt of value of 100 écus de marc and asks Salviati (C), his correspondent in Lyon, to pay the value of 100 écus de marc to Sertino (D), to Giulio's local proxy. Giulio sends Sertino (D) the original bill and Bernardo sends a copy

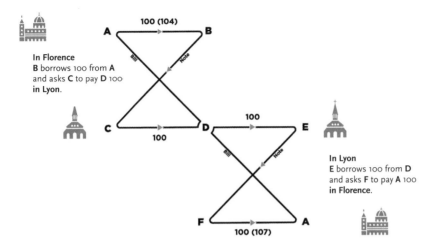

In Florence
B borrows 100 from **A**
and asks **C** to pay **D** 100
in Lyon.

In Lyon
E borrows 100 from **D**
and asks **F** to pay **A** 100
in Florence.

Currency arbitrage with debts.

to Salviati. When the bill and its copy get to Lyon, Salviati pays 100 écus de marc to Sertino.

In Lyon, Piero (E) borrows from Sertino 100 écus de marc. Piero gives Sertino a bill of exchange acknowledging the debt of 100 écus de marc and asks his correspondent in Florence (F) to pay Giulio (A) the value of 100 écus de marc. When the bill and its copy reach Florence, the trade is closed.

The price of remitting 100 écus de marc from Florence to Lyon is 104 Florentine scudi, while the price of remitting the same 100 écus de marc from Lyon to Florence is 107 Florentine scudi. The two trades yield a 3-Florentine-scudi profit. The two transactions are an arbitrage trade between the cost of remitting 100 écus de marc from Florence to Lyon and the cost of remitting 100 écus de marc from Lyon to Florence. The difference between the prices of the two remittances is the gain from the trade.

As I say, the diagram explains it rather better, clearer and quicker.

But let's make it absolutely clear what the diagram demonstrates, which is how and where money flows, and what it implies. What Davanzati's diagram reveals is the simple truth, the secret of arbitrage and what it does – which is simply to exploit the difference in prices of an asset or a trade in two different markets. Simple, deceptively simple, because when that happens, the opportunities for profit outweigh the risk of a loss.

Today, traders at investment banks do similar trades all the time. They use high-speed computers and sophisticated algorithms, but the goal of the trade is exactly the same: to exploit the difference in price of the same asset in two different markets. Not only is the goal the same, but so is the strategy: buy where the price is low and sell where the price is high. It's the oldest financial trick in the book.

At the time of Davanzati, with no computers or advanced software, as the diagram reveals, it was the bill of exchange, both debt and order of payment, which was the ideal security to arbitrage between the price of moving value across time and space between markets. The profit from each trade may have been small, but the trade could be done repeatedly for as long as the difference in the prices of the remittances held. Traders may not make much money with arbitrage, but they don't risk much either. And that's why they find them attractive.

Volatile Trades

Let's return to the diagram. It shows Bernardo buying and selling a currency, the écu de marc, for another currency, the Florentine scudo, in two different markets. Now, let's say that wrapping up this two-way trade takes two weeks. In those fourteen days, the value of the écu de marc *vis à vis* the Florentine scudo in Lyon may well change and turn Bernardo's gain into a loss. This is the risk. Trading debts in more than one currency is risky, even today with high-speed hardware and sophisticated software.

In the early modern era, it was much riskier. Currencies were incredibly volatile. Money was coins and the precious metal content of a nation's coins affected the price of its currency and sovereigns often changed the precious metal content of the coins they issued. In

France, for example, between 1295 and 1490 the silver currency was debased no fewer than 123 times. You wouldn't have wanted to have been an exchange banker during one of those 123 times. England fared rather better during the same period, when debasements were fewer, but the luck of the English did not hold. From 1542 to 1551, English silver currency was debased ten times, losing a full 83 per cent of its metal content. Again, good luck if you were trading under those circumstances.

So, the monetary policies of kings and princes were difficult to predict and debasements impacted the price of the currency at the exchange fairs; in that context, in such circumstances, arbitraging the value of the écu de marc in different markets seems not so much a good bet as a bit of a gamble.

You might think that this would be a deterrent, or that bankers' profits would have suffered, but here's the extraordinary thing: the records of the exchange bankers in Lyon between the middle of the sixteenth century and the end of the seventeenth century show that they earned plenty of profits buying écu de marc in one market and selling it in another. How were they able to achieve this? How did they maintain their steady profits, given that the game of trading debts in different currencies looks rather like roulette?

Écu de Marc

The answer lies in the nature of the écu de marc. The écu de marc was a private currency. It was created and managed by bankers for the purposes of exchange trades. This allowed it to be reasonably insulated from the monetary policies of princes, kings and emperors. The bankers then pegged the value of this écu de marc to the price of gold, which was no mean feat.

Only a very few states had ever managed to mint gold coins that contained the same amount of gold over very long periods, hundreds of years, and which therefore retained their value. There was the Spanish

Empire's scudo, plus the gold coins of the Kingdom of Naples and the republics of Venice, Genoa, and Florence; just five stable gold coinages in five different places; five kinds of supremely value-retaining gold coins. Looking at the evidence of history, the exchange bankers bet that those states were not going to be changing their coinage policies any time soon, with debasements leading to devaluing, so they stipulated that they would happily exchange the écu de marc with any of those states' coins at a fixed rate at any exchange fair.

Just like any bank, the exchange bankers at the exchange fairs had given their écu de marc, which was a form of bank money, the purchasing power of a given weight of pure gold by pegging the écu de marc to the stable gold coins of Spain, Naples, Venice, Genoa and Florence. And this peg-to-gold worked absolute wonders: the price of the écu de marc was reasonably stable up to the first quarter of the eighteenth century. The exchange bankers of the early modern era had thus put together a brilliant scheme to enable them to execute lots of arbitrage trades over time with confidence. The price of at least one of the two currencies they bought or sold was going to be stable in any market, and it was only the price of remitting the other that changed. It was audacious. It was brilliant. And it worked.

Like Mercury around the Sun

As Davanzati puts in his essay, currencies at the exchange fairs behaved rather like Mercury and the Sun in the solar system. The Sun (the écu de marc) stayed still, while Mercury (the local currency) revolved around it, moving constantly but never increasing the distance. By agreeing to exchange the écu de marc for the same weight of pure gold, bankers had given their private currency the purchasing power of gold in any European nation; in other words, they were making true supranational bank money.

For anyone who knows anything about the history of more recent monetary policy and, in particular, the international monetary agreements finalised at Bretton Woods in 1944, this might all sound rather familiar.

Towards the end of World War II, forty-four nations got together to develop a structure capable of providing the necessary stability to the post-war international monetary system. Like the exchange bankers four centuries earlier, they decided it might be a good idea to peg the value of their currencies to gold. To do that, the delegates, John Maynard Keynes among them, first chose the US dollar as the dominant currency. They then pegged the US dollar to gold and all other currencies to the US dollar. And to make all the pegs work, the United States agreed to exchange an ounce of gold for 35 dollars on demand. This simple move provided relative stability to the currencies of the Bretton Woods nations up to 1973 when President Richard Nixon terminated America's commitment to the policy.

What's extraordinary is that a group of wily European exchange bankers of the sixteenth century had managed to pull off a similar stunt to that conceived by the combined talents of all the nations at Bretton Woods all those years later. The exchange bankers' private currency, the écu de marc, basically played the role of the dollar, with the exchange bankers themselves playing the role of the Federal Reserve. In both instances, with Bretton Woods and with our Renaissance wheeler-dealers, one major result of their trick – their gimmick, if you like – was to make arbitrage trades with the pegged currencies much less risky. With a currency pegged to gold, arbitrage trades offer many more profit opportunities and fewer risks, allowing bankers to profit from lots and lots of arbitrage trades. With the écu de marc, private capital quickly recognised the opportunities offered by the system of exchange fairs based on a stable currency. They started to pay commissions to the exchange bankers to arbitrage between different exchange fairs on their behalf. The amount of private capital available grew and the exchange bankers in turn could make international trade grow in order to support the policies of kings, princes and emperors. Bankers were working with states, for the benefit of both.

Diagrams in Practice

It didn't take very long for exchange bankers to refine and perfect their methods in order to come up with a winning arbitrage strategy: borrow where remitting is cheap, lend where it is expensive, have the investor put up the capital, have the banker execute the trade and then split the profits. Bills of exchange were the perfect security to be able to execute such trades.

Returning once again to Davanzati's diagram, we can see that this is exactly what Bernardo does: he borrows from Giulio in Florence, where remitting in Lyon is cheap. Then Giulio's agent lends in Lyon, where remitting to Florence is expensive. Investors, bankers and others took full advantage of the opportunities offered by arbitrage trades done this way.

To take a minor but indicative real-world example, Francesco Martinengo was an aristocrat and a professional soldier. He served in many armies and at one time had led the cavalry of the republic of Venice. But Martinengo's real passion was investing and in particular arbitraging the écu de marc. He had an account with a Venetian bank, Maffetti & Brothers. The bank had branches in many exchange centres, among them Lyon and Piacenza. Between 1605 and 1611, Maffetti executed twenty-one arbitrage trades on the écu de marc between Venice and Piacenza for the account of Martinengo. In 1605, the account had a balance of 544 écus de marc. In 1611, the final balance was 948. Martinengo had grown his capital and Maffetti had earned plenty of commissions; banker and client had done well without running too many risks. Of the twenty-one trades executed only one produced a small loss. All the others were profitable. Borrowing écus de marc in Venice and remitting them to Piacenza paid well, and proves that Davanzati's illustration worked in practice; such trading patterns were commonplace and an absolute winner.

Martinengo may have been a minor player in the world of financial affairs, but the explanation for the difference in the price of his bank's remittances between Piacenza and Venice is rather interesting and reveals the wider context of arbitrage deals using bills of exchange and other financial instruments. The difference in price in Martinengo's deals was because the Spanish Empire was using the exchange fairs for the purposes of short-term financing.

Spain and Silver

Philip II ascended the Spanish throne in 1556. And pretty much as soon as he sat on the throne, the Low Countries, the Habsburg Netherlands, rose against Spanish rule, heralding the beginning of the so-called Eighty Years' War, or the Dutch Revolt.

Spain at the time was the strongest military power in the Western world and the Army of Flanders – which is generally considered to

Mercenary troops looking for money. The sack of Antwerp by the Army of Flanders, November 4, 1576.

be the modern world's first standing army, a multinational force based in the Spanish Netherlands and loyal to the Spanish kings – was a formidable fighting force with over 75,000 professional soldiers. Spain should really have quashed the Dutch rebellion quickly. But things turned out rather differently, with the war lasting over eighty years and Spain at the end admitting defeat. What's surprising is not so much that the Low Countries kept the Army of Flanders at bay for eighty years, but that Spain was able to keep its soldiers in the field for so long.

Fighting hundreds of miles from home and deep in enemy territory was hard and the Army of Flanders was unruly – between 1572 and 1609 it mutinied no fewer than forty-five times. The mutinies always had the same cause: a lack of cash. The Army of Flanders's professional soldiers fought for money and demanded to be paid in gold and silver. When that didn't happen, they rebelled.

What's ironic is that Spain actually had plenty of coins to be able to pay them; the mines of Potosí in Peru and Zacatecas in Mexico produced vast quantities of silver and there was no shortage of hard cash. But in the 1500s, moving South American silver from the Spanish colonies to Flanders was challenging, to say the least. The metal first had to be smelted in Potosí before travelling by mule to Lima to be assayed, and from there ships would carry the bullion to Panama, where it went by sea to Havana, where it then waited for deliveries of yet more silver from Zacatecas before being loaded onto ships and, once the winds were favourable, sailing finally to Seville. Everything about this process, from the fleet arrival time to the number of ships eventually reaching Spain and the amount of silver on board, was impossible to predict. The Empire had plenty of coins. But getting them to the mutinous Army of Flanders was another matter entirely. Just about anything could happen.

And it did.

Total Fiesco

In 1568, five ships left the Spanish harbours on their way to Antwerp carrying 155 chests of silver coins for the Army of Flanders. The coins belonged to a group of wealthy Genoese merchant bankers. The fleet from South America was, of course, late, and so the bankers loaned the coins to the Empire. But now the ships carrying the merchants' silver struck bad weather in the Bay of Biscayne. They then sighted Huguenot pirates. Taking evasive action, they sailed to Plymouth and Southampton.

This was not a smart move. England was an enemy of Spain. And Queen Elizabeth I desperately needed silver, money being scarce in England, with the Mint constantly demanding yet more metal. The Queen duly had the chests brought to London and placed in the Tower of London for safekeeping; the coins and ingots were worth around £85,000 in English money, which was a lot of money. So, the English had the silver in their possession, it belonged to the Genoese merchants, and Philip II desperately needed it delivered to Antwerp in order to pay the Army of Flanders. It was what one might call a situation. The Spanish ambassador demanded that the silver be returned to Antwerp. But his demands fell on deaf ears. So Philip changed tack. He asked Tomaso Fiesco, who was himself a Genoese banker, to deal with the matter – after all, the silver belonged to the businessmen; it was they who should negotiate its return.

As it happened, Fiesco was exactly the right man for the job. He wasn't only a banker, he was also a royal steward, Philip's financial agent responsible for short-term borrowing for the Spanish Empire. He was used to representing the interests of both lenders and borrowers, bankers and the crown; quite often, he would find himself sitting on both sides of the negotiating table. This might seem rather odd today, but this was how Spain arranged its public financing and it meant that Fiesco was uniquely qualified to navigate that rather large grey area in high finance, which still exists today, where public and private interests meet. The English had their equivalent figure in Sir Thomas Gresham, who was a brilliant merchant and financier as well as a servant of Queen Elizabeth I. Gresham moved in the same circles of bankers and statesmen as Fiesco. Queen Elizabeth chose wisely in appointing Gresham to deal with the crafty Genoese banker.

The two men were evenly matched. The negotiations lasted for over a year. But eventually they found a way out of the mess. They agreed on a form of wording and a certain way of thinking about what had occurred: Queen Elizabeth had not in fact 'seized' the chests of silver from the Spanish ships; no, no, she had merely 'borrowed' them. And she would now, of course, repay the Spaniards' loan and reward the bankers for their generosity. But she would still get to keep the silver. Win, win. How did they structure that deal?

To allow the Genoese merchant bankers to profit from the proposed settlement, Fiesco and Gresham had agreed that the value borrowed was not to be returned to the bankers in silver coins but with bills of exchange. They had worked out a long chain of remittances, from one exchange fair to another, that made it possible to arbitrage between the price of these remittances. In this way, Elizabeth got to keep the silver and the bankers made a nice little profit out of the so-called 'loan'. In addition, as part of the deal, the Duke of Alba, who was the renowned Spanish general governor of the Netherlands during the early years of the Dutch revolt and who in reprisal for the seizing of the Spanish silver had seized goods belonging to English merchants in Flanders, was permitted to sell what he had seized from the merchants but had to split the profits between the Army and the English.

It was quite the arrangement, inspired, really, and an object lesson not only in negotiation but in the functioning of exchange trades, as Philip II very quickly realised. Philip was more than satisfied with the deal and was a fast learner – he realised that despite having plenty of silver, the Empire also needed to be able to move value across time and space without using coins – just like, say, Benedetto di Gondola before him – and as Fiesco and Gresham had now demonstrated was possible with their creative solution over the problem of the 'borrowed' chests of silver. Bills of exchange offered the answer. When Don Luis

De Requesens, the new commander of the Army of Flanders, begged for money, Philip replied that 'the surest and swiftest method to send you money is by bill of exchange'.

It sounded like an easy solution but supplying the Army of Flanders was rather more difficult than Benedetto di Gondola paying for his silk and jersey or even Fiesco and Gresham coming to their neat gentlemen's agreement.

The value that Philip II had to move across time and space was absolutely enormous: Spain's annual military expenses alone fluctuated between 4 and 8 million ducats. Such sums could not be borrowed and remitted with bills issued piecemeal. And besides, the good soldiers of the Army of Flanders still wanted to be paid in coins, not in bills. In order to do so, Philip would need to issue an incredible number of bills and recruit the co-operation of as many exchange bankers as he could possibly find. He would also need to use the Spanish Empire's favourite short-term lending solution, the *asiento*.

Asientos

Just as we were lucky to have had Bernardo Davanzati to guide us through the intricacies of the arbitrage deals at the exchange fairs, so too do we now need a guide to explain the vast complexities of the Spanish Empire's deals using bills of exchange and asientos (agreements). Giandomenico Peri is that guide.

Peri was a Genoese businessman. Unlike Davanzati, he led an uneventful life. He was a mildly successful businessman, making enough money to live well; nothing out of the ordinary. But he had a deep knowledge of the world of business and was able to write about it with great clarity. Today, he would probably be teaching at Harvard Business School. In the early 1600s, Peri wrote the first manual of business administration, *Il Negotiante* (1638). The book is addressed to aspiring businessmen. Peri analyses every business of his day and teaches the right way to manage them. The table of contents of the book reads like the curriculum for a masters in business administration: Finance, Bookkeeping, Accounting.

Peri devotes an entire chapter to asientos, which was the name given to the contracts between the Spanish Empire and various merchant bankers to issue debts against future crown revenues, the most famous, or notorious, asiento today being the Asientos de Negros, which provided for the supply of African slaves to the Spanish colonies. Asientos deserve to be treated extensively, Peri tells his students, because for merchant bankers they are perhaps the biggest opportunity to make money. Any aspiring merchant banker needs to know what an asiento is and how to manage it effectively.

When it came to Philip's asientos to cover the costs of the Eighty Years' War, the bankers agreed to execute a series of cross-border transactions, borrowing, lending, remitting, and foreign exchange, while in return they stipulated how much the crown might borrow, where, when, in which currency and how much had to be paid back. The asientos also detailed the exact number of coins that had to be delivered to the Army of Flanders – soldiers, remember, did not tend to accept bills of exchange; they wanted silver or gold coins that could be spent in the local taverns. Luckily, bills of exchange could do just about everything else, so all the asientos were executed with bills.

The system of asientos might seem like the perfect answer for both bankers and the state, but things did not always go entirely smoothly.

Between 1550 and 1650 the Spanish Empire defaulted on its deals six times, and four of these defaults happened during the reign of Philip II. Yet bankers kept the money flowing and no banker lost money, despite the defaults. This seems unlikely, if not impossible, and is a conundrum that has puzzled scholars for years, until two economists, Mauricio Drelichman and Hans-Joachim Voth, studied the financing of the Spanish Empire under Philip II in order to understand the history of sovereign debt. In their highly entertaining and thorough account, *Lending to the Borrower from Hell* (2014), they analyse a total of 438 asientos signed and executed by Philip II and his bankers between 1566 and 1598. One hundred and forty-five bankers contributed to the asientos but because banking was a family business, those 145 bankers belonged to just 78 families. And among those families, just ten banking families contributed 70 per cent of the total asientos. One might expect those families to have lost an absolute fortune because of Philip II's defaults. Yet Drelichman and Voth find that not one family went bankrupt. Indeed, no family lost money on the deals. All of them earned an attractive rate of return.

This was partly because the defaults were really more like the restructuring of existing debts; Philip always ended up paying something, but less than what was agreed up front. But even so, that doesn't explain the profits that the banking families continued to make. In order to explain those, one has to study the asientos in detail.

In each contract between the bankers and the state the two parties try to include everything that can possibly go wrong and then sketch out a contingency for any of these adverse outcomes. The most frequent contingencies have to do with the late arrival of the South American fleet carrying the silver from the Empire's far-flung mines. No banker would take the risk of lending on the security of the ships of silver without some additional guarantees, and the asientos set out in detail the exact source of revenues that would have to be used in order to repay the debt if the fleet was indeed late or if the cargo came up short of what the administration had anticipated. Usually, the alternative source of revenue was the cashflow of some specific taxes. But the late arrival of the fleet was not the only adverse set of circumstances that needed to be addressed – most of the asientos had several contingency clauses and appropriate remedies.

These contingencies, regulated by the asientos, certainly reduced the risk for the bankers in financing the imperial exploits of the Spanish Empire. But minimising risk is not the same as maximising profits – in order to do that, the merchant bankers were in fact following Davanzati's model. They were borrowing from investors where the price of the écu de marc was low and remitting where it was high. They were, in other words, doing exactly what a small private investor like Francesco Martinengo was doing, but on a grand scale, and for the benefit of the Empire. Once again, it was arbitrage that guaranteed the profitability of the asientos for the exchange bankers and for the state; it was arbitrage that saved Philip II and his imperial plans.

Spiritual Finance

All that busy arbitraging going on at the exchange fairs by banks and states and individuals did not go unnoticed by the good doctors of the Catholic Church. Not surprisingly, they wanted a piece of the proverbial action, and an institution that condemned and branded the act of lending a form of usury, a mortal sin, somehow managed to end up happily blessing the practice of arbitrage, to their own considerable advantage. This takes some explaining.

Running the Papal State was expensive; the Roman Curia cost a lot of money and defending the Catholic Church from the various threats posed by Protestants and Muslims did not come cheap. True, the Papal State could count on the tax revenues of the territories that were under its direct control, which were mostly in Italy. But these revenues were not nearly enough to meet the needs of the state. So, the Pope tended to rely on regular contributions from the faithful from other countries, which meant that in effect the Pope had exactly the same problem as Benedetto di Gondola and Philip II. They were all in the same boat – they all needed to move value across time and space. It wasn't easy to induce the exchange bankers to remit the Church's tithes, gifts and donations without giving them a chance to profit from these trades. But paying them was absolutely out of the question, because that would be usury. Bills of exchange offered the church an alternative method of payment and a convenient entry point to the magic world of arbitrage.

The Roman Curia came up with a form of what the church's bankers liked to call 'spiritual finance'. The ledgers of the Vatican bankers reveal exactly what was spiritual about it: absolutely nothing. Spiritual finance was a form of arbitrage done for the benefit of bankers and the Church: bankers provided the finance; the Church made it spiritual.

In the late sixteenth century, a man named Benvenuto Olivieri had replaced the Medici as the main banker to the Vatican. Olivieri regularly loaned to the Curia and was repaid with the concessions of specific tax revenues. Earning a profit from lending to the church was not easy because of the prohibition against usury, but Olivieri was a banker, he was creative, and the Curia was flexible enough so that he was just about able to make ends meet. But Olivieri understood that the really big opportunities for profits lay with spiritual finance, which involved transferring the tithes and donations of the faithful from countries elsewhere into the coffers in Rome.

The largest contribution to the Vatican's finances from elsewhere came from Spain. In 1567 alone, the money due from Spain was equal to 9 million ducats – remitting all of that to Rome would be a great way to make money. So, Olivieri followed the tried and tested path: he arbitraged the écu de marc via the exchange fairs of Lyon. Like di Gondola, the Pope's bankers had accounts with the firm of Salviati in Lyon. Through bills of exchange, they remitted the Spanish tithes to Lyon and from there onward to Rome. In fact, in order to be able to earn even more, they did not follow the most direct route, but rather the most profitable – the ledgers show lots of debts moving from Castille to Lyon and then going to Naples or Palermo before ending up in Rome. The multiple arbitrages suited both partners: the bankers could earn their profits with lots of little accumulated deals and the Church could get money without violating its stance on usury.

And how exactly did the Church justify this use of arbitrage? Theologians debated for some time whether the art of exchange was, in fact, usurious. Did a bill of exchange put one in danger of eternal damnation? After all, the first sentence in a bill of exchange is an acknowledgment of a debt and bankers made money by borrowing and remitting. Quite a few theologians argued that exchange was just a thinly disguised form of usury. But after much lengthy and acrimonious debate, the Church eventually reached a compromise. If the exchange was executed by three or more actors, and it involved borrowing and remitting in more than one location and in different currencies, then it was permitted. The reason being that the gain from trading under these circumstances, in different currencies and in more than one market, was just too risky to be considered usurious. It was a brilliant compromise that effectively blessed arbitrage and absolved any risk-loving Vatican bankers who practised it.

How much this position was influenced by the financial needs of the Church and how much it was really a correct understanding of the risks involved in exchange trades is difficult to establish, though the evidence from the ledgers of the Church bankers seems to suggest that the risk was perhaps rather more in the minds of the theologians than in the reality of trading.

The Power of Paper

So, over time, bills of exchange became one of Europe's greatest contributions to modernity. For centuries, merchants used them to trade goods, bankers used them to mobilise capital, and states, governments and the Catholic Church used them to finance their various activities. Not bad for what are really just a few sentences on a slip of paper.

Yet even these numerous and various examples might seem rather abstruse and far-removed from everyday life for anyone not already involved in the world of banking. So, let us look finally at a couple of examples that not only prove the versatility of bills of exchange but also bring them down to earth.

We'll start with the story of one of Italy's greatest and most celebrated explorers: the Florentine Giovanni da Verrazzano. Christopher Columbus made Verrazzano extremely envious. He dreamt of succeeding where Columbus had failed: Verrazzano wanted to become the one who discovered the Northwest passage. He believed

The Dance of Death: skeletons and merchant bankers.

that discovering a shorter route to China would make him not only famous but also wealthy. And he sorely needed money. Verrazzano had planned his expedition while serving in the French navy. He had asked the King to finance the expedition, but Francis I refused to foot the bill. So Giovanni then went to Lyon, the biggest market for capital of the day.

Bankers liked Verrazzano's idea of finding a shorter route to China more than the King did; they could see the potential. Verrazzano quickly secured 600 Ecus from French merchant bankers, but this was still way short of the 4,000 he needed. Then he approached Antonio Gondi, a Florentine banker who ran the Lyon branch of the family bank. Antonio also liked Verrazzano's plan, but 3,400 Ecus was a lot of money and he didn't want to bet the bank on Verrazzano's dream. But Antonio was canny and ambitious, and he put together a bit of a scheme: if a group of bankers with branches in different markets used bills of exchange to be negotiated and cleared at the exchange fairs of Lyon, then they might not need too many coins to be able to assist Verrazzano. It was doable. Using bills of exchange would save a lot of trouble, and a lot of silver and gold.

In no time at all, Antonio had managed to persuade nine other financiers, familiar with arbitrage trades among the exchange fairs, to back Verrazzano's plans. He then gave Verrazzano the green light and opened an account for him at the Gondi family bank. Verrazzano busily set about buying supplies for his expedition in Nantes, Rouen, Dieppe and Paris, the perfect set-up for using the flexible security. When Verrazzano needed to pay for supplies for the journey, he paid with bills of exchange on the bank, then the bank debited the members of the syndicate and cleared the debts at the next exchange fair. That way the risk was spread, and the use of coins was reduced.

But not all the payments could be done with debts; some had to be done with cash. While the evidence in the ledgers of the Gondi is incomplete, it looks like less than half of the cost of the expedition was paid with gold and silver to Verrazzano, but much was remitted with bills and then cleared at the Lyon fairs. Therefore, it was bills of exchange in écus de marc that enabled Giovanni da Verrazzano to pursue his dreams and sail west. Alas, in the end he only got to the Hudson Bay and not to Cathay. Verrazzano may have been disappointed, but the citizens of New York were grateful. In 1956, they named a bridge over the bay after him, which connects Brooklyn and Staten Island. For a long time, it was the longest suspension bridge in the world and a gateway to New York City. I have travelled across that bridge many times, all thanks to bills of exchange.

Empirical English Bills

Another, final example, and this time from the realm of the empirical English rather than the romantic Italian.

I spent 2017 as a fellow at the Yale International Center for Finance, on Whitney Avenue in the center of New Haven. The atmosphere at the center was informal; fellows and scholars interacted freely. Among the scholars was Gary Gorton, one of the world's great economists and a Professor of Finance at Yale. During my time there I was lucky enough to be able to spend time with Gary, talking about arbitrage, bills of exchange and, of course, Bernardo Davanzati.

Gary's research at the time concerned the question of how and why and under what circumstances private actors such as merchants, manufacturers, ordinary citizens, anyone other than banks, are able to create money. English 'inland bills', which are bills of exchange both drawn in a country and paid in the jurisdiction of that same country (hence, 'inland') proved a perfect test case for Gary's investigations. Inland bills in England were not issued by bankers and they were not used to arbitrage between currencies and markets. So, they didn't look like money, they didn't smell like money, but they seemed to behave like money. So what exactly were they? And how did they work?

Gary was not the first to ask that question. Since 1695, the English Parliament, bankers and economists had been arguing about what inland bills really were and what role they played in the economy. A couple of simple examples of their widespread use illustrate their delightfully uncertain status.

In the 1700s, money was still scarce in the north of England. Coins were few, the bank notes of the Bank of England circulated mostly in London and the opening of new banks was restricted. Up north, banks were sparse and thinly capitalised. Yet the counties in the north, the towns and cities, were the cradle of England's Industrial Revolution, and increasing production and manufacturing without money was not easy. Fortunately, the entrepreneurs in the industrial north were rather creative. Sir Samuel Fludyer, for example, was a merchant in Yorkshire who sold fabric and cloth. In 1738, he opened a warehouse in London to be closer to his clients; this way he knew which fabrics and colours were fashionable and he could have his network of suppliers back at home produce and deliver what sold well. Among his suppliers was a man named Floodshire, who was a dyer, and a certain Daniel Packer, who was a clothier.

Soon the jolly Yorkshiremen, the merchant Fludyer, the dyer Floodshire and the clothier Packer, all owed money to each other and to their own suppliers, just like the various counterparties that we studied in Pisa a few centuries earlier. And in just the same way, the clothier wanted to pay the dyer with the debt of the merchant that was owed to him. But alas, in the north of England the three partners could not simply walk into their local bank or visit the marketplace to exchange promises with a banker. They had to find other ways to pay with other people's debts. So how did they do it?

They used bills of exchange. In England, two types of bills circulated. One was the international bill, which was not much different from those issued and cleared at the exchange fairs of Lyon – four players, two markets, two currencies. Then there were the inland bills: securities which were denominated in pounds sterling and which circulated only within England – one currency, one market.

The inland bill may not have been designed to arbitrage between currencies and markets, but it absolutely fitted the purposes of the three partners up in Yorkshire. Packer wrote bills to Fludyer, who owed him money for the cloth he had purchased, directing him to pay Floodshire, who had dyed the fabrics for him. Inland bills were the perfect security to settle the mutual indebtedness of all the partners in the supply chain.

But manufacturers and merchants also had to pay people wages, which was rather more difficult than paying suppliers with bills: workers, like the mercenary soldiers of the Army of Flanders, preferred coins or something similar. Nonetheless, English entrepreneurs once again found a way round the problem by using bills of exchange. Rowland Park, a businessman from Kirby, was especially resourceful. He wrote off some of the wages of his workers against the bills of a doctor named Loxam, who was the physician who treated them and their families, and Park then wrote a bill of exchange to the wholesaler who handled his goods, directing him to pay Loxam. In England, millions of pounds' worth of inland bills such as this circulated at any one time, with no one using them to arbitrage between currencies and markets. So what purpose did they really serve? Were they actually money?

No consensus had been reached by the nineteenth century. Two bankers, Henry Thornton and Thomas Tooke, argued convincingly that bills were part of the currency of England because people used them as means of payment to increase their purchasing power beyond that of the available coins and bank notes: the larger the monetary base, which was made up of coins, bank debt and private debt, the greater the country's economic growth. This was enough for Thornton and Tooke to conclude that inland bills were indeed a part of the currency of England and should be considered as such.

Gary Gorton took a different approach. He wanted to find out if inland bills were money and, if so, *exactly* why. To do that he examined a sample of about 500 bills issued and circulated in England between 1775 and 1855. Many people issued and circulated bills of exchange during that period. He found that in 1775, inland bills constituted about 58 per cent of the country's total money supply. And in 1855, they still made up around 40 per cent of the money supply. And when the bills changed hands, they did so at par: bills therefore had the purchasing power of gold sovereigns or bank notes of the Bank of England. And they circulated well. Viewed up close, these inland bills do indeed function like money. In England, it seems, individual businessmen could create money in much the same way as the Mint and the banking system.

This is unusual, to say the least; we usually understand money creation to be one of the attributes of sovereignty and it is normally only banks that are allowed to create it, with special charters and under the strict controls of states, governments, emperors and kings. Yet it does appear that in England during this period, private individuals, simply by issuing bills, could create money. And that they could do so at all is because of the very special qualities of the security that they used to create that money: the bill of exchange.

When Samuel Fludyer drew a bill on Packer, asking him to pay Floodshire, he acknowledged his debt to the latter and promised to pay him. And when Packer accepted the bill, he also acknowledged his debt to Floodshire and promised to pay him. Since early 1600, the English courts had made the acceptor of a bill of exchange liable for the debt jointly and severally with the individuals that accepted it before and after him. Thus, the debt of Fludyer now had become the debt of Floodshire and Packer, a much safer security. And if Floodshire accepted it, three businessmen now became liable for that obligation; the more signatures, the more likely that the bill could turn into a gold coin at expiration. All the bills in Gary Gorton's sample, for instance, were endorsed by more than one person and several by more than ten people.

It was this multiple endorsement that made the bill function like a bank note. A bank note is the banker's promise to pay, and that promise is backed by all the debts of the customers of the bankers. Since inland bills were in effect debts backed by other debts, they, too, were part of the currency of England. That was Gary's conclusion.

The ability of individual businessmen to create money by issuing inland bills of exchange was key to the development of the Industrial Revolution in England. Indeed, it wasn't until the restrictions on banking were made less strict in England that bank money became the currency of the nation and bills of exchange became no longer as essential a part of English everyday financial life. Bills made the Industrial Revolution.

Our Fantastic Reality

Davanzati really did deserve to be at that Brussels exhibition about the books that made Europe. His brief essay on exchange trades, with that beautiful diagram, explains exactly how exchange bankers in early modern Europe could meet the financial needs of their clients and how they came to build a vast financial architecture, as grand and as all-encompassing as some fortified city, based on exchange fairs, on a stable private currency, the écu de marc, and a super-flexible security, bills of exchange.

With this architecture and with these foundations, a small group of bankers executed multiple arbitrage trades over centuries in order to help popes, kings and Italian explorers move value across time and space, yielding a steady stream of profits that attracted mobile capital from all across Europe to support the economic growth and the nation building of the modern era, our fantastic reality.

CHAPTER 6

American Dreams:
E Pluribus Unum

God bless the U.S.A., so large, So friendly, and so rich.

W. H. Auden
'On the Circuit' (1965)

O N October 2, 1704, a young woman named Sarah Kemble Knight, a teacher, recently widowed, left Boston, Massachusetts on a five-month round-trip to New Haven in neighbouring Connecticut, in order to visit relatives. Travelling on horseback, she kept a diary of her trip. *The Journal of Mme Knight*, first published in 1825, has become one of the most celebrated chronicles of early Colonial America.

It is also important evidence in the history of the emerging nation's great financial revolution: the creation of an entirely new kind of monetary system, without the use of coins; a banking system established with the express purpose of supporting the state; and the eventual establishment of a truly national bank with a national currency, engineered from bank debts and promises.

Intricate Ways of Trade

After the death of her husband, Sarah Kemble Knight took control of her financial affairs: having begun her career as a schoolteacher, she eventually became a property investor and successful businesswoman. Her trip's purpose was to settle the inheritance of a wealthy cousin; it also proved to be a useful education in financial literacy. She recorded vivid descriptions in her journal of the characters she encountered during her journey and made detailed notes on the nature and use of money in Colonial New England.

A few days of hard riding after her departure, Knight crossed into Connecticut, near New London, where she spent some time lodging at the house of a local merchant. Curious about how others conducted their business, she closely observed her host. When locals and travellers came into the merchant's store looking for wares, he would ask them how they wanted to pay. 'What do you want to pay in?' he would ask. To Knight's surprise, the prices varied according to their answer.

In one instance, Knight describes in detail the haggling over the price of a penknife. When a customer offered 'pay as money', the

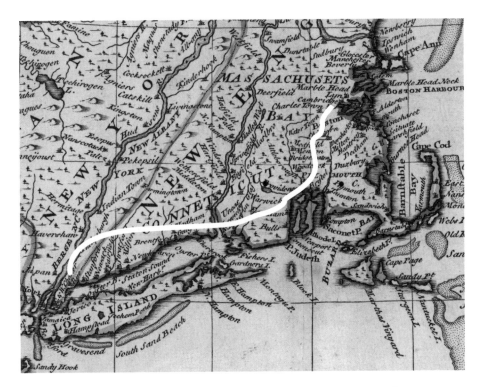

Sarah Kemble Knight's journey on horseback (1704–5), crossing Massachusetts, Rhode Island and Connecticut. Twice.

price of the penknife was twelve pence. But with 'pay', the penknife could be had for eight pence. And if the customer had coins, they could have the knife for a sixpence. 'It seems a very intricate way of trade,' Knight commented in her journal. She wanted to understand the intricacies. It turned out that there were basically four different types of money in use between Boston and New Haven: pay, coins, pay as money, and trusting.

> Pay is grain, pork, beef, etc. at the prices set by the General Court that year. Money is pieces of eight, ryalls or Boston or Bay shillings (as they call them,) or good hard money as sometimes silver coin is termed by them; also Wampum Indian beads which serves for change. Pay as money is provisions, as

aforesaid one third cheaper than as the Assembly or General Court sets it; and trust as they and the merchant agree for time.

Without quite knowing it, Knight was witnessing a new system of money – as debt – emerging in colonial America.

Coins had always been in short supply back in Knight's home town of Boston, but the General Court, as the Massachusetts legislature was called, did not want the colony to become a barter economy; the assemblymen believed bartering made trading inefficient, which slowed down economic growth. So, the court had chosen to stick with English money, pounds, shillings and pence, as the currency of the colony. At the same time, it had legislated a system that made it easy to settle debts with goods instead of coins, up to a limit, by stipulating exactly what each good was worth in English money. For instance, a bushel of corn was worth four shillings, but corn could legally settle debts only up to a value of forty shillings. Musket balls were less valuable, a farthing each – they settled debts up to twelve pence. Native American wampum – beads made of seashells – was small change. Thus, produce was allowed to settle debts by force of law, but only up to a threshold; above the threshold, acceptance was voluntary.

Using English money, along with pay and pay as money, was certainly better than bartering, but the early colonists in Massachusetts, as well as in Connecticut, tended to prefer paying with debts, or what Sarah Kemble Knight had described as 'trust', and in time, it was *this* practice of using debt as a means of payment that would extend far beyond merchants and businesses to most of the early colonial governments.

As the Massachusetts General Court tried to develop a monetary system that could work smoothly without coins by valuing goods according to a common standard – using debt as a means of payment – other colonial legislatures were doing exactly the same.

It was the sheer scarcity of coins that pushed the North American colonies into collectively establishing a coherent monetary system without the use of coins to represent money, something not done on such a large scale before. And it was this unique experience that eventually gave birth to the American dollar; a currency made of debts.

Debt as Money

Thomas Hancock was a man who knew all about using debt in business dealings. After starting his business in 1724, he became one of the most successful colonial merchants. In part, this success was due to his ability to employ debts in transacting business, and his ledgers reveal how he carried on trading despite the scarcity of coins.

As a prosperous merchant, Hancock liked to dress the part. He commissioned a local master tailor to make his trousers, jackets and waistcoats. When Hancock bought clothes from the tailor, he debited himself, on the ledger, the price of the clothes. When the tailor bought supplies at Hancock's store, Hancock debited him the price. Then he cleared the reciprocal indebtedness on the ledger. Paying for purchases by clearing debts became widespread in the colonies and by 1774, country folk, city dwellers, merchants and colonial leaders were all accustomed to paying with debts instead of coins. The practice was soon adopted by local governments to pay for public goods, including defence against skirmishes with French colonials and Native Americans.

Defence spending was particularly important to the colonies. In the 1600s, the colonists' clashes with French colonials and Native Americans were frequent, leading to Massachusetts assembling an expeditionary force against Quebec in 1689. The government of Massachusetts, however, did not have enough coins to pay for the expenses of the war, so they intended to compensate their troops with the booty from Quebec. Alas, Massachusetts's expedition was defeated, so no booty was to be had, and the colony lacked the resources to pay the defeated soldiers. To appease the troops, who were of course citizens of Massachusetts, the legislature paid them with bills of credit that they could later use to pay taxes. The citizen soldiers then gave the bills back to the local tax receiver when their tax was due, and the town treasurer cleared the mutual indebtedness on its ledger.

It's easy to imagine how the soldiers felt about this arrangement. Still, it worked reasonably well. It was what Sarah Kemble Knight would have called pay as trust, debt as money – or as close as you can get to it without banks.

Square Paper Bills

This was only the beginning. The Continental Congress, which governed the independent colonies – later, states – from 1775 to 1789, soon enlarged the practice of paying with debt by issuing bills of credit to public officials. Those officials could then pay for supplies, guns, uniforms, and rations with the bills, which were simply square pieces of printed paper. Each bill was a promise by Congress to pay a Spanish milled dollar, a heavy silver coin minted in Mexico and Peru and commonly used throughout North and South America, Europe, and Asia. Congress's square paper bills were basically primitive public debt securities intended to work as money.

And for a while they worked well. The problem, as we've seen with so many kinds of public debt security, was that their success led to an inevitable erosion in their purchasing power.

Paper money issued in 1690 by the Colony of Massachusetts. The bill is a debt of the colony that can be used by the holder to pay taxes.

The Continental Congress planned to clear people's debts against tax revenues. But the politics around the Articles of Confederation, agreed to in 1776, did not encourage tax compliance. The payment of taxes was seldom enforced and most of the square dollars were not returned to the tax receivers, remaining in circulation instead. With Congress and the former colonies requiring resources to fight the English, they then had to print yet more bills. And still they did not enforce the payment of taxes. Each newly issued bill increased the number of square dollars in circulation. But each additional bill in circulation also reduced its purchasing power. In an effort to break the inflationary cycle, the Continental Congress issued levies to be paid in silver and gold coins, and published depreciation tables that set the value of square dollars in each new issue compared with the previous ones. These arrangements, perhaps not surprisingly, were ineffective, and the purchasing power of the bills of credit continued to erode.

Delegates to the Continental Congress, representatives from the thirteen colonies that ultimately became the United States of America, were aware that the continual issue of bills was a problem, but felt they had no choice. What else could they do? What would really help, they recognised, was access to a banking system, a business that many of the delegates, as pioneering merchants and businessmen, well understood. Congress could then exchange public debts for bank debts, and since bank debts have the purchasing power of coins, this would allow them to buy more supplies to fight the so-called Redcoats, the British, enemies of the revolution, without fear of an erosion in value.

There was only one problem: there were no banks in the colonies. Enter: John Hancock.

The House of Hancock

Before the war, colonial merchants like well-dressed Thomas Hancock, and his brother John, had made extensive use of bank money despite the lack of domestic institutions. The House of Hancock, as their business was known, was one of the most vital in the colonies – they sold everything from pickled pork to household wares and from gunpowder to whale oil. Upon John's death, his son – also, confusingly, John Hancock, and the famous signer of the Declaration of Independence – went to live with Thomas. The younger John went on to learn the rudiments of business from his uncle, becoming instrumental in the company's overseas affairs, until eventually becoming one of the wealthiest men in the colonies when his uncle died and he inherited the business. His experience with the House of Hancock served him and the emerging nation well.

The House of Hancock had prospered by swapping promises to pay with English banks. The firm exported commodities, including whale oil and potash (a form of salt) to England. A man named Francis Wilks, the Hancocks' agent in London, sold their goods and kept the sales' proceeds. When the company purchased manufactured goods, they paid with bills of exchange. Those bills instructed Wilks to pay for the goods in London.

The Hancocks often issued bills of exchange to Wilks for more money than they had left with him, and to keep the Hancocks as clients, Wilks asked his bank to pay the bills. The bank then swapped Hancocks' debts with its own. The debts of the English bank circulated as money in most countries, and with those debts the House of Hancock became the biggest merchant in Boston.

In 1775, John Hancock was chosen as president of the Continental Congress. He and his fellow congressmen realised that they could take what they had learned as merchants dealing with English banks and use this knowledge against the British. There may not have been banks in the newly founded colonies, but there were plenty in those European nations hostile to England: France, Spain and Holland. The Congress believed, rightly, that these nations would be willing to support them in their war effort against their common foe. Congress therefore did exactly as John Hancock and other colonial merchants had done, dispatching envoys to various European cities, issuing their delegates with international bills of exchange. It instructed the delegates to exchange the bills for bank debts, creating substantial amounts of bank money that could be used to buy more cannons and muskets back home. It was up to the envoys to persuade the local foreign banks to accept the exchange.

Congress believed that their best chance to make their strategy work would be in France, so in March 1776 they sent a man named Silas Deane – now known as one of the original Founding Fathers, and a shrewd merchant from Connecticut – to Paris. Deane's role in helping to bankroll his new nation was certainly significant, but shortly after his arrival in Paris, a certain Benjamin Franklin joined him as another representative of Congress. And Franklin's role, as so often in his extraordinary life, was game-changing.

French Money

Franklin took residence in Passy, on the outskirts of Paris. He rented a home near a certain Alphonse Ferdinand Grand. Grand was Swiss, and like the French Finance Minister, Jacques Necker (the two were friends), he was a banker. He was the Managing Partner of Grand & Cie, a merchant bank based in Paris and Antwerp. A number of states and countries banked with Grand; Holland and Sweden were among his clients. Grand & Cie also traded the public debts of France, while raising funds for the kingdom; Grand knew exactly how banks could profit from helping governments. And his new neighbour Benjamin Franklin knew that in Grand he had found the right partner to help him and his fellow colonists fight their war in America.

Grand kindly explained how banks create money by exchanging debts – or promises, as he called them – and proposed to Franklin some of the ways in which his bank could create promises that the Continental Congress could use as money, bank money that would be backed by the public debt of the colonies. Grand's memos to Franklin setting out his ideas are a pleasure to read: short, clear and entirely to the point. And Franklin was a fast learner. Together, the two friends hatched a plan to create bank money for use by the Continental Congress – yet another version of the old story of states and banks exchanging debts and promises.

So, by 1778, things were looking pretty positive for Franklin and the American representatives to France. The King of France, Louis XVI, and his Foreign Minister had agreed to support the United States; the Finance Minister, Necker, was already on board. But getting cash from a sovereign state is always a struggle: persuading donors takes time, prying cash out of bureaucracies is far from easy, quibbling makes the outcome uncertain, and gifts suddenly become loans. The cash that finally reaches the recipient is often late and insufficient. French aid to the colonies was no exception. France's public debt was huge and the French treasury was short of coins.

Also, Grand was cautious as well as ambitious. He had dealt with sovereign nations, those that were more established than the fledgling United States, plenty of times. He knew the perils of relying on the promises of sovereigns and he was not going to 'bet the bank' on the promises of either France or the North American colonies fighting for independence. The colonies weren't even a nation yet, despite the Continental Congress declaring it the 'United States of America' in September 1776, and with all the bills of credit in circulation, it was already awash with debts.

Grand's considered proposal was therefore to issue bank debt to the Continental Congress on the requirement that both America and France promised to pay his bank first. But the French Finance Minister, Necker, was reluctant to give explicit royal guarantees, so the negotiations stalled. At which point, Grand and Franklin came up with a new proposal: special promissory notes, written promises to pay.

These were a success. Between 1779 and 1782 Benjamin Franklin signed promissory notes, each one for an amount ranging from 250,000 to 800,000 livres. In this way, over the course of just a few years, Franklin was able to secure no less than 18 million livres in funds for the Continental Congress. And Franklin, being Franklin, designed and printed the notes himself at his printing press in Passy, putting his characteristic flair and care into their design and reproduction.

The wording on these radical promissory notes indicates precisely the nature of the scheme that he and Grand had concocted to get the colonies the purchasing power they so desperately needed. Each note was signed by Franklin on behalf of the Continental Congress and each of the thirteen colonies, jointly and severally; they were therefore the obligations of each and every American sovereign entity. Also, on the notes, Franklin promised to pay Grand & Cie, on January 1, 1785, for the benefit of the French Royal Treasury, which meant that Necker thus felt safe and secure to promise to also pay the bank for the benefit of the United States.

It was the linking of sovereign promises that did the trick: France was now indebted to the bank for the benefit of the United States, and the United States was indebted to the bank for the benefit of France. With the two sovereign promises in his pocket, Grand happily issued debts to the United States, bank money that the Continental Congress could spend right away. He had successfully gained a new client without endangering the future of Grand & Cie.

In this process, Grand, Necker and Franklin had basically come up with the sovereign version of an 'accommodation bill', through which two parties guarantee each other promises to pay one bank. That bank then feels safe to issue debts for the benefit of one party. Historically, accommodation bills have been used by aggressive financers to get banks to issue debt to them and such schemes have often been criticised as one of the main reasons why banks fail and why bank money is unsafe. Adam Smith, for example, the great Scottish economist, advised banks not to accept accommodation bills. They were way too risky. Nonetheless, that's exactly what Grand, Necker and Franklin did in 1785: two sovereign nations using aggressive financial engineering to support a fight for independence – a fine example of truly daring financial dealing between states and banks.

Not surprisingly, several other banks in Europe had got word of the Continental Congress's needs and were also busy going after their business. But they approached the process in a different way than Grand, trying to make a quick buck. Luckily for the future United

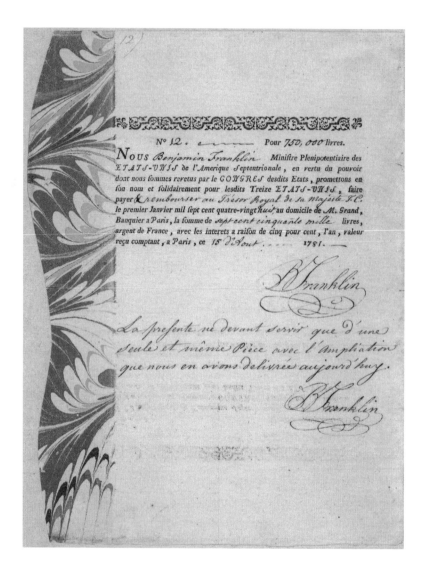

A promissory note written, printed and signed by Benjamin Franklin while he was Plenipotentiary of the Continental Congress in France. It is a promise to pay the bank of Ferdinand Grand for the benefit of the French Treasury.

States, both Franklin and Grand were able to take the long view, with Grand, in particular, knowing that his bank would profit more for a longer period of time if the colonies succeeded, becoming a truly sovereign nation with debt, the perfect client.

Bills of Exchange

But Grand wasn't the only businessman working hard to help the new republic. Though his bank was happy to exchange U.S. debt for his bank's promises and, occasionally, gold and silver coins, Grand & Cie was based in Paris and Antwerp. Back in the colonies, the army needed more money and resources than Grand and France had promised – and they needed it fast. The needs of George Washington's army were great. They required shoes, blankets, rifles, cannons, everything, and these supplies had to be sourced from multiple countries. Agents bought these goods wherever possible, whether in Europe, South America or the West Indies.

In June 1777, when Congressmen were debating exactly how to exploit Grand's bank money, they decided to take a page from the colonial merchant's playbook once again, by issuing bills of exchange payable in Paris for more than the French Treasury had promised to Grand. The strategy had worked well for merchants like the Hancocks, so they reasoned it should work well for the United States. Of course, the Continental Congress was not a trading house, issuing bills of exchange was not easy and each colony wanted a share in the bills of exchange in French currency to benefit its own residents, so squabbling ensued, but Congress eventually agreed on a solution.

First, Congress had to approve each and every issue of the bills. The president of Congress then signed each set and the bills were split among the thirteen colonies. The Continental Loan Officer of each state countersigned the bills of its state, which were then dispatched by ship to representatives in the European nations. Ships could sink or be captured by enemies or pirates, so four copies of each bill were

Bill of exchange in Spanish dollars issued by the Continental Congress in 1780.

printed and shipped separately. Congress figured that at least one of the copies would get into the right hands.

Congress was doing exactly what the colonial merchants had done. It issued debts for more than Franklin, Grand & Cie and the French Treasury had promised to each other, and relied on its agents to get Grand & Cie to issue enough bank money to cover the bills. While some bills paid for military supplies in Europe, Congress and the states also sold some to businessmen who needed funds overseas. The Continental Congress had the same goal as the leaders of Venice in 1619, England in 1694, and Spain and Naples at the end of the 1500s – all of them wanted to buy more goods with the same amount of public debt. They were able to do so by swapping state promises to pay with bank promises, giving public debt the purchasing power of gold.

Congress was able to make ends meet by exchanging its debts with Grand & Cie, but the deal did not fix the fundamental flaw in the taxation system in the states and the new nation. The Continental Congress could issue its own bills of credit but the power to tax belonged to each state, who were reluctant to raise taxes, and who kept what little revenue they raised in taxes for themselves. The arrangement finally became untenable in 1779, when Congress and the states voted to reform the nation's currency, making it difficult for Congress to print more square dollars without the backing of new taxes. The plan was sound, but implementing it required time, negotiations, and compromises.

And it came at entirely the wrong moment.

A Bank that Doesn't Make Money

The year 1780 did not start well for the American cause. Charleston fell to the British; the southern army was in tatters. The winter was harsh and George Washington's troops lacked food. They urgently needed 3 million rations and 300 hogsheads of rum. But the currency reform of 1779 had made it impossible to print more bills of credit to buy the rations. So once again, Congress needed cash.

Philadelphia stepped forward to assist. There was plenty of money in Philadelphia: coins, bills of credit and bills of exchange in many currencies. Most of the money was in the hands of merchants, who were true patriots but also hardheaded businessmen. Patriotic fervour ran high in the city, and its citizens debated among themselves how best to help Washington's hungry army. Two men – Thomas Paine and Robert Morris – came up with a plan to turn Philadelphia's patriotism into money. Paine and Morris were an odd couple, to say the least. Paine was a one-time teacher, tobacconist and corset-maker from England who had emigrated to Philadelphia after a chance encounter with Benjamin Franklin. In the New World, Paine had reinvented himself as a philosopher and pamphleteer. Morris, meanwhile, also originally from England, was a cunning businessman, slaver and shipping magnate who became known as the 'Financier of the Revolution'. Together, they developed a plan to get enough cash to help George Washington and his army.

Paine and Morris planned to open a bank of sorts and in doing so, they laid the groundwork for the first American public bank. Crediting the Bank of England as their model, they named their institution the Bank of Pennsylvania, even though it little resembled the Bank of

Left: Thomas Paine, with Robert Morris, was behind the scheme for the Bank of Pennsylvania. Right: Robert Morris, Superintendent of Finance.

England, or indeed any other bank. The Bank of Pennsylvania was really nothing more than a syndicate, a temporary alliance of citizens coming together to achieve a single and simple goal. Supporters pledged to lend the bank enough money to buy the rum and rations for Washington's army, and the bank pledged to return the loan and pay a low interest rate, 6 per cent, in six months.

The Bank of Pennsylvania wasn't going to sell supplies to Washington and his men – all they were going to do was buy and deliver; they weren't going to lend, only borrow. But without selling anything, without lending, the bank would have no revenues, only costs, and no self-respecting businessman in Philadelphia was willing to fund such an enterprise. Potential subscribers may have been willing to lend cheaply, but not to lose their capital entirely. So, in order to get their plan off the ground, Morris and Paine asked Congress to post collateral with the bank – hard money, not bills of credit – in order to offer security to the lenders. Morris, helpfully, was on the Congressional committee for the Treasury and helped broker an agreement.

The deal was as follows. Congress would deliver the new bank some bills of exchange, in Spanish dollars, French livres, and Dutch guilders, equal to the amount loaned to the bank. These bills, in hard currencies, provided the kind of security the subscribers needed. In return, Congress demanded full oversight of any deals. For example, in order to return money to its lenders, the bank would have to sell some of the bills to merchants and businessmen trading overseas – and Congress would have to have full approval of the sales. The arrangement made sense for all parties: the bank could offer security to their subscribers; Congress could have the oversight it felt it deserved and wanted; and Washington's troops would get their food and drink. And so with these terms agreed upon, and the bills of exchange duly delivered, the first bank in the continental United States began operations.

The Bank of Pennsylvania was certainly an oddity – a corporate body set up to supply the army, with capital made not of equity but 100 per cent debt, and with a loan backed by bills of exchange in hard currency. Also, although the United States is often regarded as the home of 'free banking', its very first bank was very far from free; the Continental Congress essentially controlled the bank, meaning

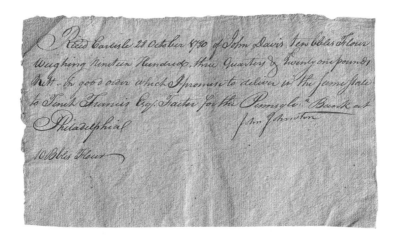

A promise by John Johnston to deliver to Tench Francis, factor of the Bank of Pennsylvania, 10 barrels of flour that the bank purchased for the Washington army.

that the North American legislature had much more power over the bank than Parliament did over the Bank of England. Only Congress could allow the sale of the collateral to reimburse the subscribers, and it also checked on all the procurement and delivery of rations and rum.

Nonetheless, despite or because of its highly unusual foundations and structure, the Bank of Pennsylvania fulfilled its singular mission, and Washington's army lived to fight another day, fed and watered on the funds raised in Philadelphia.

Plans for a National Bank

But, of course, the citizens of Philadelphia, and indeed across the emerging republic, soon wanted more. They wanted a *real* bank, not just some one-off syndicate; they wanted a bank that could make money exchanging the debts of clients for its own. Morris and Paine were well aware of the limitations of the Bank of Philadelphia. They had proceeded with their plan because it was the best way to get rations to the army in a hurry. But they knew that only a true bank could turn public debt into money, something the young country

The Battle of Monmouth between Washington's Army and the British forces, 1778.

The Bank of North America handing a wad of bank notes to George Washington.

desperately needed. When Morris became Congress's first, and only, Superintendent of Finance in 1781, he quickly set about meeting those needs.

In 1781, the aspiring new nation still had lots of debts and few coins. But like any financier who properly understands how debt works, Morris viewed these debts as assets first, then liabilities. In 1782, he told Congress that 'debt is a species of property, or stock', and if it was used properly, it would generate income and purchasing power. Morris wanted to establish a bank that would deal only in short-term debts, a commercial enterprise that would earn money exchanging the debts of clients for its own. He believed that such a business could quickly turn the mountain of public and private short-term debts in the colonies into purchasing power, a purchasing power that would make both the state and its citizens wealthier. The bank's clients could use the debt of the bank as money, paying for taxes and filling the public coffers with the bank's promises to pay, and the government could also become a client of the bank, exchanging chunks of public debt for bank money. The purchasing power of public offices would grow, and eventually bank money could replace bills of credit as the national currency. No such bank had existed in North America before, but Morris was absolutely convinced that his plans for a national bank could work.

There was only one thing standing in his way.

There were certainly plenty of debts, private and public, in the new nation, but gold and silver coins continued to be limited. And the new bank would need plenty of gold and silver to get off the ground. Without those reserves, Morris would be unable to persuade wealthy merchants, farmers, and consumers that bank debt was truly money, the kind that could be exchanged for coins day in, day out, on demand. The bank needed liquidity. Without coins, Morris believed that his plans would not work.

Alexander Hamilton's Alternative

But Morris wasn't the only person developing plans for a national bank. There were those with other ideas. A young man named Alexander Hamilton was one of those busy drawing up plans of his own.

A bold thinker and a brave soldier, in his twenties Hamilton was serving as aide de camp to George Washington. 'Aides de camp are persons in whom entire confidence must be placed and it requires men of abilities to execute the duties with propriety and dispatch,' wrote Washington. Hamilton excelled in his duties and eventually went on to become a successful lawyer, politician, and indeed, the hero of a rap musical. But while working for Washington, he spent much of his spare time studying European banking systems. It was time well spent.

A fierce patriot, like Morris, Hamilton believed that in order for the emerging nation to prosper it would need a strong national bank, capable of issuing lots of bank money. But Hamilton believed that the new United States would need a much larger bank than even Morris envisaged, with capital of at least 3 million Spanish milled dollars, a spectacular sum. In Hamilton's opinion, only such a well-capitalised bank could issue enough debts to make a difference in the new nation he imagined. A bank that just sold shares for coins would never reach capital of 3 million, so Hamilton proposed that the bank sell shares for a mixture of coins, land, and European debt securities.

In mid-May 1781, while still only in his mid-twenties and on Washington's staff, and while lobbying to secure command of his own infantry company to fight the British, Hamilton sent his alternative blueprint for the National Bank to Morris.

Alexander Hamilton, first Secretary of the Treasury of the US.

Morris praised the creativity of the plan, but rejected it as unrealistic. Morris did not intend to take any risks with bank liquidity. He was determined that bank shareholders should pay for their shares only in coins; he wanted a bank with liquid assets and liquid assets only on the balance sheet – bills and short-term securities and enough coins as a reserve. In Morris's opinion, Hamilton's plan would not provide the bank with enough coins to be able to exchange notes with silver and gold on demand; land and long-term debt, by nature not highly liquid, were poor assets for a bank in the new America. Morris's plan was to start small, with a high level of liquidity, using starting capital of only 400,000 dollars rather than Hamilton's estimated 3 million.

Yet for all their differences, the two plans had one important feature in common: they both agreed that any new national bank would need public as well as private shareholders. Morris was determined that Congress should buy the first shares. He believed that gold and silver flowing from the state to the bank would persuade merchants and planters to part with their cash as well. Of course, this had implications: he needed to find enough coins to pay for Congress's shares, before asking citizens to get involved. So, in late May 1781, he asked Congress for permission to import more silver into the United States, allowing Congress to buy shares of the bank and give comfort to private capital.

At the time, the best place for the new government to get silver was in Havana. For 200 years, Spain had shipped the silver minted in Mexico and Peru to Cuba, where boats waited in the ports of Havana for the right weather to cross the Atlantic to Europe with their precious cargo. With Cuba's proximity to continental North America, Morris reasoned, it should be possible to bring the coins home from there without much trouble. In order to obtain the silver, Morris planned to sell bills of exchange to Havana, payable in Europe. He commandeered a frigate, the *Trumbull*, and delivered the bills of exchange to the ship's captain, James Nicholson, a war hero who had outfoxed many English ships before, and the ship set sail to Havana.

Though the first few months of Morris's tenure as Superintendent were undoubtedly trying, perhaps no single day in office was worse for him than August 28, 1781. On that day, English cruisers surprised the *Trumbull* off the coast of Florida. The Royal Navy overpowered the ship, Nicholson surrendered, and the English seized the cargo, including the bills of exchange for 500,000 Spanish dollars, signed by Morris. For a moment, it looked like Morris's plans for a national bank were in jeopardy.

But all was not lost. Two weeks later, a French ship, the *Resolute*, entered Boston Harbour with the equivalent of 463,000 dollars in silver coins, a shipment from Congress's old friend, the French Treasury. John Hancock signed the receipt for the coins and took possession of the cargo. Shortly after, Morris managed to transport the French silver safely to Philadelphia, having snuck it across British lines. And with French coins worth 254,000 Spanish dollars, and Congress's permission, he bought 60 per cent of the shares of the First Bank of North America, the nation's first true public bank.

Morris's plan was back on course.

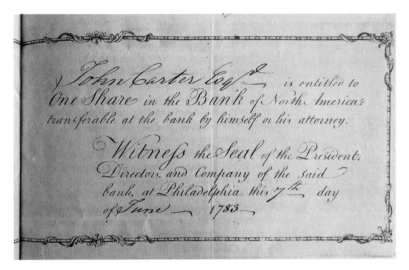

A share in the Bank of North America issued to John Carter, the brother-in-law of Alexander Hamilton.

The Bank of North America

Morris hoped to create a national currency made entirely of bank notes and deposits. He planned to replace the bills of credit – public debt – with the debts of banks as money. But a corporation with capital of only 250,000 dollars was unable to issue very much debt without going bust. What Morris called the Bank of North America therefore needed yet more coins and assets. Merchants, farmers, and business-men could supply both, but they were still resistant to paying coins for bank shares. So, Morris made yet another daring move: he struck a deal with the lenders to his first bank, the Bank of Pennsylvania.

The Bank of Pennsylvania's directors still held bills of exchange for 70,000 Spanish dollars in hard currency. They wanted to stick to the agreement they had with their lenders and sell those bills to return hard coins to them. But the directors in Philadelphia needed congressional approval in order to make any such move. And Congress refused; starved for coins of its own, it withheld permission. In Philadelphia, the bank's creditors were getting impatient; they wanted their money back. So, it was a standoff. The atmosphere throughout the city was tense. Morris, always the deal-maker and determined to succeed, saw his chance. He brokered an agreement between Congress and the creditors in which Congress authorised the selling of the bills and the returning of the coins to the lenders, but *only if* they used those coins to buy shares in the Bank of North America.

In brokering this audacious deal, Morris received both more coins and more private shareholders for his bank. Even though the capital was still short of the planned 400,000 dollars, the national bank could now start operating, and on January 7, 1782, less than a year after Morris had become Superintendent of Finance, the Bank of North America opened its doors on Chestnut Street in Philadelphia. And that very same day it got its biggest client: the Continental Congress of the United States.

But, of course, Morris immediately needed yet more bank debts. For months he had pushed Grand, Congress's French banking partner, to issue more. But Grand had resisted. Grand & Cie was stretched to the limit. He may have promised to pay all bills of exchange issued by Congress, but they kept coming and Grand & Cie now had far too much government debt on its balance sheet. And in the end, Grand refused to issue any more debt to the Continental Congress.

This meant that Morris had no choice but to exchange American public debt with American bank debt, rather than with the French; the foreign banks had let him down. So he handed the Bank of North America a six-month promissory note for 100,000 dollars, on behalf of Congress. The bank kept 3,000 dollars as commission and gave Morris bank notes for 97,000 dollars. These bank notes could be exchanged on demand for the silver dollars in the bank's coffers. That guarantee meant that the bank notes, in theory, should have kept moving from hand to hand, at par with the coins. Fortunately, they did. The bank notes kept their value and the Office of the Superintendent gained a massive amount of purchasing power from the deal.

Yet whatever the deals, and however many of them, there was never enough money, and Morris was soon exchanging with the bank another promissory note for 100,000 dollars in bank money. And then another. And when the first promissory note came due, he replaced it with another. The two parties repeated this transaction over and over again – every time Congress received the bank notes for 97,000 dollars, the bank received 3,000 dollars. Morris got his bank debts, the directors of the bank earned a good return, and they all helped the Continental Congress pay for the war. The state promised to pay the bank, and the bank promised to pay the state, with the bank delivering on its promise by giving the public Treasury debts rather than coins, and the state gained debts that would not depreciate, a debt-exchanging partnership much the same as that found between the Venetian Senate and Banco Giro, and Parliament and the Bank of England. As always, when the alchemy of banking was working, everyone benefitted, except that the balance of power tilted toward the bank. The country was flooded with depreciating bills of credit, so public debt was still not worth much, while bank debts continued to have the purchasing power of coins. The Bank of North America was thriving.

By October 1782, the Bank of North America held promissory notes of the Congress's office of finance for 400,000 dollars, which was more than the bank's paid-in capital. The finance office had paid suppliers with many different kinds of promises: bills, mandates, orders. The creditors then went to the bank and exchanged these debt instruments with bank debts, causing public debt securities to make up the largest share of the Bank of North America's assets. Things were going well, but the bank's directors grew nervous. The alchemy of banking works only if a bank's ledger is balanced. If the public debt that the bank held as assets lost value, the liabilities would be worth more than the assets, and the bank would fail (which, by the way, at the time of writing, is *exactly* what happened at the Silicon Valley Bank in 2023). The risks of exchanging obligations with Congress's finance bureau exceeded the potential profits. The bank chairman therefore asked Morris to redeem some of the promissory notes with coins. Despite its exposure to public debt, the bank was prospering and there was demand for its shares – which meant that Morris had no real choice.

He sold all the government stock in the bank for over 250,000 dollars. This meant that the Continental Congress was no longer the controlling shareholder in the bank, merely a client and a regulator. The Bank of North America was effectively now a private corporation. And there were plenty of private debts in the new country that the bank could benefit from: merchants and manufacturers exchanged the debts of their partners and customers for the bank's. Bank notes and deposits grew fast, and the bank's customers used them more and more. Despite this fast growth, the bank debts continued to hold their value, circulating at par with coins. Unfortunately, the same could not be said for the bills of credit of the Continental Congress, which kept losing purchasing power.

In order to help Congress, and in his never-ending pursuit of bank money, Morris then moved to the final stage of his plan: to convince citizens to pay their taxes with bank debts. He instructed tax collectors to favour bank notes over any other means of payment, helping both the bank and Congress. Bank money flowed into the public purse, and Congress's purchasing power grew again, as did the demand for bank debts. The bank prospered, and a virtuous circle began. As bank notes moved into the hands of citizens and public coffers, Morris's dream of a continental currency made of bank money was becoming a reality.

The Trouble with Pounds, Shillings and Pence

This new currency made of bank debts, however, was a mess. The American colonies had inherited currency practices of the motherland, and old habits die hard. Most states still counted their money in pounds, shillings, and pence, just as England did; 12 pence made one shilling, and 20 shillings made 1 pound. But each colony valued these shillings, pounds, and pence differently in terms of other currencies. A shilling was not worth the same amount of foreign currencies in, say, Georgia, as it was in New Hampshire. And when Congress had chosen a unit of money different from that of England – the Spanish milled dollar – in 1775, it had only added to the confusion. Though the dollar was the currency of the United States, it was not worth the same in every colony. Each colony treated the congressional currency as foreign. In Georgia, 1 dollar was worth 5 shillings; in New Hampshire, Massachusetts, Rhode Island, Connecticut, and Virginia it was worth 6. Meanwhile, 7 shillings and 6 pence got you a Spanish dollar in Delaware, New Jersey, and Pennsylvania; and one could be had for 8 shillings in New York and North Carolina. South Carolina, on the other hand, was off the chart – there, 1 dollar equaled 32 shillings because the value of the South Carolina shilling was so low. These varying values obviously hampered cross-border transactions, causing trade between the states to suffer. Something had to be done.

In January of 1782, at the same time as the Bank of North America began operation, Congress established a five-man committee 'to consider the state of money in the United States, and report thereon'. Robert Morris and his assistant Gouverneur Morris (no relation) took the lead. Despite having lost a leg in a carriage accident, resulting in his famous peg leg, Gouverneur Morris was a *bon vivant* and a ladies' man. Well-known for his role in writing the Preamble to the Constitution and renowned for his aristocratic manner, Gouverneur had always been interested in money. He had excelled in mathematics while at college and loved playing with numbers. Recognising his skills, Robert Morris suggested that Gouverneur figure out how to create a common national currency. The two men reported their findings to Congress on January 15. Robert Morris described the challenge to Congress as such:

A farmer in New Hampshire, for instance, can readily form an idea of a bushel of wheat in South Carolina, weighing sixty pounds, and [placed] at one hundred miles from Charlestown; but if he were told that in such situation it is worth twenty one shillings and eight pence, he would be obliged to make many enquiries, and form some calculations before he could know that this sum meant, in general, what he would call four shillings; and even then, he would have to enquire what kind of coin that four shillings was paid in, before he could estimate it in his own mind according to the ideas of money which he imbibed.

Members of Congress wanted to help both the New Hampshire farmer and his buyer in South Carolina, and in principle they all favoured a standardised currency. But each member had his own ideas about which money should be used as the national currency.

The Morrises had a hard task at hand. They didn't want to privilege the money of any one state over another, and anyway the Articles of Confederation did not give Congress exclusive power to create money or to dictate a common currency. The differences between the states on the question of a national currency were based largely on sectoral disparities. Farmers, for instance, wanted means of payment that were easy to use and widely accepted, while wealthy merchants did not want to upset the existing monetary habits of their partners and customers, practices that were based on the involvement of banks in clearing mutual indebtedness.

The new nation was at loggerheads.

Thomas Jefferson's Coins

Gouverneur Morris was forced to make a deal with Thomas Jefferson, who had been working on a system of coinage – among many other things – for many years. Jefferson advocated switching to an arithmetic of money based on the decimal system. It was agreed that the money of the United States would use the Spanish dollar, denominated in Jefferson-style decimal-based units. So far, so good. But the process didn't end there. Now Gouverneur had to figure out how to convert shillings into dollars in a way everyone would accept, coming up with a rate that would be easy to use and would not favour one state's valuation of the shilling over the others.

Gouverneur then struck upon a brilliant, if rather complex, idea. It was truly a mathematician's solution. The Spanish dollar was worth either 60, 72, 90 or 96 pence across the country. (The only exception was still South Carolina, with its 384 pence for a single dollar.) Ignoring South Carolina, the least common multiple of the four values was 1,440. That number, Gouverneur believed, was the answer to all of the problems: the fraction 1/1,440 would become the unit of the national currency, requiring a simple calculation to convert dollars into the shillings of each state. Since the shilling was worth 12 pence everywhere, this made things easier. Thus, in Georgia the shilling would be one-fifth of a dollar, while in Virginia a shilling would be one-sixth of a dollar. This new monetary arithmetic would make it somewhat easy to compare prices across the nation. A good priced at 20 cents of a dollar would be worth one shilling in Georgia and 14 pence in Virginia. Farmers and merchants in any state would welcome the national currency.

Gouverneur had devised a national currency that did not upset local habits and pride; the national money was decimal, just as Jefferson had suggested; and the convenient fraction made conversion into state money perfectly straightforward. Robert Morris believed the plan would fly through Congress, and that this new money would become national in a heartbeat.

This did not happen. The scheme had a major flaw, perhaps obvious to anyone who was not a financier, an aristocrat or a wealthy merchant. The proposed system may have made bookkeeping and clearing debts easier for merchants, but it didn't help small farmers and consumers in villages and towns across the nation. The way in which yeoman farmers bought goods hadn't changed much from the time Sarah Kemble Knight had observed rural commerce in Connecticut more than half a century earlier. The first question rural and small-town merchants asked prospective customers was still: 'What do you pay in?' Small farmers and traders looked at the means of payment in their pockets, not at the arithmetic of money on paper. They wanted coins to buy goods at the local store without discounts, coins that held their value and were widely accepted.

The basic monetary unit proposed by Morris was a fraction and therefore too small to be made into a coin. The Morrises had planned to mint pieces worth more than a fractional unit, of course, but valuing the coins would have been fiendishly difficult. The proposed new currency would have made clearing debts on ledgers easy, but paying for a penknife at a country store would have been much more complicated.

Thomas Jefferson spotted this flaw right away and proposed an entirely different approach, stressing physical money as means of payment. Instead of focusing on debts, as Robert Morris always had, Jefferson focused on the coins. Less interested in helping merchants and bankers trade debts across state borders, he wanted to give the new republic a shared coinage, composed of silver pieces, suitable for farmers, city dwellers and all other citizens to buy goods and wares. With this goal in mind, he suggested a radically simplified monetary plan to Congress.

Jefferson believed that a coinage system with just a few pieces and only decimal multiples and subdivisions would lead to a standardised national currency. He praised Gouverneur Morris's overall strategy, but criticised the plan to make a small fraction the monetary unit. In Jefferson's plan, he ignored the complexities of converting the Spanish dollars into the shilling of different states, the bedrock of Robert Morris's and Gouverneur Morris's proposal. Instead, the national coinage Jefferson proposed was straightforward and easy to understand: just five main silver coins, made up of the dollar, half-dollar, one-fifth dollar, one-tenth dollar, and one-twentieth dollar. Copper coins would be small change worth less than one-twentieth of a dollar. Gold pieces would represent dollar multiples.

The two plans were fundamental expressions of two fundamentally different worlds. The Morrises came from the world of the financial class and merchants, so their main concern was making the squaring of debts in merchants' ledgers easy. Jefferson was not a merchant; he was a landowner. The two plans also represented different approaches to the new nation's money. The Morrises were seeking a national standard of value that also worked with the accounting used by the merchants of the former colonies. Jefferson, part of the landed gentry, was suspicious of large-scale trading and finance, which is why he focused on physical means of payment, specifically the coins circulating among freemen and small farmers.

This difference between the two plans mirrors the split that has animated the American republic for centuries. Nationalists like Alexander Hamilton and the Morrises embraced national standards and systems, promoting large-scale banks, industry, national investment in infrastructure, and an increase in cross-border trade. For them, debts – not coins – were money. Debts were what corporate actors used, and they wanted to make the process of payment easy for them. Decentralists like Jefferson embraced small town values; they cared about the coins farmers and townsfolk used every day to conduct business and to buy what they needed, not the debts of merchants and bankers in big cities like Boston and Philadelphia. These two rival viewpoints brought the national debate on a national currency to a standstill.

As a result, the United States wouldn't mint its first coins until 1793, more than ten years after Jefferson and the Morrises proposed their plans to Congress. Luckily for the banks, this stalemate meant that more and more Americans used bank money as means of payment. During that time, Hamilton again raised his concerns about scale to Morris: he believed the Bank of North America was just too small. And he had a point. The institution wasn't able to issue enough bank money to meet the needs of the new nation. Some states therefore began chartering state banks in the mould of the Bank of North America.

The Bank of New York, for example, sponsored by Hamilton, was founded in 1784. And Massachusetts was not far behind. The promises of bankers under the supervision of state assemblies became the most widely used currency, while a true national currency languished. Though the Constitution of 1787 introduced a national money made of coins and bank debts, the nation still didn't have a mint – and without a mint, a national currency made of coins is not possible. Merchants, bankers and consumers kept using bank debts as money. But they were no longer using 'national' bank money from the Bank of North America. They were using the debts of local banks, which were chartered and supervised by state legislatures.

E Pluribus Unum

Time passed. And U.S. banks continued to be incapable of issuing bank money that could circulate on a truly national scale. It was Alexander Hamilton – Washington's old aide de camp – who eventually took it

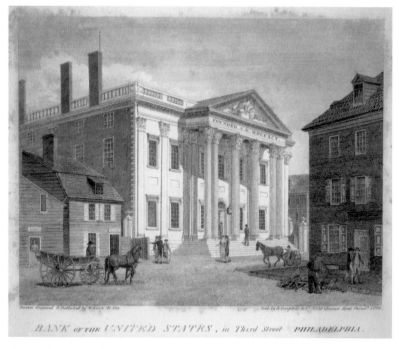

The headquarters of the First Bank of the United States, Third Street, Philadelphia.

upon himself to try to rectify the situation. When he became Secretary of the Treasury in 1789, he was able to implement his own plan for a national currency made up of one coinage, supported by one national bank. It was through Hamilton's extraordinary efforts that Congress approved a coinage close to the one Jefferson had first proposed and also established a national mint and a national standard of value. And it was Hamilton who also set up the Bank of the United States, with capital of 10 million dollars, many, many times more capital than Morris's Bank of North America began with, and with enough coins to support a national bank money.

Yet even though Hamilton's bank would end up lasting longer than Morris's, it still wouldn't be able to provide the nation with a monetary system based on the debts of a single national bank. More and more states chartered their own banks, and entrepreneurs built their own institutions. It took a long time for the United States to develop a national currency made of the debts of one national bank, and they got there through a process unlike any other seen throughout history.

The great American project, financially and otherwise, was and remains unique, the result of innovation wrought in the crucible of creating a new republic, a context entirely distinct from aristocratic republics, multinational empires, totalitarian states, and parliamentary systems. And yet the basic deals remain the same: states exchanging public debts for the debts of banks. Truly, *E Pluribus Unum*. Out of Many, One.

CHAPTER 7

Bolshevik Bank Money: Ready-Made from Capitalism

Without big banks, socialism would be impossible.
The big banks are the 'state apparatus' which we need to bring
about socialism, and which we take ready-made from capitalism;
our task here is merely to lop off what capitalistically mutilates this
excellent apparatus, to make it even bigger, even more democratic,
even more comprehensive. Quantity will be transformed into
quality. A single State Bank, the biggest of the big, with branches
in every rural district, in every factory, will constitute as much
as nine-tenths of the socialist apparatus. This will be country
wide book-keeping, country-wide accounting of the production
and distribution of goods, this will be, so to speak, something in
the nature of the skeleton of socialist society.

Lenin
Can the Bolsheviks Retain State Power? (1917)

I N THE WORDS OF THE GREAT Russian historian Dmitri Volkogonov, Vladimir Ilyich Ulyanov (V.I. Lenin) 'may have described
himself as a Russian when filling in forms', but his background
'reflected the face of the entire empire [...] Russian, Kalmyk, Jewish,
German and Swedish, and possibly others, symbolising Russian history, as it were: a Slavic beginning, Asiatic expansion, a Jewish accretion
to the national intellect, and German or West European culture.'

Lenin's mother, Maria Alexandrovna Ulyanova, was from German
Lutheran stock, so it may be that it was to her, rather than to any of his
other ancestors, that he owed the solidity, the ruthless efficiency and
the unrelenting focus that made him the most successful revolutionary
leader in history. Maybe. Who knows? Certainly, like many great leaders – Alexander, Caesar, Hannibal, Frederick the Great, and Winston
Churchill – Lenin was blessed with the gifts of extraordinary energy,
steady nerves, charm, charisma, and complete and utter ruthlessness.
Highly intelligent, adaptable and able to seize an opportunity when
he saw one, Lenin was also a stubborn creature of habit.

It can be difficult to distinguish between fact and fiction when
discussing Lenin, the Soviet cult of personality having obscured and
exaggerated aspects of his life and work, but apparently even as a child
at school the young Volodya (Vladimir) was calculating and methodical.
If not a prodigy, he was at least massively diligent and yet, notably,
according to the English historian Robert Service, in his biography
of Lenin, 'much more destructive than the other Ulyanov children'.

After leaving university and having become involved in radical
politics, Lenin was exiled to Siberia for revolutionary activity and
eventually sought refuge in Western Europe, moving between Munich,
London and Geneva. In Geneva, Lenin – he had adopted the name
in 1901, after the River Lena, or perhaps a character in a novel by
Tolstoy – spent most evenings at the Café Landolt, a popular hangout
for Russian exiles, on the corner between Rue De-Candolle and Rue
du Conseil-Général, in the bohemian Plainpalais district, near the
university. The Landolt, in the words of one historian, 'had become

an unofficial headquarters for multiple movements that sought to reimagine life in Russia and beyond'. This was the gathering place for Zionists, anarchists, socialists and every other kind of Russian and Mitteleuropean activist, visionary and dreamer. At the Landolt, characteristically, Lenin always sat at the same table, his supporters and followers, the Bolsheviks, joining him to eat, drink and argue. Indeed, Lenin's regular attendance at the Landolt was so reliable, so predictable, so much in keeping with his habit, that someone at some time had etched the word 'LENIN' on his table. Sixty years later, that table was still there or, at the very least, there was still a table at the Landolt purporting to be Lenin's table, with the name LENIN gouged deep upon it.

I know, because I was there.

The Lesson of the Communards

It was the early 1970s. May 1968 was still fresh in everyone's mind. Revolution was chic. Everyone was reading Marx and Mao. Lenin was a hero. And I was a research student, a post-doc at the University of Florence, part of a consortium of European universities. Our research team, investigating workers' rights movements, would gather in Geneva to compare notes, and in the evening we would go to the Landolt, just like the Bolsheviks and the other émigré utopians, to eat, drink and argue. But we weren't revolutionaries. We were just a bunch of social science nerds; we argued about how to conduct successful research rather than how to overthrow governments and stage successful coups and insurrections. But it was fun discussing social science at Lenin's old table.

All traces of Lenin's years in Geneva have long since disappeared; 1968 was a long time ago, and 1917 is even longer ago. The Landolt has long since changed hands – it became a pizzeria, then a Japanese restaurant. Nobody knows what happened to Lenin's table. I have tried and failed to find it.

During the day, just like us, when he wasn't at the Landolt, Lenin would go to Geneva's university library, where he would read for hours. Lenin read in exactly the same way he wrote: totally functional, ruthless, like a good post-doc; his aim not so much to expand his sympathies or ideas but to simply accomplish the task at hand. All he wanted from the books he read were the ideas and principles that he could use to get the job done – theory he could turn into practice.

The year was 1914. Lenin was convinced that a communist revolution in Russia had finally become possible. He was busy studying Marx's pamphlet, 'The Civil War in France', an address to the General Council of the International Working-Men's Association on the recent failure of the two-month radical revolutionary government in France, the Commune de Paris (the Paris Commune). Do you want to know what the dictatorship of the proletariat looks like, famously asked Engels, some years later: 'Look at the Paris Commune. [...] That was the Dictatorship of the Proletariat.' And *that*, like any other dictatorship, did not end well.

Lenin wanted his communist revolution to be a success. In order to achieve that, he was determined that the Bolsheviks should avoid the mistakes made by the Communards. Marx's pamphlet was therefore invaluable. It was a warning from history. Marx had been in close touch with the insurrectionists in Paris; he knew exactly what had happened there; he knew exactly where things had gone wrong. According to Marx, one of the biggest mistakes the Communards had made was to leave the banks alone, free to continue in their business of making and issuing money while the Communards busily set about hoisting the red flag, closing schools and churches, banning newspapers, abolishing child labour and toppling the famous Vendôme column, memorial to Napoleon's victory at the Battle of Austerlitz. The banks simply carried on, bided their time and then used the money they had issued to pay for the guns and for the soldiers who ruthlessly quashed the Commune during *la semaine sanglante*, the Bloody Week, during which thousands of Communards (some recent scholars suggest as many as

20,000) were killed. 'The hardest thing to understand', Marx wrote, indignant, was 'the holy awe with which they [the Communards] remained standing respectfully outside the gates of the Bank of France. This was also a serious political mistake. The bank in the hands of the Commune – this would have been worth more than 10,000 hostages.' Ultimately, it was bank money that killed the Communards. Ignoring the banks, allowing them just to do what they do, was a catastrophic error. Lenin had no intention of making the same mistake.

Finanzkapital

At the Société de Lecture (the Reading Society of Geneva), another favourite hangout, we know that Lenin also laboured through *Das Finanzkapital* (*Finance Capital*), by a man named Rudolph Hilferding. Hilferding is one of history's great forgotten finance polymaths, an Austrian physician-turned-economist who eventually became Finance Minister of the Weimar Republic.

Hilferding was many things: a paediatrician, newspaper editor, close friend of the philosopher Karl Kautsky, and one of the founders of that strain of Marxist thought known as Austromarxism, with its emphasis on nationalism and social democracy; what Hilferding undoubtedly was not, however, was a great writer. At first glance it's difficult to see why Lenin was so enamoured of Hilferding's book. *Finance Capital* makes *Das Kapital* read like Charles Dickens; it is wordy, dense, full of abstract arguments and statements, not at all the kind of book one might expect to provide an impatient revolutionary like Lenin with new ideas, let alone a road map to power. But if one gets to the final chapters of the book, it becomes clear why Lenin admired *Finanzkapital*, as much as he might have disagreed with the good Dr Hilferding's reformist and social democratic tendencies:

The socializing function of finance capital facilitates enormously the task of overcoming capitalism. Once finance capital has brought the most important branches of production under its control, it is enough for society, through its conscious executive organ – the state conquered by the working class – to seize finance capital in order to gain immediate control of these branches of production. [...] Even today, taking possession of six large Berlin banks would mean taking possession of the most important spheres of large-scale industry, and would greatly facilitate the initial phases of socialist policy during the transition period, when capitalist accounting might still prove useful.

While the Communards provided Lenin with the evidence from history, Hilferding provided Lenin with the theory that bankers and banks might be a dangerous enemy, but they are also a powerful tool, perhaps *the* most powerful tool in the early stages of a revolution. If one wants to build a communist commonwealth quickly, like Lenin, one needs not only to nationalise industry and the land, and to social-ise, organise and govern the distribution of goods and commodities, but one also needs to use the banks. You have to seize finance capital. By the time Lenin boarded that fateful train in Zurich on April 9, 1917, bound for the Finland Station in St Petersburg to finally join the Revolution, he had long since absorbed both the lessons of the Communards and of Hilferding's *Finance Capital*. 'Can the Bolsheviks Retain State Power?' he asked in the title of his famous pamphlet, published in October 1917. Yes, was the loud answer. And how, exactly? By using the banks, of course.

The '*skeleton*' of a socialist society, in Lenin's phrase, the structural framework of the nation, consists of 'countrywide book-keeping' and 'countrywide accounting', by which he means not the mere passive registration of the financial outcomes of transactions; he means the *actual* execution of those transactions, the kind of bookkeeping that banks do when they exchange their debts for those of their clients in their ledger and then clear those debts by setting them one against the other. To be absolutely clear: Lenin did not want to get rid of banks and banking – no, not at all; he wanted a *bigger*, better, more comprehensive bank, 'A single State Bank, the biggest of the big, with branches in every rural district, in every factory', which 'will constitute as much as nine-tenths of the *socialist* apparatus'. Lenin's vision of the communist state was to have this one giant bank keeping a giant ledger in which it

Lenin and Trotsky addressing a crowd in St Petersburg in 1917.

executed every single transaction, balancing the nation's ledger; in this way, this super, this supra-bank could manage and supervise the whole economy. With the assistance of this all-powerful bank, balancing its all-knowing, all-powerful ledger, Lenin would be able to make the communist economy work smoothly, effectively and, indeed, without money. It would be Marx's dream come true, the communist paradise, built using a tool, the banking system, ready-made from capitalism.

Things did not work out exactly as Lenin planned.

Seizing the Banks

The Smolny is a large Palladian complex in the centre of St Petersburg. Built in 1805, it had once hosted a finishing school for the daughters of the Russian aristocracy, the Society for the Upbringing of Well-Born Girls. In 1917, Smolny, with its Grecian pillars and grand reception hall, became the Bolshevik headquarters, home to the Bolshevik Revolutionary Committee and the Military-Revolutionary Committee. 'It was,' Trotsky wrote in *The History of the Russian Revolution* (1930), 'as though the Winter Palace and Smolny had changed places.'

In October, Smolny was a frenzy of activity; this was the very nerve centre of the revolution. Outside, armed Soviets fanned out into the city to occupy key government buildings; inside, Bolshevik leaders moved from one room to the other, organising the revolution. Lenin arrived at the Smolny on the evening of October 24, 1917, disguised as a workman, wearing a wig, a bandage and make-up. The moment to seize power had arrived. 'There can be no delay!' he told the Bolshevik Central Committee. On October 25, Lenin addressed his comrades in the Smolny's main hall: 'The old state apparatus will be destroyed at its roots and a new apparatus of administration will be created in the form of the soviet organisations.' There was work to be done. It was time to seize the banks – because the banks *are* the state apparatus needed to bring about socialism. This was not France. And the Bolsheviks were not the Communards.

The story goes that soon after arriving at the Smolny, Lenin was wandering down a corridor and came across a man sleeping on a couch, a label pinned to it: 'People's Commissariat of Finances'. Lenin recognised the slumbering form: Vyacheslav Rudolfovich Menzhinsky, a Polish Bolshevik from a noble family who had worked for a while at the Crédit Lyonnais in Paris and whom the party had therefore put in charge of finance. Vyacheslav was not a man who was universally admired – a dilettante, poet, novelist and brilliant linguist, he was renowned for playing Chopin on a grand piano at the Smolny, much to the annoyance of his fellow Bolsheviks. Trotsky later wrote of him: 'The impression he made on me could best be described by saying that he made none at all.' But Vyacheslav at least dressed like a banker – three-piece suits, a derby hat, pince-nez – and Lenin was keen to put him to work. It was Vyacheslav whom Lenin instructed to take control of the State Bank – Russia's central bank, the biggest of the big, in charge of managing money and overseeing the country's banking system. Others may have been preparing to storm the Winter Palace; Vyacheslav was the man who was chosen to seize the keys to the state apparatus.

The State Bank was just a few blocks from the Smolny. The plan was simple: Vyacheslav and his armed guard would arrive and ask the bank's director to hand over the keys to the establishment, plus a cool 10 million roubles in cash. Vyacheslav would then take the keys and the money and hand them over to Lenin, and his mission would be complete; he could then presumably return to his couch and to his Chopin. The only trouble was, when Vyacheslav arrived, the bank's director point-blank refused to hand over either the keys or the money. So Vyacheslav threatened him – at which point, the director and his whole staff promptly went on strike. This presented a problem for the hapless Vyacheslav: no self-respecting Bolshevik would use violence against a fellow worker exercising their right to strike. It was a classic Russian stand-off, utterly absurd and yet somehow entirely mundane, like something out of a story by Gogol or Goncharov: a handful of armed Bolshevik soldiers and sailors occupying the headquarters of the State Bank, unable to take it over because the employees were on strike. Stalemate.

So, poor Vyacheslav had to go back to Smolny, where he arranged for the Commissariat of Finance to issue a decree that replaced the director of the bank with a rather more obedient Bolshevik, who would do exactly what he was told. This newly appointed director duly complied, enabling Vyacheslav to provide Lenin with the keys to the Russian banking system, plus a truckload of cash. And so the takeover of the State Bank was finally complete. It was, in its way, an episode entirely typical of the 1917 revolution: part tragedy, part farce. And 100 per cent catastrophic for the future of the Russian people. 'The Bolshevik Revolution,' in A. J. P. Taylor's memorable phrase, 'was not a fully orchestrated piece with the music already composed. It was compounded, like most other events, of confusions and misunderstandings, of human endeavours and human failures, where the outcome surprised the victors as much as it stunned the defeated.'

Lenin was perhaps less surprised than others. He had spent decades planning and theorising the revolution and he now had the state apparatus he needed to be able to change the way in which Russia produced and consumed goods and commodities: he had the bank. And he quickly set about executing his plan. Having nationalised the State Bank, the Bolshevik leadership renamed it the People's Bank; this People's Bank then took over every banking and quasi-banking establishment in the country; the Commissariat of Finance was then merged with the People's Bank; and thus the nation's banking system soon became the Central Budgeting and Accounting Administration of Soviet Russia, the keeper of the ledgers that registered and cleared all the debts and claims in the economy.

So far, so good. The grand plan was working.

There was just one problem: reality.

The Red Square and the Sukharevka

In February 1990, I moved to Moscow. I went there to close a deal: the privatisation of AvtoVAZ, the USSR's automobile manufacturer, best known for the Lada, the most popular car in all of Soviet history. It was Fiat who had originally built the AvtoVAZ manufacturing plant in 1966 and who had then turned it over to the Soviets, and in 1989, the Chairman of the board of Fiat and Mikhail Gorbachev, the last and only president of the Soviet Union, signed a memorandum of understanding for the privatisation of AvtoVAZ through a sale of 50 per cent of its equity back to Fiat. The general terms of the deal had been agreed. All that was required was someone to dot the I's and cross the T's. I was working for Fiat and the job fell to me. With the USSR disintegrating, the only way to get the job done was to actually go to Russia and stay there.

To assist me, I needed a guide and mentor. I was lucky enough to find one in Vladimir Yakovlev. Then aged just thirty-one, Vladimir was the Editor-in-Chief of *Kommersant*, a weekly magazine of business and public affairs. *Kommersant* was the New Russia's version of the *Economist*. The original *Kommersant* had been an influential weekly before the October Revolution, but the Bolsheviks then closed it down in 1917. Seeing an opportunity, Yakovlev had dusted it off and started publishing it again, taking advantage of Gorbachev's *perestroika* ('reconstruction') and all that it promised. I could not have been blessed with a better mentor – Vladimir taught me how to make sense of what was happening and how to survive and operate as the great Soviet system began to crumble, crack and collapse.

To make things simple, Yakovlev explained to me that since 1917, Russia had effectively been running two economies, each taking its name from a Moscow landmark. The first was the Red Square economy; this consisted of the state-owned companies run according to communist party principles and guidelines by the state institutions housed in the Red Square. The second was the so-called '*Sukharevka*' economy; this took its name from the centuries-old open-air market in Moscow, where peddlers, hawkers and bagmen plied their wares, trading anything and everything. Cash was king in the Sukharevka economy; here, it was profit rather than ideology that motivated the participants, who were self-styled businessmen and women, entrepreneurs, peasants, farmers, hucksters, hawkers, mongers, what the English might call 'grafters', 'duckers and divers' or 'wheeler-dealers', and ordinary everyday decent Russian citizens. The Sukharevka is perhaps the ultimate laissez-faire free market. (Not surprisingly, perhaps, the actual Sukharevka market was shut down in 1925, Lenin believing it to be a 'breeding ground for speculation', which is exactly what it was.)

In the Red Square economy, it was administrators and bureaucrats who ruled; in the Sukharevka, it was traders. The respective size and importance of the two economies had varied in the seventy-odd years of the Soviet Union, but never had one economy been able to do without the other. Like rival siblings, or a long-suffering husband and wife, the Red Square and the Sukharevka existed alongside one other and made arrangements that made it possible for each of them to thrive and survive if not exactly together, then at least in parallel. And in order to get anything done in Russia, Vladimir told me, one had to be able to work with both of them. For an outsider like me, it was a hard lesson to learn. And it was exactly the same lesson for Lenin and the Bolsheviks.

Not only had the Red Square economy changed little over the years of Soviet rule, in the 1990s, the Sukharevka worked exactly in the way an observer had described it back in the 1920s. 'Everywhere you look is an agitated, noisy human crowd, buying and selling. The various types of trade are grouped together. Here currencies are bought and sold, there the food products, further along textiles, tobacco, cafes and food stands, booksellers, dishes, finished dresses, all sorts of junk. The merchants cry to people walking by: "Citizen, what are you looking to buy? Hats here, the best in the whole Sukharevka."'

The privatisation of AvtoVAZ and its sale to Fiat were firmly in the province of the Red Square economy – the deal had to be done according to the endless rules and procedures of the sclerotic communist bureaucracy. But with the USSR collapsing, these rules and procedures were a complete mess. From the start, closing the deal seemed not only difficult but nigh-on impossible; no one knew what was happening, or how to make it happen. I tried for two years while the USSR slowly died around me and the Russian republic was born. I was there for the 1991 Soviet *coup d'état* attempt, the August coup, and then when Gorbachev was replaced by Boris Yeltsin, who confirmed his intention to go forward with the AvtoVAZ plans. And again, I tried to close the deal. But all in vain. Splinters of the old Soviet system rebelled against Yeltsin, who repressed the insurrection. Everything was chaos. The standard of living for the average man and woman on the street was deteriorating rapidly. Things were falling apart. And meanwhile, in St Petersburg, a little-known but ambitious former KGB officer named Vladimir Putin became head of the Committee for External Relations of the Saint Petersburg Mayor's Office, with responsibility for promoting international relations and foreign investments, making the Smolny – Lenin's centre of operations – his office. The privatisation of AvtoVAZ was quietly shelved. Defeated and frustrated by the Red Square economy, I eventually left Russia. During my time there, it was the traders in the Sukharevka who kept me supplied with what was essential for daily survival.

* * *

Twenty years later, to my great surprise, I found myself back in Moscow to head up the Goldman Sachs office in Russia. I had changed. I was no longer working for Fiat. And I was far from the naïve young post-doc student researching the social sciences back in the 1970s. I was a banker. And the country had changed; the Sukharevka economy had grown and the power of the Red Square had diminished. But they were still very much in operation and working together.

Understanding the Red Square and the Sukharevka, these fundamental, seemingly immutable features of the Russian economy, is essential for making sense of the first few extraordinary years of Bolshevik rule, the role that money and the banks played in the Bolshevik experiment, and what exactly went so wrong – and so right – with Lenin's plans.

The Murder of Trade

At all times, in all places, all socialist movements tend to be more hostile towards private traders than towards private manufacturers. Traders are always the enemy; they're an easy target. The Bolsheviks despised trading of all kinds: they viewed buying low and selling high as the most despicable kind of degenerate capitalist profit-seeking. This aversion to the ethos of trading, it should be said, had clear ethnic under- and indeed overtones; Asians, Jews, Armenians and Greeks were often defined as 'trading' people. When the Bolsheviks prosecuted traders, along with other class enemies, what they were effectively doing was targeting certain ethnic groups.

But if the Bolsheviks wanted to kill trading, they had their work cut out for them, because trading in Russia was, and remains for people of *all* ethnicities and backgrounds, not just an occupation but a way of life. It is difficult to explain to anyone who has never lived or worked there, but Russians trade all the time – bargaining, bartering, haggling, negotiating. Like it or not, traders and trading dominate the economy, historically and geographically, all the way from the ancient Silk Road routes, from Southern Siberia to the Northern Caucasus, to the Sukharevka, to the rise of the oligarchs, to the current planned Arctic Silk Road route.

Back in 1917, much of the everyday trade in Russia took place in the large metropolitan shops, called *magaziny*, from the French 'magasin', which had first been introduced in Russia around the 1870s. Then there were what Americans would call the mom-and-pop shops, the little one-man or one-woman enterprises. These made up the rest of official retail sales in Russia; they might have an average turnover of ten roubles per day. Then there were the markets, the Sukharevka, the outdoor trade fairs and street vendors, which remained an important part of trade in Russia long after their decline in Western Europe. (In the early twentieth century, hawkers and peddlers were everywhere on the streets and squares of Russian cities; some estimates suggest that no less than 20 per cent of all Muscovites were involved in trade.) In the countryside, meanwhile, trading was even more pervasive, as Lenin knew only too well. In his early economic work, *The Development of Capitalism in Russia* (1899), he had documented in great detail the recent changes in the rural economy and the growth of individual rather than communal property ownership. Despite these changes, the manufacturing and trading unit in the countryside remained the family, with agricultural production often being combined with the production of goods for the market: handicrafts, textiles and lace – everyone in the family was involved. In one way or another, Mother Russia was a trading nation.

For the Bolsheviks, their hostility towards all these forms of trading went hand-in-hand with one of the major goals of a communist revolution: getting rid of money altogether. Trading needs money, but money without trading is superfluous – who needs money if there is no trade? If they were able to eliminate trade, the Bolshevik leadership reasoned, they would also be able to get rid of money. Which would be a major step toward full communism, that final, paradisal state of humanity in which all needs are met. Bukharin and Preobrazhensky, in a pamphlet first published in 1919, *The ABC of Communism*, the Bolshevik primer and textbook for the Russian people, and the most widely read work in pre-Stalinist Soviet Russia, were absolutely explicit and unequivocal: 'Communist society will know nothing about money.'

This is all well and good in theory. But for better and for worse, the exchanging of goods and services is an essential feature of any human society. Even the smallest and most egalitarian societies have some form of exchange of goods and services; we need to be able to exchange in order to fulfil our most basic needs. Much more complex societies – like Russia, say – with more complex needs have to be able to exchange all sorts of goods and services in order to be able

Crowds flocking to Market Square, now Red Square.

to function. And traditionally, this is what money is for; money is not in itself a good or a service; it greases the wheels; it is a means of making the exchange and distribution of goods and services work smoothly. So, the challenge for the Bolsheviks was how to turn their theory into practice. How do you exchange goods without money in a society like Russia?

Marx provided the answer. Marx thought a lot about money. Money, according to his essay on 'The Jewish Question', was the 'alienated essence of man's work and existence'. This essence 'dominates him and he worships it'. Money was all-powerful:

It changes fidelity into infidelity, love into hate, hate into love, virtue into vice, vice into virtue, servant into master, stupidity into intelligence and intelligence into stupidity.

(*Economical and Philosophical Manuscripts*, 1844, trans. T. Bottomore, 1963)

Marx had read most of the important works on money, including Ferdinando Galiani, David Ricardo and Adam Smith, and while in London he had covered for the New York *Daily Tribune* the parliamentary debates on the Bank Act that reformed the Bank of England in 1844. All of his reading and observations had convinced him that the two main functions of money, as a means of payment and as a measure of exchange value, should be dealt with separately, and in his own writing and thinking, of course, he focused on money as a measure of exchange value (and in particular the labour theory of exchange value).

Many of the Bolsheviks, not just Lenin, had read Marx. And even if they hadn't, they, too, were obsessed with the problems of money, markets, trade and exchange: 'the problem of markets very much interested all us young Marxists', recalls Nadezhda Konstantinovna Krupskaya, Lenin's wife and life-long companion in her book, *Memories of Lenin* (1930). (The couple first met, romantically, in St Petersburg in 1893 when someone gave Nadezhda 'an exercise-book containing a screed '*On Markets*', containing Lenin's thoughts on the subject.) The Bolsheviks believed that to smoothly and effectively exchange goods and services in a communist society, all that was required was a stable measure of exchange value, shared by all members of society. Basically, if the state were to fix the price of goods, those prices would become the stable measure of the exchange value. The State Bank – the bookkeeper for the whole society – would then be able to execute the trades in its ledgers, credits and debts would balance, and in this way, trading and cash would quickly disappear. This is the system, the thinking, that Lenin attempted to put into practice.

By Exchange Alone: Mandatory Commodity Exchange

Inspired by Marx and directed by Lenin, the Bolsheviks decided to replace trading with mandatory commodity exchanges at prices fixed by the Supreme Council for the National Economy – a perfectly rational, organised system for a perfectly rational, organised society. Agricultural trading, for example, was instantly overhauled with a system of mandatory commodity exchange.

As soon as the Congress of Soviets had announced the nationalisation of land, village communities were ordered to manage this land according to the principles of 'real socialism'. This meant that at every level – local, regional and national – agricultural goods had to be distributed to consumers and in return, industrial products had to reach agricultural communities *by a process of exchange alone*. Fabric, clothes, boots, tobacco, tea, and other consumer goods were transferred to a state agency to be exchanged in return for grain and other foodstuffs. At first, the state simply devised the exchange ratios; one unit of fabric, for example, was exchanged for five units of grain. But the Bolshevik leadership soon moved to a system of requisitions and exchange, again at prices set by the Supreme Council. Thus, in one fell swoop, trading with money had been abolished.

The Powdered Milk Manufacturing Problem

This sudden shift to mandatory commodity exchange brought with it problems. Simply exchanging food for manufactured goods may have been difficult, but it was not impossible, and it was certainly nowhere near as difficult as exchanging manufacturing inputs for other manufacturing inputs or outputs, or indeed simply acquiring manufacturing parts by exchange. The equations and calculations here were not as straightforward as, say, X amount of grain equals Y amount of tobacco. Manufacturing involves a lot of literal and metaphorical moving parts – it is complex, with all sorts of supply chains and forms of specialisation enabling production at scale. Just imagine

Adam Smith's pin factory or Henry Ford's Model T manufacturing plant, with no means of purchase or income except by exchange, in Russia, in 1917.

One man who faced the logistical and mathematical nightmare of implementing mandatory commodity exchange in a complex manufacturing environment in a vast nation was Robert Axelrod, a Swiss engineer, the son of a family of Russian Marxists who had moved to Geneva. His father Pavel had often argued with Lenin at the Landolt. Axelrod Senior's arguments had not prevailed. What Axelrod Junior now faced was the logical outcome and consequences of those arguments.

In 1917, Robert Axelrod believed that he should devote his skills to a more noble cause than merely working as a Swiss industrial engineer, so he moved to Russia to join the Revolution. He went to work in Vologda, an industrial city on the Volga, and there found a job as the production manager of a factory making powdered milk. Things started well. But one day a powdered milk machine broke down. Production stopped. It was no big deal. As production manager, Axelrod just needed to acquire a spare to replace a broken part. But the procurement of a spare part, an input into the manufacturing process, now had to be done by way of mandatory exchange. And the office in charge of executing such exchanges was in St Petersburg. Which was fine. To expedite the process, Axelrod sent his best and most enterprising mechanic to St Petersburg. If anyone could get the job done quickly, it was he. The necessary procedures and protocols were clear. The mechanic had to visit the mandatory commodity exchange office, where all exchanges were recorded in the ledger; the powdered milk factory was to be debited for the price of the spare and the producer of the spare would be credited. With the ledger duly balanced, the exchange could take place, the powdered milk factory would get its part, and manufacturing could resume. Of course, the powdered milk factory first had to be authorised to be debited the spare by the exchange office; this took three days. In the meantime, the mechanic, who was good, had already located the spare part that he needed at the Putilov iron works in St Petersburg and had requested that his counterpart there apply for authorisation for their claim to be entered in the mandatory commodity exchange office's ledger. He applied, the two vouchers of authorisation were entered in the book, the debt was credited and cleared, the spare changed hands and Axelrod's mechanic boarded the train to come home. Job done.

Axelrod was Swiss *and* he was an engineer. So, naturally, he noted every step of this process of exchange: the time it took, how much it cost, the whole thing. The spare part cost 60 roubles. That was the amount the company was debited. On paper, that was what it cost. But the milk powder factory had lost fourteen days of production. And the mechanic's trip had cost over a thousand roubles. Axelrod added it all up and published a little pamphlet setting out his findings, which is how we know the calculations. Mandatory commodity exchange may have worked, but it was far from simple and efficient. It was expensive and it was time-consuming.

For a little while, Axelrod just about managed to cope with all this. But sometime after the first machine part breakdown, the powdered milk factory ran out of containers for the milk. They needed 300 more. This meant that Axelrod would have to apply for mandatory exchange for 300 new containers, so, back to St Petersburg and back through the whole process again. This seems to have been the straw that broke the engineer's back; it was just too much for him. He returned to Switzerland; mandatory exchange was not his cup of tea. Quite a few people felt the same. Mandatory commodity exchange never quite thrilled people in the way the Bolsheviks expected. Industries and individuals required swift and simple solutions to the problem of exchange – mandatory commodity exchange offered neither.

The Trouble with War Communism

During this initial period of what is now known as War Communism, the economic and political system implemented during the early stages of the Russian Civil War – from roughly 1918 to the spring of 1921 – the two Russian economies, the Red Square and the Sukharevka, functioned separately. The Red Square economy consisted of the socialist state-owned firms, with their planned production and the distribution of goods through mandatory collective exchange. Exchanges were entered and settled by the Council of the National Economy or the Commissariat of Finances. Goods were exchanged at fixed prices and the transactions that were authorised by the Council or the Commissariat were mandatory. The only role that money played in these exchanges was to allow the squaring-off of debits and claims on the books as a measure of exchange value.

The Sukharevka economy, meanwhile, continued to thrive throughout the country among the small producers of goods, with farmers, artisans and small firms trading between themselves and others. In the Sukharevka economy there were no banks, no councils and no committees, and there was no mandatory commodity exchange, so money was still needed to trade goods. Prices were negotiated and agreed between the partners to the trade; goods changed hands when cash was handed to the seller. So, naturally, most of the cash circulating in Russia ended up in the Sukharevka – all of the coins, all of the notes, tszarist and Provisional Government money, foreign money, and indeed all the local currency printed by independent regions. This cash economy wasn't just small street-corner trading; this was the daily exchange and movement of huge amounts of cash across the country between vast numbers of buyers and sellers, the ordinary Russian people. A contemporary correspondent in the *Izvestia*, the official Bolshevik newspaper (and Russia's official national newspaper to this day), described how this economy functioned in Kiev and its surroundings, with some disdain: 'A sort of grey caterpillar moves along the rails – this is the train, completely covered with a grey mass of bagmen. Under them neither the cars, not the engine, not the roofs nor the space between the cars are visible. Every space is occupied, filled in. But as the train slows down in its approach to the Kiev station, its grey skin begins to slip off.' That 'grey skin', the poor Russian traders who had clung to the rail cars, then spread out into Kiev to sell their wares in the streets and squares, in return purchasing goods to bring back home and to sell there. The great grey caterpillar of commerce, crawling endlessly on.

The separation between the Red Square and the Sukharevka economies seriously impacted the Bolsheviks' ability to manage Russia as a whole. This was especially the case in the relationship between the cities and the countryside. The cities needed food and the farmers needed manufactured goods, but industry was in the Red Square economy and the farms occupied the Sukharevka – and mandatory commodity exchange, as Robert Axelrod knew only too well, did not work well in facilitating smooth and swift exchange. So, what, to borrow a phrase from Lenin, is to be done?

The Paradoxical Sovznak

Paradox abounds in the history of the early years of Bolshevik rule: a people's revolution leading to terror and civil war; the restructuring of the economy leading to widespread shortages and famine; and strong central government that was often unstable and out of control. For economists, another of the great Bolshevik paradoxes is the rise of inflation during War Communism. From 1917 to 1921, Russia had among the highest inflation rates in Europe. Usually, inflation is associated with excessive growth of the money supply, so how on earth, one might ask, could the money supply be growing if the Bolsheviks' stated aim was to make money disappear? And if goods were traded through mandatory commodity exchanges?

It's a good question. And the simple answer is surprisingly obvious: inflation was rising because the money supply *was* growing, money was indeed being printed in Russia at the maximum possible speed. To paraphrase Mark Twain, the reports of money's death at the hands of the Bolsheviks were greatly exaggerated. What is to be done? Print more money but call it something else.

The reality was that killing money was going to be a long and drawn-out process, even for an all-powerful government dedicated to its total elimination. The Bolsheviks may have questioned the value and necessity of money, but when faced with the immediate and urgent need to purchase, say, powdered milk machine parts, or simply to exchange manufactured goods for foodstuffs, they found that they needed to use money. In order to survive and to thrive, in order to ease and sustain the relationship between the cities and the countryside, the state needed money. And so the Bolsheviks came up with an inventive solution: the *sovznak*.

Before the revolution, the State Bank was in charge of issuing currency either directly or through the banking system. The amount of money that was put in circulation was based on the needs of its clients who exchanged their debts with those of the bank. The issuing of currency was regulated and backed by assets and reserves. The State Bank issued bank notes which were effectively state credit notes, public debt. On demand, the bank would exchange the notes with a fixed amount of minted gold; and for that purpose, the State Bank kept a reserve of gold coins. The ratio between the circulating bank notes and the gold reserve was set by law. Only the Bank of England had a higher ratio of reserves to currency. In 1914 the gold reserves of the State Bank in Russia exceeded the total value of the notes in circulation; the purchasing power of the rouble was therefore that of gold – which is to say, very stable.

After the Revolution, all the banks were merged into the People's Bank, which became the bookkeeper that cleared debts and credits arising from the mandatory commodity exchanges. The People's Bank did not make money by exchanging debt any more and individuals and firms paid taxes in kind. With payments in kind, the revenues of the state had drastically shrunk, and the state was left with little or no currency. In the Sukharevka, meanwhile, goods were still traded for cash, and the state desperately needed cash in order to procure in the Sukharevka economy what it needed. So, in order to square the circle, the Commissariat of Finance started to print its own circulating notes, Soviet settlement tokens – *Sovetskiye znaki*, or *sovznak* for short. These tokens were not exchangeable into gold coins, but they worked well as a kind of currency in the short term – sovznaks enabled the Bolsheviks to bring together the two economies. The Commissariat started to print more and more of these useful little settlement tokens. And then more. And more again. And more: the amount of circulating sovznaks increased constantly, month by month. The face value of the circulating tokens was a multiple of what tszarist money had been in 1914, and their purchasing power was a small fraction. Between 1914 and 1921 the rouble depreciated between five and six *thousand* times. Sovznaks may have been an interim solution, but they were not sustainable.

Bolshevik Inflation: Destroying the Value of Money

After World War I, inflation raged across western and central Europe, especially in Germany, Austria, and Hungary. Inflation was not just a Russian problem, but the Bolsheviks initially adopted a very different approach to the problem. As Western governments scrambled to contain inflation, the Bolsheviks didn't seem bothered by it at all. Indeed, the party's left wing welcomed inflation as a powerful force in the drive to abolish money entirely. Leon Trotsky, the most prominent leader of the left, in a speech at the Second Congress of the Communist International in 1920, linked Soviet inflation to the decline of money relations, and this, he said, was entirely to be welcomed.

Lenin was rather less extreme than Trotsky on this matter, at least, but he also welcomed runaway inflation. In an interview reported by the *New York Times* in 1919, he was quoted as remarking on the fact that 'hundreds of thousands of rouble notes are being issued daily by our Treasury' and that 'this is done not in order to fill the coffers of the State with practically worthless paper, but with the deliberate intention of destroying the value of money as means of payment. There is no justification for the existence of money in the Bolshevik state where the necessities of life shall be paid by work alone.' This was fighting talk. But behind the scenes, the Bolshevik leadership was having to come up with a plan to deal with the immediate problem of hyperinflation and the fundamental problem of exchange in an economy divided between the Red Square and the Sukharevka.

NEP! NEP!

Armand Hammer, the larger-than-life American businessman often referred to as Lenin's chosen or favourite capitalist, and whose entire life story reads like a novel, was not himself a communist, but his father was one of the founding members of the American Communist Labor Party and a friend of Lenin. The family connection had helped Hammer to secure a concession to trade with the Bolsheviks on favourable terms and he was a frequent visitor to Moscow both before and after the Revolution. Hammer's memories and recall of that period may or may not be entirely accurate or reliable, but they are certainly colourful. Remembering August 1921, having been away from Moscow for only a month, he recalls that he couldn't quite believe what he was seeing upon return – the gloom was gone; the streets that had been deserted were now thronged with people; everyone seemed to be in a hurry, full of purpose; scarce goods were being unloaded into shops from wagons; the curse of inflation seemed to be lifting. Hammer asked what had happened in his absence. And everyone he asked gave the same answer: 'NEP! NEP!'

NEP was the acronym for the New Economic Policy, which Lenin fought hard to impose on the Bolshevik left. Lenin, adaptable as ever, argued that the NEP – which he called 'state capitalism' – may have been one small step back from socialism, but it was necessary to take two giant steps forward towards communism. In essence, the NEP meant that large-scale industry was still owned by the state, but that other areas of the economy were to be allowed a mix of private and communal ownership; the Red Square economy would shrink a little and the world of the Sukharevka would be allowed to grow, all in the interests of providing the 'missing material prerequisites' of modernisation and industrialisation in order to achieve the Bolsheviks' long-term goals.

The biggest change made by the NEP was in the Sukharevka economy. Requisitions of goods and commodities, especially in the agricultural sector, were abolished and replaced with a tax in kind. Peasants paid to the state a fixed proportion of the goods they produced, and they were allowed to sell whatever was left for cash with no restrictions. The new policy was aimed at increasing the productivity of the land, allowing producers to trade freely; in reality it was, in the words of E. H. Carr in *The Bolshevik Revolution 1917–23*, a simple recognition of 'what had never ceased to exist'. As bankers, economists and some political leaders know only too well, denying reality can work for a while, but not forever. Fortunately for the Bolsheviks, facing reality worked; under the NEP, Russian trade came back with a vengeance – which was good, but all that trade needed money. And the sovznak was not up to the job.

Money, Signs and Symbols

As much as anything, the sovznak had an image problem. The various Russian revolutionary regimes understood very well the power of symbols and the profound effect of the simple repetition of certain images and representations: red flags, red stars, hammers and sickles. They were also well aware that money, too, carries meaning. Early on, after the February Revolution in 1917, for example, which had toppled Tsar Nicholas II, the Provisional Government had changed the appearance of Russian bank notes.

The novelist Maxim Gorky was put in charge. He assembled a committee made up of architects, painters and sculptors to design the new bank notes. To symbolise the new regime's aspiration to create a socialist democracy, the new currency bore images of the Tauride Palace, the seat of the Duma, the Russian Parliament.

After the end of the Provisional Government and the death of parliamentary democracy in October 1917, the Bolshevik Department of Currency Production continued to print this Duma money for a while, but they soon realised that the currency needed a new look and a different name, hence the sovznak, whose appearance was distinct from both the notes both of the Tsar and of the Provisional Government. The hammer and sickle appeared on most sovznak notes; Marx's image appeared on others. One bank note had the motto 'Proletarians of the World Unite' emblazoned upon it – in eight languages.

But now, the NEP reformers decided that they needed something different again: a new kind of cash for a new era, bearing a symbol capable of inspiring everyday Russian citizens to have faith in the stability of the new regime. In Russia, icons had long been an effective means of spreading faith and belief; the NEP reformers recognised that they needed a currency whose iconic power was as important as its technical features and capabilities. So they started searching Russian monetary history for a suitable icon of stable money.

Chervonets Reborn

They found it in chervonets. Russia had minted gold since the 1500s, with the early coins duplicating the appearance of the Venetian ducat. Peter the Great was the first to mint a truly Russian 'national' coin in the early 1700s, called chervonets (*chervonnoye zoloto*, meaning 'red gold'). Chervonets had been the name attached to every Russian gold coin since; to Russian eyes, the chervonets was *the* icon of stable money. The last Tsar, Nicholas II, had also minted chervonets, coins containing seven point seven grams of pure gold with a face value of ten roubles, making the purchasing power of the rouble equal to the purchasing power of a fixed weight of pure gold.

The Bolsheviks therefore chose the chervonets as the monetary unit of the paper currency to be issued by the new State Bank. To be faithful to tradition, each chervonets, just like Tsar Nicholas II's, had a face value of ten roubles and the purchasing power of seven

A note for 1,000 roubles issued by the Commissariat of Finance in 1919. On the bank note is written the exhortation from the Communist Manifesto 'Proletarians of the World Unite' in eight languages: Russian, German, French, Italian, Greek, English, Arabic and Chinese.

point seven grams of pure gold. Fixing the purchasing power of the new currency was easy; implementing it was a totally different story. On the international market, the State Bank was able to maintain parity to gold by the selective purchase of other currencies linked to gold (mostly dollars and pounds sterling). But the most difficult task was keeping the purchasing power of the chervonets stable inside Russia. The bank notes were not convertible into gold on demand. The decree that fixed the value of the new currency had made some vague promises about making the notes exchangeable with gold at a later stage, but nothing more. So it was up to the bank how to work out how to keep the reborn chervonets as stable as its ancestor, the good old Russian gold coin.

To allow the State Bank to make the chervonets stable, the reformers made the new State Bank – the Gosbank – as similar as possible to a central bank of a capitalist country. Indeed, they selected the Bank of England as their model. Two men in particular were responsible for steering the fate of the chervonets and the Gosbank: Leonid Naumovich Yurovsky, a brilliant young economist from the St Petersburg Polytechnic Institute, who became a Member of the Board of the Commissariat of Finance; and Grigory Sokolnikov (real name, appropriately, Girsch brilliant), who became the People's Commissar

A gold chervonets minted in 1980.

of Finance. Yurovsky and Sokolnikov realised, to their credit, that the bank needed to be self-supporting and profitable and that it should therefore get paid to issue debt to its clients, that it should hold enough assets (the debts of its clients) to balance its books, that the assets held by the bank should be good and liquid, and that a fixed percentage of its assets should be in bullion or foreign exchange.

Yurovsky and Sokolnikov had the right idea. It wasn't a perfect set-up, but it was a pretty good start for the Gosbank – it would be able to meet the needs of its clients and keep the purchasing power of the chervonets stable on the international and domestic market.

A Tale of Two Currencies

The only trouble was, there was already a currency in place and in widespread use: the sovznak. The Bolshevik government had needed cash to purchase goods and services, most of its taxes were now paid in kind, the cash revenues accruing to the state were small and certainly a lot less than what was needed to buy the goods and services required to keep the state working, and the public deficit had to be filled somehow. In order to fill the gap, the Treasury kept on printing its settlement tokens, the sovznaks. And once it had started, it simply could not stop.

But now, with the appearance of the chervonets, Russia would effectively have two parallel currencies issued by two different institutions, the State Bank and the Treasury, with no fixed exchange ratios between them. Moreover, the settlement tokens, the sovznaks, were the only legal tender. Acceptance of the chervonets was voluntary. It looked like the new monetary system was going to be yet another disaster.

To everyone's surprise, it wasn't – the unusual arrangement worked better than anyone could have possibly expected. At first, the separation between the Red Square and the Sukharevka helped: in the beginning, chervonets were used mostly in the Sukharevka, while large industries received the sovznak settlement tokens from government departments

A note for 3 chervonets with Lenin's portrait.

and used them to pay their workers, as many of their input requirements were procured by way of mandatory exchange. The public viewed the chervonets more as a security than as an actual means of payment – traders and consumers bought them with spare cash and sold them when necessary. This strategy made sense, since the value of the sovznaks, issued in increasingly large numbers, kept depreciating. The chervonets bank notes, however, were of high denomination and bank money was issued in limited amounts, so it kept its purchasing power.

What happened next was perhaps both inevitable but also extremely fortunate: the state began accepting chervonets in payment for taxes. This meant that bank money rather than Treasury money was becoming established in the Red Square economy. Government offices happily received the chervonets bank notes in tax payments and with them they paid for goods and services; bank money soon stopped functioning merely as a security and became a means of payment.

The chervonets depreciated a little, but on the whole, they kept most of their purchasing power. The NEP was working – both the Red Square and the Sukharevka economies were growing. Trade of all kinds was spreading into the realm of the Red Square; businesses needed more and more money and they naturally chose the currency that was more stable: the chervonets. And as businesses paid more tax, the state was required to print fewer sovznaks; bank money was triumphing in Bolshevik Russia.

By 1924, the Bolshevik leadership was ready to reform the currency yet again.

The Triumph of the Bank

The time had come to choose between chervonets and sovznaks, between bank money and the Treasury settlement tokens. No surprises; the Bolshevik leadership decided to make bank money the main currency. The sovznak was dead – the currency issued by the Treasury had become a subsidiary of the chervonets. This meant that when it came to making money, the bank led and the Treasury followed; the monetary policy of Soviet Russia was now effectively managed by the State Bank. Both the Red Square and the Sukharevka economy benefitted from the new arrangement. Stable money helped both to grow. Trade between agricultural and industrial regions worked smoothly. Farmers supplied the food and manufacturers manufactured.

Moreover, the Russian economy became more integrated with the world economy. Most of the trading partners of Bolshevik Russia were on the gold exchange standard; de facto, Russia now had a similar system with a currency that had a fixed exchange ratio with gold and most gold-based currencies. The chervonets was traded in the world market at par with the US dollar and pound sterling. Western firms and entrepreneurs returned to Russia, the likes of Armand Hammer among them.

Yurovsky and Sokolnikov had pulled off an incredible feat: they had engineered a successful monetary reform and had stood Gresham's Law on its head; in Bolshevik Russia, of all places, good money had literally driven out bad.

For a while, the reformers were celebrated both at home and abroad – until Stalin. Then Sokolnikov and Yurovsky were first side-lined, then tried as traitors and in the end, of course, executed.

The Soviet Bookkeeper Supreme

But there is a final twist to the tale, a final accomplishment wrought by the Bolsheviks that proves once again that in different cultures, at different times, under different regimes, and yet in very similar ways, states and nations deal with banks to achieve their purposes and goals, paying for goods with banks' promises to pay.

After the triumph of the chervonets, the Gosbank not only had the power of issuing money, but it remained the authority that managed every substantial transaction in the country in its ledger; the nation's all-seeing, all-knowing supreme bookkeeper, in the same way that the omnipotent Gosplan planned the Soviet economy and the omnipresent Gossnab eventually allocated goods.

Every institution in the country, from manufacturing firms to commodity producers to service providers and citizens' associations, held two accounts at the Gosbank, what one might think of as a Sukharevka account and a Red Square account. The first was a current account from which the account holder withdrew the cash they needed, mostly for wage payments and minor transactions. The second was the so-called settlement account. This was where the debts and credits of the account holder were cleared. The bank checked every significant transaction proposed by the account holder. If satisfied, it entered the financial aspect of the trade as a debit or a credit, then cleared them; the settlement account mirrored the financial position of any and every institution in Russia, how much they owed and how much they were owed.

This obviously made the bank enormously powerful. The Bolshevik leadership realised that with this power, they could do something similar to what the Venetian Senate had managed to do in the early seventeenth century and what the British parliament had done later that same century: they could use the bank to make money out of public debt for the benefit of the state.

In some ways, it was almost too easy. In 1925, the Treasury issued a public loan for economic reconstruction and forced companies to subscribe to it from their current account, where they kept the money, rather than the settlement accounts, where the bank cleared debts and credits. Since no company had enough in their current account to pay the Treasury, the State Bank agreed to lend them the money to buy the loan, using the bonds as collateral. This ingenious trade unfolded in five simple steps.

1. The company subscribed and purchased its share of bonds from the Treasury but did not pay for them right away.
2. The company posted the bonds with the bank as collateral for a loan.
3. The bank issued new money and deposited into the cash account of the company.
4. The company paid the Treasury for the bonds.
5. And then once the company had accumulated enough cash, it repaid the loan to Gosbank.

Genius. The whole process was designed to allow the bank to turn public debt into money for the benefit of the state.

So, the Bolsheviks had come full circle. Not only did they not make money die or disappear, they made good money drive out bad *and* they had established a banking system that made money out of public debt for the benefit of the state, using the same kind of means and methods as Western, capitalist models. Quite an irony. Rudolf Hilferding had criticised Western capitalism because it allowed banks to accumulate too much power. Then Lenin had seized Hilferding's analysis and turned it into an action plan, and the outcome was the all-knowing and all-powerful State Bank, a bank that was at once the bookkeeper that managed the transactions in the country *and* made money out of public debt for the benefit of the state. *No* financial institution has ever had that kind of power in a capitalist country. The story of the relationship between the state and the banks in Bolshevik Russia in many ways reflects the wider story of the Bolsheviks' triumph in Russia; Lenin's émigré fantasy had become a reality – degraded, exaggerated and immense, but a reality nonetheless. Bolshevik banking, the great irony: not only ready-made from capitalism, but truly bigger and more comprehensive.

Indebted

THE SEVEN EPISODES IN *Money and Promises*, describing the relationships between seven states and banks, during seven different periods of long duration, are not the only instances when banks and states have co-operated with each other. But I believe that they are representative of the complex system of interdependence that has developed over time.

In our examples, the various states have been quite unlike the others: aristocratic republics, a parliamentary system, a centralised empire, a federal republic, and a Bolshevik dictatorship. The banks we have studied have also been different: charities, for-profit corporations, branches of the state. But in all these cases, in every deal and every transaction, states and banks have swapped debts and both partners have gained something from the exchange: the state supplies more public goods; banks get the power to create money. This is the alchemy of banking. This is the mysterious work of Lady Debt.

That work, that magic and that process of exchange continue to this day; the debts of banks become the national currency and make up the money supply; sovereign debts make up a substantial portion of the banks' assets; and the fortunes of public debt therefore affect both the banking system and the national currency. Today, the purchasing power of every actor in society – every individual, every organisation, and the state itself – is effectively bank debt.

For many centuries, things were relatively simple; money was a creature of the state. When money was coins, the state determined and governed the two basic functions of money, as a measure of value and as a means of payment: the state minted the coins and determined the purchasing power of those coins by decree. But over time there developed a separation: the state kept the power to manage the measure of value, but banks came to determine and operate the means of payment. The two fundamental functions of money therefore became governed by two different entities whose interests nonetheless remain entwined and whose fates remain intimately linked. This is why, for example, the state tends to bail out the banks in a crisis, because the debts of banks *are* the currency of nations. As we have seen, again and again, and as recent financial crises continue to show, the exchange of debts between banks and states presents as many challenges as it does opportunities. Lady Debt is a fickle and a hard mistress.

In sketching this extraordinary history, with all its ups and downs, in tracing the connections between the development of banks and bank money, and in trying to understand the relationship between banks and the destiny of nations, I have been informed and inspired by my own experience as a banker, by my reading and researching in the archives over many years, and by a number of great teachers.

One of my first teachers was Giovanni Sartori, the Italian political scientist. One day, when I was a graduate student at the University of Florence, Sartori called and asked me to visit him at home. Sartori was a man renowned for his sharp tongue, but he was also a tremendous mentor to his students, so I had no idea what to expect – either a dressing-down or a detailed discussion of some theoretical point about concept formation in the development of constitutional design, one of his favourite topics. When I arrived in the grand surroundings of his home, he sat me down for a chat.

'I have been thinking, Zannoni,' he said, 'that perhaps you do not have the personality to thrive as an academic here in Italy.' For me to succeed, he explained, he would have to try to help me find a job at some obscure university where I would then have to work for at least ten years doing research for a professor before ever getting the opportunity to devote myself to my own work. 'I don't think that would suit you, Zannoni,' he said. I agreed.

'Good,' he said, 'because I have decided that you should go to Yale.' And so he sent me to Yale, where I became a student of scholars that have shaped social sciences: Doug Rae, Joe la Palombara, Ed Lindlom and the great Robert Dahl.

Dahl was one of the fathers of modern political science, a theorist of democracy and power relations in political systems, the author of *A Preface to Democratic Theory* (1956) and *Polyarchy: Participation and Opposition* (1971). He was a Boston Brahmin figure, brilliant and charming; among my peers, as graduate students, we referred to such professors as 'the greyhounds'. When I was searching for a suitable focus for my PhD, Dahl pointed me towards the work of another greyhound, James Tobin.

At the time, Tobin was a man in his prime; Sterling Professor of Economics, a consultant and advisor to the US Treasury and the Federal Reserve, and a former Director of the Cowles Foundation for Research in Economics at Yale. I met with Tobin and he sent me away with a roughly photostatted copy of a paper he had published, Cowles Foundation Discussion Paper No.159, first published in 1963, titled 'Commercial Banks as Creators of "Money"'.

'This might prove an interesting topic for your PhD', he said, 'and in particular, what might be the consequences for the state if this theory were correct, that commercial banks were creators of "money"? What might this mean?' At the time, I had no idea. I never finished my PhD; indeed, I barely got started. Before long, I left academia, went to work in business and never looked back.

Now, looking back, a lifetime later, I see that Sartori's ideas about the importance of concepts and the need for terminological exactitude, plus Dahl's various notions about democracies and power and combined with Tobin's crucial insight into the role of banks as creators of money, have helped to form my own ideas about the relationship between banks and the state, and the importance of understanding exactly what we mean when we talk about 'debt' and 'money'. So, this book is perhaps the PhD that I never wrote, plus fifty years of reading and experience.

✳ ✳ ✳

My learning continues. Only recently, I became familiar with the work of Ralph George Hawtrey, a member of the so-called Cambridge Apostles, and a close friend of John Maynard Keynes. Hawtrey was a brilliant mathematician who worked at the UK Treasury. In 1919, Hawtrey published a book, *Currency and Credit*, which according to Keynes in his review of the book in *The Economic Journal* in 1920 'is one of the most profound and original treatises on the Theory of Money which has appeared for many years'. Keynes was correct. Hawtrey's is a beautiful, eccentric book, written in a style one could only ever hope to emulate. 'Money,' it begins, 'is one of those concepts which, like a teaspoon or an umbrella, but unlike an earthquake or a buttercup, are definable primarily by the use or purpose which they serve.' If only all books on finance were written with such charm. Hawtrey defines the use and purpose and money as 'the means established by law (or custom) for the payment of debts', and over the course of the book he returns again and again to various comparisons with umbrellas and umbrella-makers to make his various points about debt, money, banks and the workings of financial systems.

An umbrella-maker might pay wages by creating a debt from himself to his workmen, but, in order that his workmen may *spend* their wages, the liability must be transferred to other shoulders than those of the umbrella-maker, for he can sell them nothing but umbrellas.

The solution of this difficulty is to be found in the intervention of someone who *deals in debts*. The umbrella-maker can sell to this "dealer in debts" the debts due to him for the umbrellas which he has sold, and in return the "dealer in debts" can take on himself the liability for the umbrella-maker's debts to his workmen. If every creditor assigned his rights as against his debtors to the dealers in debts, the setting off of debts against one another would be enormously facilitated.

A dealer in debts or credits is a full-time *Banker*. The debts of the whole community can be settled by transfers in the banker's books or by the delivery of documents, such as bank notes, representative of the banker's obligations. So long as the bankers remain solvent, their obligations supply a perfectly adequate means for the discharge of debts, because a debt can be just as well cancelled against another debt as extinguished by a payment of money.

The complex, intimate relationship between individual states and banks that I have attempted to describe in this book is brilliantly sketched and summarised here in just a few paragraphs by Hawtrey. For what are states but umbrella-makers, metaphorically speaking? And what is a banker but a dealer in debt, an ally to umbrella-makers, now and forever?

Money and Promises has been my *apologia pro vita sua*, certainly. But it is also an acknowledgement of those who taught me, years ago, and everything I have learnt since from my lifetime's work with banks and states. I am no longer a banker, but I remain indebted, as do we all, for better and for worse, as citizens and as nations.

About the Author

Paolo Zannoni is the President of Prada Holding and International Advisor to the Executive Office of Goldman Sachs International. He is also a member of the Advisory Board of the Jackson Institute and the International Center for Finance for Global Affairs at Yale University. With a global financial career, his former positions include Partner of Goldman Sachs, President of Fiat USSR and President of Fiat USA. Before venturing into the financial world, Zannoni studied at the universities of Bologna, Florence and Yale. *Money and Promises* is his first book.

Acknowledgements

Many thanks to everyone who read and commented on drafts of this book, including Will Goetzmann, Gary Gorton, Joseph La Palombara, Doug Rae, Geert Rouwenhorst, Jan Shapiro, Victor Halberstadt, Dante Roscini, Paolo Battaglia, Claudio Marsilio, Paola Avallone, Valerie Tomaselli, Zach Gaiewsky and Andra Zappulli.

Many people helped me to conduct research in the State Archives of Venice, Naples, the Bank of England Museum, London, Philadelphia and Medina del Campo. Among them Maria Giulia Pesavento, Ned Downing, Orazio Abbamonte, Sergio Rioli, David Brigham and Andrea Zappulli.

The manuscript would not be readable without the efforts of Ian Samson, who read it over and over again. It would not have been published without Anthony Cheetham, Nic Cheetham, Karina Maduro and all the team at Head of Zeus, and without my agent, Irene Baldoni at Georgina Capel.

Bibliography

Chapter 1

Monica Baldassarri, *Zecca e monete del Comune di Pisa: Dalle origini alla Seconda Repubblica*, XII century–1406, vol. 1 (Pisa: Felici Editori, 2010).

Francesco Balducci Pegolotti, *La pratica della mercatura* (Cambridge, MA.: The Medieval Academy of America, 1936).

Marta Battistoni, *L'Opera del Duomo di Pisa: il patrimonio e la sua gestione nei secoli XII-XV* (Pisa: Pacini Editore, 2013).

Robert-Henri Bautier, *Commerce méditerranéen et banquiers italiens au Moyen Âge*, Variorum Collected Studies (Abingdon-on-Thames: Routledge, 1992).

Carlo Maria Cipolla, *Studi di storia della moneta: i movimenti dei cambi in Italia dal secolo XIII al XV* (Pavia: Università di Pavia, 1948).

Carlo Maria Cipolla, *Money, Prices, and Civilization in the Mediterranean World: Fifth to Seventeenth Century* (New York: Gordian Press, 1967).

Carlo Maria Cipolla, *The Monetary Policy of Fourteenth Century Florence* (Berkeley, CA: University of California Press, 1982).

Benedetto Cotrugli, *The Book of the Art of Trade*, edited by Carlo Carraro and Giovanni Favero (London: Palgrave Macmillan, 2017).

Flaminio Dal Borgo, *Raccolta di scelti diplomi pisani* (Pisa: 1655).

Raymond de Roover, *The Medici Bank* (New York: New York University Press, 1948).

Keith Devlin, *Finding Fibonacci: The Quest to Rediscover the Forgotten Mathematical Genius Who Changed the World* (Princeton, NJ: Princeton University Press, 2017).

Marc Flandreau, 'Le système monétaire international: 1400–2000', in *La Casa di San Giorgio: il potere del Credito* (Genoa: Società Ligure di Storia Patria, 2004).

Maria Ginatempo, *Prima del debito. Finanziamento della spesa pubblica e gestione del deficit nelle grandi città toscane (1200–1350 ca)*, Biblioteca storica toscana, series I, vol. 38 (Florence: Olschki, 2000).

William N. Goetzmann, 'Fibonacci and the Financial Revolution', in *NBER. National Bureau of Economic Research* (March 2004), working paper 10352.

William N. Goetzmann, *Money Changes Everything: How Finance Made Civilization Possible* (Princeton, NJ: Princeton University Press, 2017).

David Herlihy, *Pisa in the early Renaissance* (New Haven, CT: Yale University Press, 1958).

Charles Jenkinson Earl of Liverpool, *A Treatise on the Coins of the Realm in a Letter to the King* (Oxford: Oxford University Press, 1805).

Nobuhiro Kiyotaki – John Moore, 'Evil Is the Root of All Money', in *American Economic Review*, 92 (2002).

Pompeo Litta, *Famiglie celebri italiane* (Milan: Luciano Basadonna, 1866–1871).

Robert Lopez – Irving Raymond, *Medieval Trade in the Mediterranean World* (New York: Columbia University Press, 1955).

Robert Lopez, *The Dawn of Modern Banking* (New Haven, CT: Yale University Press, 1979).

Nicholas Mayhew, 'Money in England from the Middle Ages to the Nineteenth Century', in Robartus J. van der Spek – Bas van Leeuwen (eds.), *Money, Currency and Crisis: in Search of Trust, 2000 BC to AD 2000* (Abingdon-on-Thames: Routledge, 2018).

Federigo Melis, *Note di Storia della Banca pisana nel Trecento* (Pisa: Società Storica Pisana, 1955).

George O'Brien, *An Essay on Mediaeval Economic Teaching* (London: Longmans Green and Company, 1920; reissued 1970)

Lucio Papa D'Amico, 'Titoli di credito di antichi mercanti italiani', in *Annali del Credito della Previdenza* (Rome: Tipografia Eredi Botta, 1885).

Abbott Payson Usher, 'The Origins of Banking: The Primitive Bank of Deposit, 1200-1600', in *Economic History Review*, vol. 4 (1934).

Raffaele Pisano – Paolo Bussotti, 'Fibonacci and the Abacus Schools in Italy: Mathematical Conceptual Streams – Education and Its Changing Relationship with Society', in *Almagest* (November 2015).

Angela Redish, *Bimetallism: An Economic and Historical Analysis* (Cambridge: Cambridge University Press, 2000).

Yves Renouard, *Les hommes d'affaires italiens au Moyen Age* (Paris: A. Colin, 1949).

Niccolò Rodolico, 'Il sistema monetario e le classi sociali nel Medioevo', in *Rivista. Italiana di Sociologia*, vol. 8 (1904).

Giuseppe Rossi-Sabatini, *L'espansione di Pisa nel Mediterraneo fino alla Meloria* (Florence: Sansoni, 1935).

Armando Sapori, 'La cultura del mercante medievale italiano', *in Rivista di Storia economica*, II (1937).

Armando Sapori, *Studi di storia economica medievale* (Florence: Sansoni, 1946).

Armando Sapori (ed.), *Libro Giallo Della Compagnia Dei Covoni* (Milan: Istituto Editoriale Cisalpino, 1970).

Thomas J. Sargent – François R. Velde, *The Big Problem of Small Change* (Princeton, NJ: Princeton University Press, 2003).

William Arthur Shaw, *The History of Currency: 1252–1894* (London: Wilsons and Milne, 1895).

Pietro Silva, 'Intorno all'industria e al commercio della lana in Pisa', in *Studi storici*, vol. 14 (1910).

Marco Tangheroni, *Politica, commercio e agricoltura a Pisa nel Trecento* (Pisa: Edizioni Plus, Università di Pisa, 2002).

Elisabetta Ulivi, 'Masters, Questions and Challenges in the Abacus Schools', in *Archive for History of Exact Sciences*, vol. 69 (2015).

Franca Maria Vanni, *Pisa gloriosa: Le monete della zecca di Pisa* (Pisa: CLD Libri, 2010).

Cinzio Violante, *Economia, società, istituzioni a Pisa nel Medioevo* (Bari: Dedalo, 1980).

Gioacchino Volpe, *Studi sulle istituzioni comunali a Pisa: Città e contado, consoli e podestà, secoli XII-XIII* (Florence: Sansoni, 1970).

Chapter 2

Most of the surviving original documents on Banco Giro are at the ASV (Archivio di Stato di Venezia). They can be found in two different collections: *Senato, Delibere, Banco Giro* and *Senato, Delibere, Zecca*.

The ledger for the first six months of the Banco's operation is in *Senato, Delibere, Banco Giro.*

A few documents are also at Fondazione Querini Stampalia, Venice. Among these, a complete list of debts, credits and coins of the Banco Giro for the first ten years of operation.

Carlo Beltrame – Marco Morin, *I cannoni di Venezia. Artiglierie della Serenissima da fortezze e relitti* (Florence: All'Insegna del Giglio, 2014).

Fabio Besta, *Bilanci pubblici generali della Repubblica di Venezia* (Venice: Visentini, 1912).

Guido Candiani, *I vascelli della Serenissima. Guerra, politica e costruzioni navali a Venezia in età moderna, 1650–1720* (Venice: Istituto Veneto di Scienze, Lettere ed Arti, 2004).

Roberto Cessi, 'Il problema bancario a Venezia nel secolo XIV', in *Atti della R. Accademia delle Scienze di Torino*, vol. 52 (1916).

Roberto Cessi, 'Studi sulla moneta veneziana. La coniazione del ducato aureo', in *Economia*, vol. 2, 1 (1924).

David Chambers – Brian Pullan (eds.), *Venice: A Documentary History 1450–1630* (Toronto: University of Toronto Press, 2004).

Carlo Maria Cipolla, *Guns and Sails in the Early phase of European Expansion 1400–1700* (London: Collins, 1965).

Girolamo Costantini, *Delle monete in senso pratico, e morale. Ragionamento diviso in sette capitoli* (Venice: Simone Occhi, 1751).

Robert Cotton, 'A Speech Touching the Alteration of Coin', in William Arthur Shaw, *Select Tracts and Documents Illustrative of English Monetary History 1626–1730* (London: Wilsons and Milne, 1896).

Raymond de Roover, 'Cambium ad Venetias: Contribution to the History of Foreign Exchange', in Raymond de Roover – Julius Kirshner (eds), *Business, Banking and Economic Thought in Late Medieval and Early Modern Europe* (Chicago: University of Chicago Press, 1974).

Raymond de Roover, 'New Interpretation of the History of Banking', in Raymond de Roover – Julius Kirshner (eds.), *Business, Banking and Economic Thought in Late Medieval and Early Modern Europe* (Chicago: University of Chicago Press, 1974).

Charles Dunbar, 'The Bank of Venice', in *The Quarterly Journal of Economics*, VI (April 1892).

Luigi Einaudi, 'Teoria della moneta immaginaria da Carlo Magno alla Rivoluzione Francese', in *Rivista di storia economica*, vol. 1 (1936).

Luigi Einaudi, *The Medieval Practice of Managed Currencies*, in Arthur David Gayer (ed.), *The Lessons of Monetary Experience. Essays in Honour of Irving Fisher* (New York: Farrar & Rinehart, 1937).

Alberto Errera, *Storia dell'economia politica negli stati della Repubblica Veneta* (Venice: Antonelli, 1877).

Francesco Ferrara – Francesco Lampertico, *Gli antichi banchi di Venezia. Il credito* (Palermo: Fondazione culturale Lauro Chiazzese della Cassa di Risparmio, 1970).

William N. Goetzmann, *Money Changes Everything: How Finance Made Civilization Possible* (Princeton, NJ: Princeton University Press, 2017).

Ettore Inclimona, 'Le origini del Banco Giro', in *Giornale degli economisti*, vol. 46 (February 1913).

Frederic Lane, *Venice and History* (Baltimore, MD: Johns Hopkins University Press, 1966).

Frederic Lane – Reinhold C. Mueller, *Money and Banking in Medieval and Renaissance Venice* (Baltimore, MD: Johns Hopkins University Press, 2020).

Elia Lattes, *La Libertà delle Banche a Venezia dal secolo XIII al XVII secondo i documenti inediti del R. Archivio dei Frari* (Milan: Valentiner e Mues, 1869).

C. G. Londonio, 'Dei banchi pubblici e privati', in *Giornale dell'I.R. Istituto Lombardo di scienze, lettere ed arti* (1843).

Gino Luzzatto, 'L'oro e l'argento nello politica monetaria veneziana dei secoli XIII e XIV', in *Rivista storica italiana*, vol. 54 (1937).

Gino Luzzatto, *Studi di storia economica veneziana* (Padua: Cedam, 1954).

Domenico Malipiero, *Annali Veneti dall'anno 1457–1500* (Florence: Vieusseux, 1843).

Giulio Mandich, 'Formule monetarie veneziane del periodo 1619–1650', in *Studi in onore di Armando Saponi* (Milan: Istituto Editoriale Cisalpino, 1957).

Giuseppe Maranini, *La costituzione di Venezia: dalle origini alla serrata del Maggior Consiglio* (Florence: La Nuova Italia, 1927).

Jan Morris, *The World of Venice* (San Diego, CA: Harcourt Brace, 1993).

Reinhold C. Mueller, 'Bank Money in Venice, to the Mid-Fifteenth Century', in Vera Barbagli Bagnoli (ed.), *La moneta nell'economia europea secoli XIII-XVIII* (Florence / Prato: Le Monnier / Istituto Internazionale di Storia Economica F. Datini, 1981).

Luciano Pezzolo, *Il fisco dei veneziani. Finanza pubblica ed economia tra XV e XVII secolo* (Verona: Cierre Edizioni, 2003).

Luciano Pezzolo, 'Bonds and Government Debts in Italian City States, 1250–1650', in William N. Goetzmann – K. Geert Rouwenhorst (eds.), *The Origins of Value: The Financial Innovations that Created Modern Capital Markets* (Oxford: Oxford University Press, 2005).

Vito Piergiovanni, *The Growth of the Bank as an Institution and the Development of Money-Business Law*, vol. 12 of *Comparative Studies in Continental and Anglo-American Legal History* (Berlin: Dunckler and Humblot, 1993).

John Richards (ed.), *Precious Metals in the Later Medieval and Early Modern Worlds* (Durham, NC: Carolina Academic Press, 1983).

Amadeo Soresina, *Il Banco Giro di Venezia* (Venice: Fratelli Visentini, 1889).

Alan M. Stahl, *Zecca: The Mint of Venice in the Middle Ages* (Baltimore, MD: Johns Hopkins University Press, 2000).

Ugo Tucci, *Il Banco della Piazza di Rialto, prima banca pubblica veneziana in Idem, Mercanti, navi, monete nel Cinquecento veneziano* (Bologna: Il Mulino, 1981).

Ugo Tucci, 'Convertibilità e copertura metallica della moneta del Banco Giro veneziano', in *Credito, Banche e investimenti. Secoli XIII–XX* (Florence / Prato: Le Monnier / Istituto Internazionale di Storia Economica F. Datini, 1981).

Abbott Payson Usher, 'The Early History of Deposit Banking in Mediterranean Europe', in *Harvard Economic Studies*, vol. 75 (Cambridge, MA.: Harvard University Press, 1943).

Chapter 3

Few of the tallies issued by the Exchequer survive. Thirty-nine tallies varying from complete to fragments are in the vaults of the Bank of England. Some of them are related to the first trade between the Bank of England and the Exchequer July–August 1694. Those tallies were examined by D. L. Evans before 1950; he detailed the results of his examination in a report now at the bank. The first trade was entered on page 1 of the *General Cash Book*, July 17, 1694 – January 17, 1695, Adm. 42/2.

Robert Ashton, *The Crown and the Money Market* (Oxford: The Clarendon Press, 1960).

Bruce Carruthers, *City of Capital: Politics and Markets in the English Financial Revolution* (Princeton, NJ: Princeton University Press, 1996).

C. D. Chandaman, *The English Public Revenue, 1660–1688* (Oxford: Oxford University Press, 1975).

John Clapham, *The Bank of England: A History*, vol. 1 (Cambridge: Cambridge University Press, 1970).

William Deininger, *Calculating Values* (Cambridge, MA.: Harvard University Press, 2018).

Christine Desan, *Making Money: Coin, Currency, and the Coming of Capitalism* (Oxford: Oxford University Press, 2014).

P. G. M. Dickson, *The Financial Revolution in England: A Study in the Development of Public Credit, 1688–1756* (Farnham: Ashgate Publ. Co, 1967).

Albert Edgar Feavearyear, *The Pound Sterling: A History of English Money* (Oxford: Clarendon Press, 1963).

Edmund B. Fryde, 'Materials for the study of Edward III's credit operations, 1327–1348', in *Bulletin of the Institute of Historical Research*, vol. XXIII, issue 67 (London: 1950).

Edmund B. Fryde, *William de la Poole: Merchant and King's Banker (d.1366)* (London: Hambledon Continuum, 1988).

John Giuseppi, *The Bank of England: A History from Its Foundation in 1694* (Chicago: H. Regnery Company, 1966).

Michael Godfrey – William Paterson, *A Brief Account of the Intended Bank of England* (London: Randal Taylor, 1694).

John Gray, *The Social System: A Treatise on the Principle of Exchange* (Edinburgh: William Tait, 1831).

Eric L. Hargreaves, *The National Debt* (London: Frank Cass & Co. Ltd., 1966).

J. Keith Horsefield, *British Monetary Experiments 1650–1710* (New York: Garland, 1983).

Hilary Jenkinson, 'Exchequer Tallies', in *Archaeologia, or Miscellaneous Tracts relating to Antiquity*, vol. 62 (London: Society of Antiquaries of London, 1911).

Hilary Jenkinson, 'Medieval Tallies, Public and Private', in *Archaeologia, or Miscellaneous Tracts relating to Antiquity*, vol. 75 (London: Society of Antiquaries of London, 1925).

Mervyn King, *The End of Alchemy. Money, Banking and the Future of the Global Economy* (Boston: Little, Brown Book Group, 2016).

Richard Kleer, *Money, Politics and Power: Banking and Public Finance in Wartime England, 1694–96* (London: Routledge, 2017).

John Law, *Money and Trade Considered: With a Proposal for Supplying the Nation with Money* (Glasgow: R&A Foulis, 1750).

Thomas Levenson, *Money for Nothing* (New York: Random House, 2020).

Moshe A. Milevsky, *King William's Tontine: Why the Retirement Annuity of the Future Should Resemble its Past* (Cambridge: Cambridge University Press, 2015).

Tony Moore, *'Score it upon my taille': The Use (and Abuse) of Tallies by the Medieval Exchequer*, Reading Medieval Studies (Reading: University of Reading, 2013).

Anne Murphy, *The Origins of English Financial Markets: Investment and Speculation before the South Sea Bubble* (Cambridge: Cambridge University Press, 2009).

Colin Nicholson, *Writing and the Rise of Finance: Capital Satires of the Early Eighteenth Century* (New York: Cambridge University Press, 1994).

Ellis T. Powell, *The Evolution of the Money Market (1385-1915)* (London: Frank Cass, 1966).

Richard D. Richards, *The Early History of Banking in England* (London: PS King & Son, 1929).

Thorold Rogers, *The First Nine Years of the Bank of England* (London: PS King Publisher, 1885).

Richard S. Sayers, *Modern Banking* (Oxford: Clarendon Press, 1964).

David Stasavage, *Public Debt and the Birth of the Democratic State* (Cambridge: Cambridge University Press, 1970).

James Stevens Rogers, *The Early History of the Law of Bills and Notes* (Cambridge: Cambridge University Press, 1995).

Peter Temin – Hans-Joachim Voth, *Prometheus Shackled: Goldsmith Banks and England's Financial Revolution after 1700* (Oxford: Oxford University Press, 2013).

Eugen von Philippovich, *History of the Bank of England and its Financial Services to the State* (Washington: US National Monetary Commission, 1911).

Carl Wennerlind, *Casualties of Credit: The English Financial Revolution, 1620–1720* (Cambridge, MA.: Harvard University Press, 2011).

James F. Willard, 'An Early Exchequer Tally', in *Bulletin of the John Rylands Library*, vol. 7, no. 2 (January 1923).

Chapter 4

Between the sixteenth and eighteenth centuries, the banking charities of Naples numbered seven. Slowly they merged. By 1808, under the Napoleonic rule, they were consolidated into one. And one – Il Banco di Napoli – still survives. It is now part of Banco Intesa San Paolo, Italy's biggest commercial bank. The archives of the banking charities were also consolidated into one.

The archives are unique because the money "created" by the banking charities was unique – the pledge; then the pledge circulated. Every time the pledge changed hands, the change in the bank creditor was recorded by a note in the ledgers. When the pledges were returned to the bank by the creditor and the bank debt extinguished, they were filed. Hundreds of years of pledges – bank money – are now filed in the archives.

These ledgers and the pledges allow us to re-assemble most of the activities of the bank.

I have relied on the records of four of the seven banking charities: Banco della Pietà, Banco dei Poveri, Banco di San Eligio, Banco di San Giacomo.

Paola Avallone (ed.), *Prestare ai poveri. Il credito su pegno e i Monti di*

Pietà in area Mediterranea (XV–XIX secolo) (Naples: CNR, Istituto di Studi sulle Società del Mediterraneo, 2007).

Paola Avallone – Raffaella Salvemini, 'Between Charity and Credit: The Evolution of the Neapolitan Banking System (Sixteenth–Seventeenth Century)', in Lilia Costabile – Larry Neal (eds.), *Financial Innovation and Resilience: A Comparative Perspective on the Public Banks of Naples (1462–1808)*, Palgrave Studies in the History of Finance (London: Palgrave Macmillan, 2018).

Francesco Balletta, *La circolazione della moneta fiduciaria a Napoli nel Seicento e nel Settecento (1587–1805)* (Naples: Edizioni Scientifiche Italiane, 2009).

Francesco Balletta – Luigi Balletta – Eduardo Nappi, 'The Investments of the Neapolitan Public Banks: A Long Run View (1587–1806)', in Lilia Costabile – Larry Neal (eds.), *Financial Innovation and Resilience: A Comparative Perspective on the Public Banks of Naples (1462–1808)*, Palgrave Studies in the History of Finance (London: Palgrave Macmillan, 2018).

Lodovico Bianchini, *Della storia delle finanze del regno di Napoli* (Naples: Stamperia Reale, 1859).

Antonio Calabria, *The Cost of Empire: The Finances of the Kingdom of Naples in the Time of Spanish Rule* (Cambridge: Cambridge University Press, 1991).

Raffaele Calapietra, *Problemi monetari negli scrittori napoletani del Seicento* (Rome: Accademia Nazionale dei Lincei, 1973).

Giuseppe Coniglio, *Declino del Viceregno di Napoli (1599-1689)* (Naples: Giannini Editore, 1991).

Lilia Costabile – Larry Neal (eds.), *Financial Innovation and Resilience: A Comparative Perspective on the Public Banks of Naples (1462–1808)*, Palgrave Studies in the History of Finance (London: Palgrave Macmillan, 2018).

Domenico Demarco – Eduardo Nappi, 'Nuovi documenti sulle origini e sui titoli del Banco di Napoli', in *Revue Internationale d'Histoire de la Banque*, no. 31 (Géneve: Librairie Droz, 1987).

Luigi De Simone Rocco, *La fede di credito* (Naples: Borrelli, 1922).

Mario De Stefano, *Banchi e vicende monetarie nel Regno di Napoli 1600–1625* (Livorno: Il Tirreno, 1940).

Riccardo Filangieri, *I Banchi di Napoli dalle origini alla costituzione del Banco delle Due Sicilie (1539–1808)* (Naples: Tipografia degli Artigianelli, 1940).

Ferdinando Galiani, *Della moneta* (Naples: Raimondi, 1751).

Giuseppe Giarrani, *Il carattere bancario e l'evoluzione strutturale dei primigenii monti di pietà: riflessi della tecnica bancaria antica su quella moderna* (Milan: Giuffrè, 1957).

Marco Mastrofini, *Le usure* (Rome: Vincenzo Poggioli, 1831).

Maria Giuseppina Muzzarelli – Mauro Carboni (eds.), *I conti dei Monti. Teoria e pratica amministrativa nei Monti di pietà fra Medioevo ed Età Moderna* (Venice: Marsilio, 2008).

Michele Rocco, *De' Banchi di Napoli e della loro ragione* (Naples: F.lli Raimondi, 1785).

Umberto Santarelli, '«Maxima fuit Florentiae altercatio»: l'usura e i «montes»', in *Banchi pubblici, banchi privati e monti di pietà nell'Europa preindustriale. Amministrazione, tecniche operative e ruoli economici*, conference proceedings (Genoa: Società ligure di storia patria, 1990).

Matilde Serão, *Il ventre di Napoli* (Milan: Treves, 1884).

Richard Spear – Philip Sohm, *Painting for Profit: The Economic Lives of Seventeenth-Century Italian Painters* (New Haven, CT: Yale University Press, 2010).

Eugenio Tortora, *Raccolta di documenti storici, statistici, leggi e regole concernenti il Banco di Napoli* (Naples: Francesco Giannini, 1882).

Eugenio Tortora, *Nuovi documenti per la storia del Banco di Napoli* (Naples: A. Bellisario, 1890).

Giovanni Donato Turbolo, *Discorso sopra le monete del Regno di Napoli* (Naples: n.p., 1629).

François R. Velde, 'Neapolitan Banks in the Context of Early Modern Public Banks', in Lilia Costabile – Larry Neal (eds.), *Financial Innovation and Resilience: A Comparative Perspective on the Public Banks of Naples (1462–1808),* Palgrave Studies in the History of Finance (London: Palgrave Macmillan, 2018).

Chapter 5

Willem R. Bisschop, *The Rise of the London Money Market* (London: Routledge, 1910).

Marie-Thérèse Boyer-Xambeu – Ghislain Deleplace – Lucien Gillard, *Private Money and Public Currencies: The Sixteenth Century Challenge* (New York: M.E. Sharpe, 1994).

Edwin Cannan, *The Paper Pound 1797–1821: A reprint of the Bullion Report* (London: P.S. King & Son, 1925).

David Chilosi – Oliver Volckart, *Good or Bad Money? Debasement, Society and the State in the Late Middle Ages,* working paper (London: London School of Economics, 2010).

Read Conyers, 'Queen Elizabeth's Seizure of the Duke of Alva's Pay-Ships', in *The Journal of Modern History,* vol. 5, no. 4 (December 1933).

Carlo Cuneo, *Memorie sopra l'antico Debito Pubblico, mutui, compere e banca di S. Giorgio in Genova* (Genoa: Stamperia dei Sordi Muti, 1842).

Jacques du Puy de la Serra, *Trattato delle lettere di cambio delle più celebri piazze d'Europa* (Florence: S.A.R., 1718).

Tri Vi Dang – Gary Gorton – Bengt Holmström, *Ignorance, Debt and Financial Crises*, working paper (2020).

José Gentil Da Silva, *Marchandises et finances: Lettres de Lisbonne, 1563–1578* (Paris: SEVPEN, 1961).

José Gentil Da Silva, *Banque et crédit en Italie au XVIIe siècle* (Paris: Klincksieck, 1969).

Bernardo Davanzati, *Notizia de Cambi, Scisma d'Inghilterra con altre Operette del Sig. Bernardo Davanzati* (Florence: Nuova stamperia del Maffi e Landi, 1638).

Raymond de Roover, *Gresham on Foreign Exchange* (Cambridge, MA.: Harvard University Press, 1949).

Raymond de Roover, *L'évolution de la lettre de change. XIVe–XVIIIe siècles* (Paris: Librairie Armand Colin, 1953).

Raymond de Roover, 'Cambium ad Venetias: Contribution to the History of Foreign Exchange', in Raymond de Roover – Julius Kirshner (eds), *Business, Banking and Economic Thought in Late Medieval and Early Modern Europe* (Chicago: University of Chicago Press, 1974).

Debra Glassman – Angela Redish, 'Currency Depreciation in Early Modern England and France', in *Explorations in Economic History*, vol. 25, issue 1 (January 1988).

Gary Gorton, *Private Money Production Without Banks*, NBER Working Paper Series, Working Paper 26663 (Cambridge, MA: National Bureau of Economic Research: 2020).

Robin Harris, *Dubrovnik: A History* (London: Saqi Books, 2006).

Ralph George Hawtrey, *Bretton Woods. For Better or Worse* (London: Longmans, 1946).

Giuseppe Iacono – Salvatore Ennio Furone, *Les marchands banquiers florentins et l'architecture à Lyon au XVIe siècle* (Paris: Publisud, 1999).

Charles Jenkinson Earl of Liverpool, *A Treatise on the Coins of the Realm in a Letter to the King* (Oxford: Oxford University Press, 1805).

Patrick Kelly, *The Universal Cambist, and Commercial Instructor* (London: Lackington, Allen and Co., 1811).

Charles Kindleberger, *Spenders and Hoarders: The World Distribution of Spanish American Silver 1550–1750* (Singapore: Institute of Southeast Asian Studies, 1989).

Henri Lapeyre, *Simón Ruiz et les 'asientos' de Philippe II* (Paris: Armand Colin, 1953).

Henri Lapeyre, *Simón Ruiz en Medina del Campo. 1525–1597* (Valladolid: Cámara de Comercio e Industria de Valladolid, 1971).

Franciscus Lixaldius, *Le register* (Brussels: Kiessling, 1902).

Giulio Mandich, *Le pacte de Ricorsa et la marché italien des changes au XVIIe siècle* (Paris: Editions de l'École des Hautes Études en Sciences Sociales, 1953).

Claudio Marsilio, *Exchange Fairs and the Money Market in Early Modern Italy (1630–1650)* (Genoa: Città del silenzio, 2018).

Nadia Matringe, *La Banque en Renaissance. Les Salviati et la place de Lyon. Au milieu du XVIe siècle* (Rennes: Presses Universitaires De Rennes, 2016).

Federigo Melis, 'Uno spiraglio di luce sul finanziamento del primo viaggio di Giovanni da Verrazzano', in *Giornate commemorative. Greve in Chianti: 21–22 ottobre 1961* (Florence: Leo S. Olschki, 1970).

Reprinted in Idem, *I mercanti italiani nell'Europa medievale e rinascimentale* (Florence: Istituto Internazionale di Storia Economica F. Datini, 1990).

Sergii Moshenskyi, *History of the Weksel* (Bloomington: Xlibris, 2008).

Susan Mosher Stuard, *A State of Deference. Ragusa / Dubrovnik in the*

Medieval Centuries (University Park, Pennsylvania, PA: Penn State University Press, 1992).

Craig Muldrew – Steven King, *Cash, Wages, and the Economy of Make-shifts in England, 1650–1800* (London: Palgrave Macmillan, 2018).

Shizuya Nishimura, *The Decline of Inland Bills of Exchange in the London Money Market 1855–1913* (Cambridge: Cambridge University Press, 1971).

Giuseppe Candido Noaro, *La teoria dei cambi esteri di Bernardo Davanzati* (Rome: L'italiana, 1920).

Geoffrey Parker, *The Army of Flanders and the Spanish Road 1567–1659: The Logistics of Spanish Victory and Defeat in the Low Countries' Wars* (Cambridge: Cambridge University Press, 1975).

Cristóbal Pérez Pastor, *La Imprenta en Medina del Campo* (Madrid: Sucesores de Rivadeneyra, 1895).

Giovan Domenico Peri, *Il Negotiante* (Venice: Giacomo Herz, 1682).

James Steven Rogers, *The Early History of the Law of Bills and Notes: A Study of the Origins of Anglo-American Commercial Law* (Cambridge: Cambridge University Press, 1995).

Sigismondo Scaccia, *Tractatus de commerciis, et cambio* (Rome: Jacopo Mascardi per Andrea Brugiotti, 1619).

William Arthur Shaw, *The History of Currency, 1252–1894* (London: Wilsons & Milne, 1895).

Heinrich Sieveking, *Studio sulle finanze Genovesi nel Medioevo e in particolare sulla casa di S. Giorgio* (Genoa: Atti della Società Ligure di Storia Patria, 1907).

John Smail, *Merchants, Markets and Manufacture* (London: Palgrave Macmillan, 1999).

Henry Thornton, *An Enquiry into the Nature and Effects of the Paper Credit of Great Britain* (London: George Allen & Unwin Ltd, 1802).

Sergio Tognetti, *I gondi di Lione. Una banca d'affari fiorentina nella Francia del primo Cinquecento* (Florence: Leo S. Olschki, 2013).

Thomas Tooke – William Newmarch, *A History of Prices and of the State of Circulation from 1793 to 1837* (London: Longman, 1838).

Francesca Trivellato, *The Promise and Perils of Credit. What a Forgotten Legend about Jews and Finance Tells Us about the Making of European Commercial Society* (Princeton, NJ: Princeton University Press, 2019).

Ed Tufte, *Seeing with Fresh Eyes: Meaning, Space, Data, Truth* (Cheshire, CT: Graphics Press: 2020).

Max Weber, *Economy and Society* (Berkeley, CA: University of California Press, 1978).

Jin Xu, *Empire of Silver: A New Monetary History of China* (New Haven, CT: Yale University Press, 2017).

Chapter 6

The surviving records of the Bank of North America are now at the historical Society of Pennsylvania in Philadelphia. Unfortunately, few of the records covering the first year of operations of the bank survive: some journals, a few ledgers and an analysis of the state of the bank for the first three months of operations. These offer a (small) window onto the relationships between the continental congress and the bank.

Most of the documents on Robert Morris as Superintendent of Finance are from *The Papers of Robert Morris* edited by James Ferguson, John Catanzariti, Elisabeth Nuxoll, Mary Gallagher, and published by University of Pittsburgh Press.

William Anderson, *The Price of Liberty: The Public Debt of the American Revolution* (Charlottesville, VA: University of Virginia Press, 1983).

Rafael Arroyo Bayley, *The National Loans of the United States, from*

July 4, 1776, to June 30, 1880 (Washington, DC: U.S. Department of the Treasury Government Printing Office, 1882).

William Baxter, *The House of Hancock: Business in Boston, 1724–1775* (Cambridge: Harvard University Press, 1945).

John P. Butler, *Index of Papers of Continental Congress* (Washington, D.C.: National Archives and Records Service, 1978).

Neil Carothers, *Fractional Money: A History of the Small Coins and Fractional Paper Currency of the United States* (New York: Bowers & Merena Galleries, 1990).

Robert H. Carstens – Dale L. Flesher, 'Accounts of the Commissioners of the Continental Congress', in *Accounting Historians Notebook* (Spring 1987), vol.10, no. 1.

William F. De Knight, *History of the Currency of The Country and of the Loans of the United States, from the Earliest Period to June 30, 1900* (Washington, DC: U.S. Department of the Treasury Government Printing Office, 1900).

Alexander Del Mar, *The History of Money in America: From the Earliest Times to the Establishment of the Constitution* (New York: Cambridge Encyclopedia Company, 1900).

Ned W. Downing, 'Transatlantic Paper and the Emergence of the American Capital Market', in William Goetzmann – Geert Rouwenhorst (eds.), *The Origins of Value. The Financial Innovations that Created Modern Capital Markets* (Oxford: Oxford University Press, 2005).

Ned W. Downing, *The Revolutionary Beginning of the American Stock Market* (New York: Museum of American Finance, 2010).

Joseph Felt, *An Historical Account of Massachusetts Currency* (Boston: Perkins and Marvin, 1839).

James Ferguson, *The Power of the Purse: A History of American Public*

Finance, 1776–1790 (Chapel Hill: University of North Carolina Press, 1968).

James Ferguson – John Catanzariti – Elisabeth Nuxoll – Mary Gallagher, *The Papers of Robert Morris*, vol. 1. (Pittsburgh: University of Pittsburgh Press, 1973–1999).

Roy A. Foulke, *The Sinews of American Commerce* (New York: Dun & Bradstreet, 1941).

William Goetzmann – Geert Rouwenhorst (eds.), *The Origins of Value. The Financial Innovations that Created Modern Capital Markets* (Oxford: Oxford University Press, 2005).

Dror Goldberg, *Why Did Massachusetts Invent Modern Currency?*, working paper (Texas A&M University, 2007).

William M. Gouge, *A Short History of Paper-Money and Banking in the United States* (New York: Augustus M. Kelley, 1833 [reprint 1968]).

Charles Holdt Carroll, *Organization of Debt into Currency* (New York: Van Nostrand Reinhold, 1964).

Journal of Continental Congress, records of the daily proceedings of the Congress (Library of Congress, 1774–1789).

Sarah Kemble Knight, *The Private Journal of a Journey from Boston to New York: in the Year 1704* (Albany: F.H. Little, 1865).

Michael Antony Kirsch, *The Challenge of Credit Supply: American Problems and Solutions, 1650–1950* (Wilmington, DE: Vernon Press, 2015).

Lawrence Lewis, *History of the Bank of North America, The First Bank Chartered in the United States* (Philadelphia: T.B. Lippincott & co., 1882).

Herbert Lüthy, *La Banque protestante de la révocation de l'édit de Nantes à la Révolution* (Paris: S.E.V.P.E.N., 1959, 1961).

Cathy Madson (ed.), *The Economy of Early America: Historical Perspectives and New Directions* (University Park, PA: Penn State University Press, 2006).

Andrew McFarland Davis, *Currency and Banking in the Province of the Massachusetts-Bay* (New York: The Macmillan Co., 1900).

Andrew McFarland Davis (ed.), *Colonial Currency Reprints, 1682–1751* (Boston: John Wilson and Son, 1910).

Anne Cary Morris (ed.), *The Diary and Letters of Gouverneur Morris* (New York: Charles Scribner's Sons, 1888).

Curtis Nettles, *The Money Supply of the American Colonies Before 1720* (Madison: University of Wisconsin, 1934).

Edwin J. Perkins, *American Public Finance and Financial Services, 1700–1815* (Columbus, OH: Ohio State University Press, 1994).

George David Rappaport, *Stability and Change in Revolutionary Pennsylvania. Banking, Politics, and Social Structure* (University Park, PA: Penn State University Press, 1996).

Thomas Schaeper, *France and America in the Revolutionary Era* (New York/Oxford: Berghahn Books, 1995).

Jared Sparks, *The Life of Governor Morris. With a Selection from His Correspondence and Miscellaneous Papers* (Boston, MA: Gray & Bowen, 1832).

The Papers of Benjamin Franklin, a collaborative project by Yale University, (New Haven, CT: Yale University, from 1954).

Chapter 7

Arthur Arnold, *Banks, Credit and Money in Soviet Russia* (New York: Columbia University Press, 1937).

Alexandre Axelrod, *L'œuvre économique des Soviets* (Paris: J. Povolozky, 1920).

Alan Ball, *Russia's Last Capitalists, The Nepmen, 1921–1929* (Berkeley, CA: University of California Press, 1990).

Arup Banerji, *Merchants and Markets in Revolutionary Russia, 1917–30* (London: Palgrave MacMillan, 1997).

Nikolaĭ Ivanovich Bukharin, *Economics of the Transformation Period* (New York: Bergman, 1971).

Nikolaĭ Ivanovich Bukharin – Evgenii A. Preobrazhensky, *The ABC of Communism* (London: The Communist Party of Great Britain, 1922 [reprint by Merlin Press, London, 2007]).

Emilio Colombino, *Tre mesi nella Russia dei Soviet: relazione di E. Colombino ai metallurgici d'Italia* (Milan: Società Editrice Avanti, 1921).

Robert W. Davies, *The Development of the Soviet Budgetary System* (Cambridge: Cambridge University Press, 1958).

George Garvy, *Money, Financial Flows, and Credit in the Soviet Union* (Cambridge, MA.: Ballinger Publishing Company, 1977).

Jefferson J. A. Gatrall – Douglas Greenfield, *Alter Icons, The Russian Icon and Modernity* (University Park, PA: Penn State University Press, 2010).

William Thomas Goode, *Bolshevism at Work* (London: Allen & Unwin, 1920).

Mikhail M. Gorinov (ed.), *The Preobrazhensky Papers. Archival Documents and Materials Revolution. Volume I: 1886–1920* (Chicago: Hay Haymarket Books, 2014).

Iurii Vladimirovich Got'e, *Time of Troubles* (Princeton, NJ: Princeton University Press, 1988).

Julie Hessler, *A Social History of Soviet Trade* (Princeton, NJ: Princeton University Press, 2004).

Rudolf Hilferding, *Finanzkapital* (London: Routledge, 2006).

Leonard E. Hubbard, *Soviet Money and Finance* (London: Macmillan, 1936).

S. S. Katzenellenbaum, *Russian Currency and Banking, 1914–1924* (London: P.S. King & Son Ltd, 1925).

Mikhail V. Khodjakov, *Money of the Russian revolution: 1917–1920* (Newcastle upon Tyne: Cambridge Scholars Publishing, 2014).

Nadezhda Krupskaya, *Memories of Lenin* (Stafford: Panther Books, 1970).

Raul La Bry, *L'industrie russe et la révolution* (Paris: Payot, 1919).

Gustave Lemaire, *Le système bancaire de la Russie soviétique* (Paris: Arthur Rousseau, 1929).

Vladimir Lenin, *Imperialism, The Highest Stage of Capitalism* (London: Pluto Press, 1996).

Vladimir Lenin, *The Development of Capitalism in Russia* (Honolulu: University Press of the Pacific, 2004).

Lars T. Lih, *Bread and Authority in Russia, 1914–1921* (Oakland, CA: University of California Press, 1990).

Silvana Malle, *The Economic Organization of War Communism 1918–1921* (Cambridge: Cambridge University Press, 1985).

Karl Marx, *A Contribution to the Critique of Political Economy* (Chicago: C.H. Kerr, 1904).

Karl Marx, *Capital* (London: Penguin Books, 1992).

Karl Marx – Vladimir Lenin, *The Civil war in France. The Paris Commune* (New York: International Publishers, 1940).

V. Obolenskii-Osinskii, 'How We Got Control of the State Bank', in *Ekonomicheskaia zhizn'*, no. 1 (November 6, 1918).

Leo Pasvolosky, *The Economics of Communism: With Special Reference to Russia's Experiment* (New York: Macmillan, 1921).

Evgenii A. Preobrazhensky, *From N.E.P. to Socialism. A Glance into the Future of Russia and Europe* (London: New Park Publications, 1973).

Evgenii A. Preobrazhensky, *Paper Money in the Epoch of Proletarian Dictatorship* (Leiden: Brill, 2014).

Victor Serge, *Year One of the Russian Revolution* (Chicago: Hay Haymarket Books, [or. ed. 1930] 2015).

Stephen A. Smith, *Red Petrograd: Revolution in the Factories, 1917–1918* (Cambridge: Cambridge University Press, 1983).

Gregory Sokolnikov, 'Loan for Economic Reconstruction', in *Soviet Policy in Public Finance* (Redwood City, CA: Stanford University Press, 1931).

Boris Sokoloff, *Les Bolchéviks jugés par eux-mêmes: documents des Soviets de 1919* (Paris: Éditions franco-slave, 1919).

Leon Trotsky, *On Lenin* (London: George G. Harrap & co Ltd, 1971).

Dimitry Volkogonov, *Lenin, a New Biography* (New York: Free Press 1994).

Max Weber, *The Russian Revolutions* (Oxford: Polity Press, 1995).

Edmund Wilson, *To the Finland Station: A Study in the Acting and Writing of History* (New York: Farrar, Strauss, Giroux, 1971).

David Woodruff, *Money Unmade* (Ithaca, NY: Cornell University Press, 1999).

Yakov Yurovsky, *Currency Problems and Policy of the Soviet Union* (London: Leonard Parsons, 1923).

Yakov Yurovsky, in Naum Jasny, *Soviet Economists of the Twenties: Names to be Remembered* (Cambridge: Cambridge University Press, 2008).

Image Credits

Chapter Openers

Chapter 1: The Cathedral and Leaning Tower in the Piazza del Duomo, Pisa, *c.*1200.

Chapter 2: Venice and its galleys. Ships good for trade and for war.

Chapter 3: A view of London and the River Thames, featuring London Bridge and St Paul's Cathedral, *c.*1630.

Chapter 4: Naples with the Mount Vesuvius, Joseph Vernet Philippe Sauvan-Magnet.

Chapter 5: A view of the city and harbour of Dubrovnik. The massive walls protect both.

Chapter 6: An east prospect of the city of Philadelphia, George Heap.

Chapter 7: Red Square in Moscow.

Index

Entries with page references
in italics denote paintings,
photographs, illustrations etc.
Headings within the text are
shown with words in capital
letters

The ABC of Communism
(pamphlet) 243
'accommodations bill' 203
Alba, Duke of 176
Alexander Hamilton, first
  Secretary of the Treasury of
  the US *213*
Altamura 143–4
American Colonies
  Debt as Money 197–8
  defence spending 197–8
  Intricate Ways of Trade
  194–7
  money as debt 195–6, 197–8
  money types 195–6
  Paper money issued in
    1690 by the Colony of
    Massachusetts. The bill is a
    debt of the colony *198*
  and taxation difficulties
  206–7
American Communist Labor
  Party 253
American dollar 197
American Revolution 199,
  200–1, 205, 206
A Bank that Doesn't Make
  Money 207–10
An Essay Upon Projects (book)
  93
*Annali Veneti (Venetian
  Annals)* 51–3
Annunziata (Naples charity)
  122
Antwerp 161
arbitrage strategy 74–5
arbitrage trades 166–8, 171,
  172–3, 176, 177, 180, 181–2,
  184
'Art and Fortune' (book) 155
Articles of Confederation
  199, 220

Asientos 177–80
  Spanish Empire
  defaults and agreements
  179–80
  and Eighty Years' War 178
Asientos de Negros 178
Auden, W. H. 193
Averardo, Bishop 28–9
AvtoVAZ, privatisation of
  239, 240–1
Axelrod, Pavel 247
Axelrod, Robert 247–8

Balletta, Francesco 133–4
Banco dei Poveri 138
  The arms of the Banco
    dei Poveri (Bank for the
    Poor) in the ledger of the
    year 1600 *132*
  pledge of credit 132–3
Banco del Giro 10–11, 60–1,
  126, 128
  and the Artillery Office
  66–7, 71
  bank money 73
  Beautiful Cannons 66–7
  The Heady Years 75–7
  The Last Tab 71–2
  Leasing New Ships 67–71
  The ledger for Banco
    Giro's first six months of
    operation *62, 64*, 71–2,
    78, 97
  The main branch of Banco
    Giro *60*
  Rules and Regs 64–6
  Wily Arbitrageurs 74–5
Banco del Giro delle Biave
  58, 61
Banco della Piazza di Rialto
  54, 55, 73, 76
Banco della Pietà 146, 150
Banco di Napoli 127–8, 150
  archives *127*
  bank and state relationship
  143
Banco di Sant' Eligio 131
Banco di Santo Spirito
  (Naples) 144

Banco Salviati 160
Bank Act UK (1844) 245
Bank Money and Economic
  Growth 41–3
Bank of Amsterdam 126
Bank of England 12, 93, 128,
  187, 257
  The Bank of England and
    the Projecting Age 93–7
  The Charter Renewed
  104–5
  The English Disease 108–9
  Exchequer Tallies and the
    Bank of England 97–101
  The first page of the general
    cash book of the bank,
    July 27, 1694 *99*
  Fractional Reserve Banking
  101–2
  General Court 96–7,
  99–100, 102
  The government kisses the
    bank *107*
  invention of 93–101
  Safe Sticks, Safe Debts
  102–4
  Subscribing to the shares of
    the Bank of England *94*
  The Treasury Challenges
    the Bank 105–8
  and the War of the Spanish
    Succession 106
Bank of Hamburg 126
Bank of New York 223
Bank of North America 219,
  223–4, 225
  The Bank of North America
  215–18
  The Bank of North America
    handing a wad of bank notes
    to George Washington *211*
Bank of Pennsylvania
  207–10, 215
Bank of Philadelphia 210
Bank of the United States
  E Pluribus Unum 224–5
Banker
  a dealer in debt (or credits)
  269

banking
The inside of a medieval
bank *74*
The Ledger is the Key
32–4
Medieval banking
illustration *114*
and revolution 232–3, 234
'Banking Crises: An Equal
Opportunity Menace'
(working paper) 15
Bar-sur-Aube 159
Barcelona 33
The Battle of Monmouth
between Washington's
Army and the British
forces, 1778 *210*
Bernardo Davanzati Bostichi.
Banker and writer *164*
Bertie, Charles 100
Beyond Good and Evil (book)
123
Biblioteca Riccardiana,
Florence *25, 26*
Bibliotheca Wittockiana 165
Bill of exchange in Spanish
dollars issued by the
Continental Congress in
1780 *206*
Bills of Exchange 205–7
Bills of exchange moving
between Florence and
Lyon *165*
Biscayne, Bay of 175
Bologna 9
Bolshevik Central
Committee 236
Bolshevik Department of
Currency Production 255
Bolshevik Revolution
Revolutionary Committee
236
Seizing the Banks 236–8
*The Bolshevik Revolution
1917–23* (book) 254
Bolshevik rule
Bolshevik Inflation:
Destroying the Value of
Money 252–3
Chervonets Reborn 255–8
By Exchange Alone:
Mandatory Commodity
Exchange 246
exchange value 245

mandatory commodity
exchange 246–8
Money, Signs and Symbols
254–5
The Murder of Trade
242–5
New Economic Policy
(NEP) 253–4
The Paradoxical Sovznak
250–2
The Powdered Milk
Manufacturing Problem
246–8
The Soviet Bookkeeper
Supreme 261–3
Supreme Council for the
National Economy 246
A Tale of Two Currencies
258–60
Treasury 251, 258, 259,
260, 261–2
The Triumph of the Bank
260
Bolsheviks 231, 232
Boston 196
Bretton Woods 171
Broggia, Carlo Antonio 123
Bruges 160
Brussels 188
Bugia 24
Bukharin, Nikolai 243

Camillo & Lorenzo Strozzi
157
*Can the Bolsheviks Retain
State Power?* (pamphlet)
229, 234
Candia 70–1
Caravaggio 133
Caravaggio's Money 128–31
lost painting 130–1
The two entries in the
ledger of the Banco di
Sant'Eligio for the lost
painting by Caravaggio
130
Carr, E. H. 254
Catholic Church 136–7,
157, 159
arbitrage practice 180–2
lending at interest 116, 118
Pisa's cathedral 28–30
Spiritual Finance 180–2
The Warrior Pope 115

Cattedrale Metropolitana
Primaziale di Santa Maria
Assunta 22
Central Budgeting and
Accounting Administration
of Soviet Russia 238
Champagne region 159–60
The chapel of the Sacro
Monte dei Poveri with
the arms of the De Santis
family *126*
Charles I, King 72, 91
Charles II, King 91
Charleston 207
chervonets 255–8, 260, 261
China 158
City of London Corporation
90–1
'The Civil War in France'
(pamphlet) 232
Cologne 160
Columbus, Christopher 182
Commercial Banks as
Creators of 'Money'
(discussion paper) 267
Commissariat of Finance
238, 252, 257
Compagnia di Parazone e
Donato 10, 31–41, 42
Dealing in debts *38*
Paying for goods with
other people's debts, not
coins *36*
promises
Acquiring Cash with
Promises 39–40
Making Promises 34–5
Trading Promises 35–9
Trading Promises Pays
40–1
see also Libro dell' a di
Parazone Grasso e
Donato del maestro
Pietro
Compagnia di San Giorgio
95
Continental Congress 11,
198–9
and the Bank of North
America 215–18
and Bank of Pennsylvania
208–10
and bills of exchange
205–7, 208–9

dollar currency choice 219
French Money 201–5
international bills of
    exchange 200–1
Square Paper Bills 198–9
*A Contribution to a Critique
    of Political Economy* (book)
    125
Corporate Banking, the
    beginning of 30–1
Cotton, Sir Robert 72
Council of Ten (Venetian
    Republic) 14
Cromwell, Oliver 156
Currency and Credit (book)
    268

D'Abernon, John 85–6
    Brass rubbing of the image
        on the tomb of John
        D'Abernon *85*
D'Abernon, John (son) 86
Dahl, Robert 267, 268
Daily Tribune (newspaper)
    245
D'Aloisio, Carlo 144, 145,
    148
D'Aloisio, Luciano 144
The Dance of Death:
    skeletons and merchant
    bankers *183*
*Das Finanzkapital (Finance
    Capital)* (book) 233–4
Das Kapital (book) 233
Davanzati, Bernardo 164–8,
    170, 172, 177, 179, 179,
    185, 188
De Franchis, Antonio 132,
    138
De Franchis, Tommaso 131
Depretis, Agostino 120
Deane, Silas 201
Death in Venice (book) 48,
    78–9
Debt: The First 5000 Years
    (book) 16
Defoe, Daniel 15–16, 93
Della Moneta (On Money)
    (book) 113, 124, 125
d'Épinay, Madame 125
*The Development of Capitalism
    in Russia* (book) 243
di Gondola, Benedetto
    157–9, 160–1, 177

di Gondola family 156
Dictatorship of the
    Proletariat 232
Diderot, Denis 124
Dominican Order
    Franciscan Order, dispute
        with 115, 118–19
Donato di Pietro 32
Drelichman, Mauricio 178–9
Dubrovnik 156

East India Company 103
The Economic Journal 268
*Economical and Philosophical
    Manuscripts* 245
Economist (magazine) 239
écu de marc 11, 171, 188
Écu de Marc 169–70
Edward III, King 88
Elba 22
Elizabeth I, Queen 175, 176
Engels, Friedrich 232
England 69, 206
    bills of exchange
        inland bills 185–8
        international bills 186
    currency debasement 169
    Empirical English Bills
        184–8
    expenditure and taxes
        Parliament Takes Charge
            92–3
    Industrial Revolution 185,
        188
    Mint, the 105
    The stocks of early
        Exchequer tallies *84*
    tallies 84–6
English Civil War 91
English Exchequer 11, 86–9
    Paying taxes to the
        Exchequer *88*
    Sol and Pro Tallies as
        Private Debt Instruments
        89–90
    Tallies and Institutional
        Change 90–2
English Parliament 185
    and the Bank of England
        217, 261
Epidaurum 156
*Etymological Dictionary of the
    English Language* 156
Euro 11

European Economic
    Community 165
'Evening: Ponte al Mare, Pisa'
    (poem) 21
exchange, bills of 158–68
exchange bankers 164, 171,
    188–9
    Diagrams in Practice
        172–3
    Exchange Fairs 159–61, 171
    Like Mercury around the
        Sun 170–1
exchange trades 165–8
    currency arbitrage with
        debts *167*
The Eyes of the Mind and
    the Eyes on the Forehead
    164–8

Fabrizio di San Severino,
    Count 138, 139
February Revolution 254
Ferdinando Galiani. The
    foulest man of his century
    124
Fiat 10, 239
    Fiat USSR 10
Fibonacci 22
    abaci, schools of 32
    new mathematics 24–8
Fibonacci's Liber Abaci.
    Dating from 1290 *25*
Fiesco, Tomaso 175–7
Fifth Lateran Council 115,
    116, 118, 121, 135–6
Finanzkapital 233–6
First Bank of North America
    214
'*The* Flagellation of Christ'
    (painting) 131
Flanders 174
    Army of Flanders 173–4,
        174–7, 178, 186
Florence 9, 30, 157, 158, 164
Florence, University of 231,
    266
Fludyer, Sir Samuel Fludyer
    185–6, 187–8
Fondazione Banco di Napoli
    128
Fox, Charles 100
France
    and American Revolution
        funding 205, 206

currency debasement 169
Francis I, King of France 183
Franciscan Order
  banking charities 115,
    135–6
  Dominican Order, dispute
    with 115, 118–19
  The Monti: Renting Coins
    116–20
  see also Monti di Pietà
    (Mounds of Compassion)
Frankfurt 161
Franklin, Benjamin 11, 201
  and funding for the
    Continental Congress
    201–3, 204–5, 206
Frederick II, Emperor of
  Prussia 78
The front page of La Tabula
  della Salute. A pamphlet by
  Marco da Montegallo on
  the Monte di Pietà 117

Galiani, Ferdinando 113,
  123–8, 128, 135, 145, 147,
  150–1
Galileo Galilei 22, 166
Game of Thrones 156
Garzoni Bank 52, 53
Geneva 160
  Café Landolt 230–1, 247
  Lenin, time there 230–1,
    247
Genoa 30, 33
Genoa, Republic of 95
Genovesi, Antonio 123
Giles of Viterbo 115
Godfrey, Michael 95, 96
Goetzmann, Will 25
A gold chervonets minted in
  1980 257
gold coins, stable 169–70
Goldman Sachs International
  10
Goldman Sachs (Russia) 241
Gondi, Antonio 183–4
Gorbachev, Mikhail 239, 241
Gorky, Maxim 255
Gorton, Gary 185, 187, 188
Gosbank 258, 261, 262
  see also Russian State Bank
Gosplan 261
Gossnab 261
Gradisca, War of 55–6, 57

Graeber, David 16
Grand, Alphonse Ferdinand
  201–5
Grand & Cie bank 201, 203,
  205, 206
Gresham, Sir Thomas 175–6
Gresham's Law 260
Gundulić, House of see di
  Gondola family
Gunn, Peter 120

Habsburg Austria 61, 63
Habsburg Netherlands
  Dutch Revolt 173–4
Hague 69
Hamilton, Alexander 11, 223
  US National Bank plans
    212–14, 223
Hammer, Armand 253, 260
Hampstead Water Company
  93
Hancock, John 199–200,
  214
Hancock, John (son) 200
Hancock, Thomas 197,
  199–200
Hancock brothers
  The House of Hancock
    199–201
Havana 214
Hawtrey, Ralph George 268
Hilferding, Rudolph 233–4,
  262
The History of the Russian
  Revolution (book) 236
Hudson Bay 184

Il Negotiante (book) 177–8
Il Principe (book) 166
Ishango bone 84
Istoria e dimostrazioni (letters)
  166
Izvestia (newspaper) 249–50

Jefferson, Thomas 11
  system of coinage 220–4
The Journal of Mme Knight
  (book) 194
Julius II, Pope 115

Kautsky, Karl 233
Keynes, John Maynard 42,
  171, 268
Kiev 249–50

Knight, Sarah Kemble
  194–6, 198, 221
Kommersant (magazine) 239
Krupskaya, Nadezhda
  Konstantinovna 245

la Palombara, Joe 267
Lady Debt 16, 17, 265, 266
Lagny 159
Lanfranco (Pisa squire) 28–9
Lanificio San Casciano 41
Lateran Palace, Rome 115
Leaning Tower of Pisa
  and the Power of Debt
    28–30
Lembombo bone 84
Lending to the Borrower from
  Hell (book) 178–9
Lenin, Vladimir Ilyich
  Ulyanov 229, 230
  and communist revolution
    232
  and Das Finanzkapital
    (Finance Capital) 233–4
  Geneva Russian exiles
    meetings 230–2
  and runaway inflation
    252–3
  State Bank and the
    Bolshevik revolution
    234–8, 262–3
  see also New Economic
    Policy (NEP)
Lenin and Trotsky addressing
  a crowd in St Petersburg in
  1917 235
Leo X, Pope 115, 119
Leonardo da Pisa see
  Fibonacci
Leonardo da Pisa. Fibonacci
  24
Liber Abaci, The Book of
  Calculation 25–6
A Liber Abaci from the
  Republic of Genoa (1512)
  27
A Liber Abaci from the
  Republic of Venice, by
  Girolamo Tagliente 26
Libro dell' a di Parazone
  Grasso e Donato del
  maestro Pietro (ledger)
  31–41
Limes, Rodolfo 70, 71

Lindlom, Ed 267
Lippomano Bank 52
Lisbon 161
London 11, 69, 157, 158
London Gazette (newspaper)
102
Louis XII, King of France
115
Louis XVI, King of France
202
Lyon 160–4, 172, 181
exchange fairs 183–4, 186

Machiavelli 166
Maffetti & Brothers (bank)
172
Maggior Consiglio 59
Malatesta, Carlo 52
Malipiero, Domenico 57–8
Mann, Thomas 48, 78
Martinengo, Francisco
172–3, 180
Marx, Karl 125, 232–3,
244–5
Massachusetts, General
Court of
monetary system 196
Medici family 53
Medina del Campo 12, 161
Melis, Federico 34, 41
Memories of Lenin (book)
245
Menzhinsky, Vyacheslav
Rudolfovich 237–8
Mercenary troops looking
for money. The sack of
Antwerp by the Army of
Flanders, November 4,
1576 *173*
The Merchant of Venice (play)
48
Shylock 47
Merisi, Michelangelo *see*
Caravaggio
Michelangelo Merisi da
Caravaggio *129*
Money
states and banks 266
Montague, Charles 95, 98,
101
Monte dei Poveri 121
*Monti di Pietà (Mounds of
Compassion)* 116–20, 121,
126

Morris, Gouverneur
common national currency
219–24
Morris, Robert 207–9, 210,
211–12
and Alexander Hamilton's
bank plan 213, 223
and the Bank of North
America 215–18
common national currency
219–20, 221–3
US National Bank funding
213–14
Moscow 10
The Red Square and the
Sukharevka 239–42
Motta, Battle of 52

Naples 12, 206
banking charities 121–3,
125–8
Behind the Scenes: Sales
and Buybacks 135–9
The pledge of credit in
the 1600s *134*
The pledge of credit in
the 1700s (left). The
pledge of credit in the
1800s (right) *135*
The Rise – and Rise – of
Credit Pledges 132–5
The seal of the Bank of
the Holy Saviour (left).
The seal of St James
(right) *148*
and tax farming 142–3,
148
and the Treasury 144–5,
146–8
benevolent associations
banking 114, 121–2
Church of Santa Maria
138
The Foulest Man of his
Century 123–8
Market in Naples in the
1600s *136–7*
Mint, the 139, 149–50
Monti banking charities
121, 122, 148 (*see also
Monti di Pietà (Mounds of
Compassion)*)
Quasi-Perpetual Public
Debt 139–41

Un pezzo di cielo caduto in
terra 120–2
Vedi Napoli e poi muori
128
Naples: A Palimpsest (book)
120
Naples, Kingdom of 11, 120,
133, 136
Don Juan's Warrant 122–3
Isabella, One Sharp Trader
146–8
Liquidity, Depth – and the
Curse of Public Debt
143–6
public finances,
management of 139–41
Silver Coins and Bank
Money 148–51
Tax Farming 141–3
Napoleon 61, 63, 232
Necker, Jacques 201, 202, 203
Neirot, Melchior 69
NEP *see* New Economic
Policy (NEP)
Netherlands 69
New Economic Policy (NEP)
253–4, 259
New England
money, use of 194
New Haven, Connecticut
194
New London 194
New York 184
New York Times (newspaper)
252
Newton, Isaac 149
Nicholas II, Tsar 254, 255,
256
Nicholson, James 214
Niebuhr, Barthold Georg 78
Nietzsche, Friedrich 123–4
Nixon, President Richard
171
A note for 3 chervonets with
Lenin's portrait *259*
A note for 1,000 roubles
issued by the Commissariat
of Finance in 1919 *256*
Notizia de cambi (essay) 164,
165–8, 188

Occam's razor 118
'Of Credit in TRADE'
(article) 16

Olivieri, Benvenuto 181
'On Markets' (Lenin) 245
'On the Circuit' (book) 193
'On the Jewish Question'
   (essay) 244–5
Ottoman Empire 70–1
Our Fantastic Reality 188–9

Packer, Daniel 185–6, 187–8
Paine, Thomas 207–9, 210
Palmieri, Giuseppe 123
Parazone Grasso 32, 41
Paris
   The Lesson of the
      Communards 231–3
Paris, Commune de 232
Park. Rowland 186
Paterson, William 93, 95–6,
   97
Paulson, Hank 13, 54
People's Bank (under
   Bolshevik rule) 238, 251–2
Peri, Giandomenico 177–8
Peter the Great 255
Philadelphia 12, 214, 216
   Washington's army, funding
      for 207–10
Philip II, King of Spain 139,
   157, 173, 175, 176, 177,
   178–9, 180
Piacenza 172
Pien Collegio (Full College)
   59–61, 62, 63–4, 65–6
   Banco del Giro and bank
      money 75–7
   Pien Collegio: The
      Overseers 59–60
Pisa 10, 12, 22
   cardinals' meeting 115
   Cathedral Foundry 28–30
   Cathedral Square 30
   coin trouble 22–4
   Mint, the 23–4, 30, 42, 43
   Piazza del Duomo 30
   see also Corporate Banking,
      the beginning of; Leaning
      Tower of Pisa; Square
      of Miracles (Piazza dei
      Miracoli)
Pisa, University of 34, 41, 42
Pisani Bank 52
Plymouth 175
Pole, Richard de la 87–8,
   98–9

Polyarchy: Participation and
   Opposition (book) 267
Potosí 174
The Power of Paper 182–4
Prada 10, 157
A Preface to Democratic Theory
   (book) 267
Preite, Isabella 146–8
Preobrazhensky, Yevgeni 243
Priuli, Gerolamo 13–14
Priuli Bank 13, 52
A promise by John Johnston
   to deliver to Tench Francis,
   factor of the Bank of
   Pennsylvania, flour 209
A promissory note written,
   printed,signed by
   Benjamin Franklin while
   Plenipotentiary of the CC
   in France 204
Provins 159, 160
Prussian Mint 78
Putilov iron works 248
Putin, Vladimir 241

Quebec 197

Radolovich, Nicolo 130
Rae, Doug 267
Ragusa, Republic of 156
Ranelagh, Lord 100
Red Square economy 239,
   241, 249–50, 254, 258, 259
Reinhart, Carmen 15
Requesens, Don Louis de
   176–7
Resolute (ship) 214
Rialto (Venice) 48
Riflessioni sulla Publica Felicità
   relativamente al Regno di
   Napoli (book) 123
Robinson Crusoe (book) 15,
   93
Rogoff, Ken 15
Roman Curia 180–1
Rome 157
Romer, Gaspare 143–4
Rousseau, Jean-Jacques 125
Royal Bank of Scotland 107
Royal Gyro and Exchange
   Bank, Berlin 78
Royal Navy
   Trumbull seizure 214
Ruskin, John 83

Russian Civil War 249
Russian Provisional
   Government 249, 254–5
Russian State Bank 245, 256,
   257, 260, 262–3
   currency issuing 251

Salona 156
Salviati bankers 181
Sannazaro, Jacopo 120
Sarah Kemble Knight's
   journey on horseback
   (1704–5), crossing
   Massachusetts, Rhode
   Island and Connecticut
   195
Sardinia 22
Sartori, Giovanni 266–7,
   268
Scienza Nuova (book) 123
Service, Robert 230
Sette opere di Misericordia
   (painting) 130
'The Seven Acts of Mercy'
   (painting) 131
Seville 174
A share in the Bank of North
   America issued to John
   Carter, the brother-in-law
   of Alexander Hamilton
   215
Shelley, Percy Bysshe 21
Silk and Jersey 157–9
Skeat, Walter W. 156
Smith, Adam 203
Société de Lecture (the
   Reading Society of Geneva)
   233
Sokolnikov, Grigory 257–8,
   260
Song Dynasty 158
Southampton 175
Soviet settlement tokens see
   sovznak
Soviet Union 10
   collapse of 239
sovznak 250–1, 252, 254,
   255, 258–60
Spain 206
   Cuba, silver shipments
      from 214
   and silver to Army of
      Flanders
         Total Fiesco 175–7

Spain and Silver 173–4, 179
  Vatican financial
    contributions 181
Spanish Empire 11
  see also Asientos
Spanish milled dollar 198
Square of Miracles (Piazza
  dei Miracoli) 30
St Petersburg 234, 241, 245,
  247–8
  the Smolny 236
Stalin 260
Star Wars 156
Stevens, Antony 100
Stoke D'Abernon Church,
  Cobham 85
Streit, Hugo 78
Strozzi family 158, 160–1
Sukharevka economy
  239–41, 249–50, 252, 254,
  258, 259
Sukharevka market 240, 242,
  250, 252

Tacitus 164
Tagliente, Girolamo 26
tallies 84
  exchequer tallies and the
    Bank of England 97–106
  The longest tally issued for
    the value in the vaults of
    the Bank of England 87
  Sticks as Public Debt
    Securities 86–9
  Tallies as Financial Tools
    85–6
Tauride Palace 255
Taylor, A. J. P. 238
Thomas Paine with Robert
  Morris, Superintendent of
  Finance and the scheme for
  the Bank of Pennsylvania
  208
Thornton, Henry 187
Tobin, James 267, 268
Tonnage Act (1694) 96
Tooke, Thomas 187
Trattato de' tributi, delle
  monete, e del governo politico
  della sanità (book) 123
Treaty of Rome 165
Trilling, Lionel 155
Trotsky, Leon 236, 252

Troyes 159, 160
Trumbull (ship) 214
Turbolo, Giovanni 149, 150

Ulyanova, Maria
  Alexandrovna 230
United States
  The Bank of North
    America 215–18
  French funding 202–3
  Plans for a National Bank
    210–12
  Alexander Hamilton's
    Alternative 212–14
  Thomas Jefferson's Coins
    220–4
  The Trouble with Pounds,
    Shillings and Pence
    218–20
United States Declaration of
  Independence 200
United States Treasury 14
Unto This Last (book) 83
US dollar and gold 171
  see also American dollar
Uskok War see Gradisca,
  War of

Vatican State
  arbitrage, use of 180
Vendramin, Zuane 48–50,
  56–9, 72, 78
  and Banco del Giro 64–6
Venetian ducat 255
Venetian Republic 11
Venetian Senate 52, 53–4,
  59, 61, 61, 73, 261
  Banco del Giro and bank
    money 75–7
  and Banco Giro 217
Venice 10, 12, 157, 172, 206
  Armamento 68, 69–70, 71
  Arsenale 67
  bank ledgers 51
  Bank Money – Familiar,
    Easy to Use and
    Reasonably Safe 51–3
  The Bank of Transfers for
    Grain 57–9
  banking experiment 77–9
  'banking supervisors' 33
  Campo di San Giacomo di
    Rialto 48, 49

Confronting Bubbles 53–4
Convento dei Frari 62
currency arbitrage 74–5
Forced Loans 50–1
Grain Office 57–9, 66, 71
Mint, the 48–9, 55, 56–7,
  59, 64–6, 67, 71
Mint Money vs Current
  Money 72–3
Piazza San Marco 68
The Price of War 54–6
shipping fleet development
  68–70
Vendramin, Zuane
  A Brilliant, Self-Serving
    Proposal 56–7
Verrazzano, Giovanni da
  182–4
Vico, Giambattista Vico 123
Vieux Lyon 160–4
Vieux Lyon. The city in the
  sixteenth century 162–3
Voghet, Pietro de 66–7
Volatile Trades 168–9
Volkogonov, Dmitri 230
Vologda 247
Voth, Hans-Joachim 178–9

War Communism
  inflation rise 250–3
  The Trouble with War
    Communism 249–50
Washington, George 205
Washington DC 10
Weimar Republic 233
Welser, Marcus 166
West Riding, Yorkshire 88
Wilks, Francis 200
William of Ockham 118
Wolf bone 84
World War II 171

Yakovlev, Vladimir 239
Yale 9, 267
Yale International Center for
  Finance 184–5
Yeltsin, Boris 241
Yurovsky, Leonid Naumovich
  257–8, 260

Zacatecas 174
Zuniga, Don Juan de 122–3